LINCOLN *Emancipated*

LINCOLN
Emancipated

The President and the Politics of Race

BRIAN R. DIRCK *Editor*

ALLEN C. GUELZO *Foreword*

NORTHERN ILLINOIS UNIVERSITY PRESS

DeKalb

© 2007 by Northern Illinois University Press
Published by the Northern Illinois University Press, DeKalb, Illinois 60115
Manufactured in the United States using acid-free paper
All Rights Reserved

Library of Congress Cataloging-in-Publication Data
Lincoln emancipated : the president and the politics of race / edited by Brian R. Dirck.
   p.   cm.
Includes bibliographical references and index.
ISBN-13: 978-0-87580-359-3 (clothbound : alk. paper)
ISBN-10: 0-87580-359-8 (clothbound : alk. paper)
1. Lincoln, Abraham, 1809–1865—Political and social views. 2. Race—Political
aspects—United States—History—19th century. 3. Racism—United States—History—
19th century. 4. United States—Race relations—History—19th century. 5. Slaves—
Emancipation—United States. 6. United States—Politics and government—
1861–1865. I. Dirck, Brian R., 1965–
E457.2.L825 2006
973.7092—dc22
2006001574

CONTENTS

ALLEN C. GUELZO

FOREWORD

Was Lincoln a Racist?

Once upon a time, almost every African American home or business had, hanging on its walls, a portrait of Abraham Lincoln. Once upon a time, blacks in America supported the Republican Party, almost unanimously, as the party of Lincoln. Once upon a time, representative black leaders such as Booker T. Washington and Jackie Robinson hailed Lincoln as their model and champion.

This has now all but disappeared. Instead of the Great Emancipator, Lincoln is routinely condemned as a racist whose interest in freeing American slaves was dictated purely—and cynically—by his desire to reunite the Union, as a man who preferred, once he had freed the slaves, to deport them to a colony in central America or the Caribbean, and as a racist who believed in the supremacy of white Europeans and did not believe blacks could ever achieve civil equality with whites. In his defense, Lincoln's admirers plead that this is an example of *presentism*—measuring people and situations from the past by the standards and sensibilities of the present. A number of Lincoln's contemporaries, however, saw the issue of racism with fully as much clarity and urgency as anyone today, and that seems to leave precious little excuse for a man who is otherwise praised on all hands for his superior moral insights. Besides, the question of racism itself is important because of how much Lincoln still means to all Americans, black and white. If it turns out that Lincoln was a white supremacist with no confidence in the possibility of liberty and justice for all, then, no matter how many excuses we can manufacture for him, every other accomplishment he has woven into the warp and woof of American life falls into discredit.

WAS LINCOLN A RACIST? The term "racism" was first coined in the 1930s by Magnus Hirschfield, who made it the title of his critique of the racial philosophy of the Nazis. But, as James Leiker's essay in this collection wryly shows, in the seventy years since the Nazis came to power in Germany, the word has undergone a significant expansion, and sometimes even inflation. No longer do we confine *racist* to a full-blown philosophy. Instead, we use "racist" to describe an attitude, which can be said to have two fundamental parts:

Dishonor: the idea that members of a certain race are biologically, intellectually, and permanently inferior to one's own race, and inferior to the point that it justifies what Glenn Loury calls "racial stigma."

Enmity: in other words, that members of another race can be treated with anger, derision, or contempt. I leave to one side here the basic problem that Philip Paludan's essay tackles, whether essentializing anyone by the term "racist" is itself flawed; even the very concept of *race* contains deadly inconsistencies. It is important to bear in mind that racism can come packaged in different ways. Racism can exist as *social* racism, where racist beliefs are widely shared, but only as a sort of social assumption, without clear targets or definition, and as *institutional* racism, which describes racism as practiced as policy by specific institutions, such as schools or governments, but that may not reflect anything about an individual's opinions. Finally, racism can exist on a spectrum. It may be little more than exaggeration of what Kwame Anthony Appiah calls *racialism,* which talks about differences without implying dishonor; or it may give rise to a militant genocidal hatred that takes serious public form. There is also a question about who can be a racist, because it is often insisted that an essential element of racism, whether it involves any quantity of enmity or dishonor, is *power*. By this reasoning, even the mildest taint of enmity or dishonor in the mind of those possessing *power* becomes automatically racist, whereas racial rage on the part of the powerless can simply be interpreted as righteous anger. This is largely, I suspect, a self-exculpatory mechanism that allows racial loudmouths of various stripes to indulge as much enmity and dishonor of other races as they please while claiming to be innocent of racism because they are "powerless." This argument might have more force if a coherent and specific definition of "power" was available, but *power* is so amorphous a concept that it has almost no serious analytical use in determining what constitutes racism. So, like the question of race itself, there is no practical way to get it to bear on the business of Lincoln.[1]

So we return to the question: *was Lincoln a racist?* Certainly the social and institutional world of Lincoln's Illinois, where he came to maturity as a lawyer and politician in the 1830s through the 1850s, was so pervasively racist as to make us blush simply to read about it. For his part, Lincoln certainly opposed slavery, from his earliest speeches in the Illinois state legislature. But as a lawyer in Springfield, Illinois, Lincoln showed little enthusiasm for doing more than just opposing it. Out of the more than five thousand cases that he participated in during his professional life, only thirty-four involved African Americans, and, even in those cases, he showed little dissent from the prevailing patterns of institutional racism in Illinois. In his famous 1858 debates with Stephen A. Douglas, Lincoln insisted that, though he opposed slavery, what he meant was opposition to any further extension of legalized slavery outside the South—not the destruction of slavery in the South itself. And he was careful to add that, by opposing slavery, he was not saying anything in favor of civil rights for blacks.

As president, Lincoln actually disciplined two of his generals—John Charles Fremont and David Hunter—and a cabinet secretary—Simon Cameron—who wanted to move outright to emancipation. And when he issued an Emancipation Proclamation of his own in September 1862, the document itself sounded remote and indifferent and liberated only slaves in the rebellious Confederate states, not in the four upper South slave states—Missouri, Kentucky, Maryland, and Delaware—which had remained loyal to the Union.

If all this does not make Lincoln a racist, it certainly appears that he condoned it in others and confined his opposition to slavery to the most minimal definition of *opposition*.

IT IS, NEVERTHELESS, POSSIBLE to call too quickly for the verdict about Lincoln, and for a number of important reasons that run back to our definition of racism.

First of all, remember that racism is a lethal combination of two elements, *dishonor* and *enmity*. Much as Lincoln doubted in the 1850s that there was much likelihood for civil or political equality for blacks, his doubts were expressed in terms of the historical circumstances of slavery and the structure of American law, not on some inherent black racial inferiority. Whatever any particular polity did about articulating the *civil* rights of its members, Lincoln believed that no political community—state or otherwise—had the power to alter or disregard in any way the *natural* rights of its members. On this point, as Kenneth Winkle's essay on Lincoln's prepresidential record on race demonstrates better than anything previously written on the subject, Lincoln differed significantly from the racism of his fellow Illinoisans. Although his commitment to majority rule in a democracy meant that he would yield to a state's decision to curtail certain *civil* rights—voting, juries, and the like—for blacks, the *natural* rights of blacks to life, liberty, and happiness could not be so curtailed, simply on the basis of their common humanity with "all people of all colors everywhere."[2]

A similar corrective emerges from Brian Dirck's analysis of the judicial environment of the Emancipation Proclamation. Facing a Supreme Court top-heavy with justices, from Roger Taney on downward, who had formulated the Dred Scott decision, Lincoln had to cut the cloth of emancipation with exquisite care, lest Taney and his judicial allies find a handhold for constitutional litigation that would wreck all prospects for emancipation. It was not latent racism, from a president who manipulated emancipation purely for political advantage, that explains Lincoln's mincing step in the Proclamation, but his determination to make emancipation as Taney-proof as care could make it.

What weakens still more any suspicion that Lincoln personally subscribed to notions of racial inferiority was Lincoln's gradual movement, over the course of the Civil War, to advocacy for civil rights for the freed slaves in the newly reconstructed Southern states. Take, for instance, Philip Paludan's discussion of colonization and Lincoln's meeting with a "deputation of Negroes," a delegation of black ministers whom he invited to the White House in August 1862. Originally, Lincoln had been convinced that, in light of the pervasive social and institutional racism of his America, the only workable next step after emancipation would be the colonization of freed blacks to Africa, the Caribbean, or Central America, where blacks would find no difficulty in granting themselves the civil and political rights denied them in white America. The "deputation" had been formed on August 14, 1862, at Lincoln's request, "who had sent . . . word" to the African American clergy of Washington "that he had something to say to them of interest to themselves and to the country"—thus making Lincoln the first president ever formally to request an official meeting with an African American delegation in the White House. It is difficult for us now to grasp what a thrill of horror Lincoln must have stimulated in the minds of whites when they read that Lincoln had met them, "shaking hands very cordially with each one."[3] What he said, however, must have seemed even more radical, because it overturned the complicit silence American presidents had observed on the subject of slavery for half a century. "Your race are suffering, in my judgment, the greatest wrong inflicted on any people," Lincoln candidly admitted to the "deputation." Even if slavery were to disappear, the sufferings inflicted by racism would not. "It is a fact, about which we all think and feel alike, I and you," he explained to the black clergymen. "It is better for us both, therefore, to be separated." Lincoln could not argue with the determination "some of you" have to "remain within reach of the country of your nativity," but he would be the first to acknowledge that it was the land, and not the people, to which they owed loyalty. "I do not know how much attachment you may have toward our race. It does not strike me that you have the greatest reason to love them."[4]

The great obstacle in the way of colonization was the simple fact of the black soldier, who had been freed and enlisted to fight in the Union army by the Emancipation Proclamation. Lincoln could not ask those who had fought to save the Union to leave it, and by the spring of 1864 John Hay believed that Lincoln "has sloughed off" the "hideous & barbarous humbug." Instead, we find Lincoln nudging the governors of reconstructed Southern states to include voting rights for blacks as part of their new state constitutions. In the fall of 1864, he sent one his White House staff, William O. Stoddard, to occupied Arkansas as the new U.S. marshal and instructed him to "do all you can, in any and every way you can, to get the ballot into the hands of the freedmen!" Four days before his death, Lincoln publicly advocated the extension of voting rights and free education as part of an overall reconstruction plan in the South. True, he limited this proposal to "the very intelligent" and "those who have served our cause as soldiers," but this was exactly the portion of the black community that racists, north and south, most dreaded, and strove the most to insist did not even exist.[5]

But even if we grant that Lincoln recognized and deplored social and institutional racism, and expressed no particular belief in racial inferiority, there is still the other half of the racist proposition, and that is the expression of personal hatred toward another race. On this point, the record is even more remarkable, because Lincoln seems to have been noticeably free from any form of racial malevolence. "In all my interviews with Mr. Lincoln," recalled the black abolitionist, Frederick Douglass, "I was impressed with his entire freedom from popular prejudice against the colored race. He was the first great man that I talked with in the United States freely, who in no single instance reminded me of the difference between himself and myself, of the difference of color, and I thought that all the more remarkable because he came from a State where there were black laws."[6] Sojourner Truth, who was introduced to Lincoln at the White House in the fall of 1864, said, "I never was treated with more kindness and cordiality than were shown to me by that great and good man, Abraham Lincoln."[7]

If the test of racism is racial hatred, Lincoln passes it with high marks and is not a racist. If the test is a belief in the racial inferiority of others, Lincoln passes the test *personally*. He barely passes the test by condoning racism in *social* and *institutional* contexts, but it is a passing grade all the same, made possible largely through his movement toward black civil rights after 1863 and his candor about the evils of *social* and *institutional* racism. Lincoln frankly admitted to the black ministers in August 1862, "You are cut off from many of the advantages which the other race enjoy. The aspiration of men is to enjoy equality with the best when free, but on this broad continent, not a single man of your race is made the equal of a single man of ours. Go where you are treated the best, and the ban is still upon you."[8] We might judge him too passive and acquiescent in the racism all around him. But that is another matter entirely from describing Lincoln as a racist himself.

THE MOST CONCISE EVALUATION of Lincoln on the subject of race came from Frederick Douglass, in Douglass's most famous speech, at the dedication of Thomas Ball's emancipation monument in Washington in 1876. "I have said that President Lincoln was a white man, and shared the prejudices common to his countrymen toward the colored race," Douglass said. Whatever great deeds he did on behalf of African Americans, Lincoln was still "pre-eminently the white man's president, entirely devoted to the welfare of white men." This meant that, in the eyes of a black abolitionist like Douglass, "Lincoln seemed tardy, cold, dull, and indifferent." The critical word was "seemed." It was not a difference of historical context that, in the end, led Douglass to enter a plea on behalf of Lincoln, but a question of perspective. "Measuring him by the sentiment of his country, a sentiment he was bound to consult, he was swift, zealous, radical, and determined." Lincoln's modern racially minded critics, as well as the well-meaning historical relativists who defend Lincoln on the ground that he cannot be judged by modern understandings of race, have missed Douglass's point. What Lincoln *seemed* to be, in contrast to what he *was*, was very much in the eye of the beholder and said fully as much about the observer as it did about Lincoln. And in the eye of Douglass, Lincoln "is double dear to us, and his memory will be precious forever."[9]

Notes

1. Lawrence Blum, *I'm Not a Racist, But . . .: The Moral Quandary of Race* (Ithaca, N.Y.: Cornell University Press, 2002), 9, 32; Frederickson, *Racism: A Short History* (Princeton, N.J.: Princeton University Press, 2002), 151; Glenn

Loury, *The Anatomy of Racial Inequality* (Cambridge, Mass.: Harvard University Press, 2002), 9–11.

2. Abraham Lincoln, "Speech at Springfield, Illinois" (June 26, 1857), *Collected Works of Abraham Lincoln,* ed. Roy P. Basler (New Brunswick, N.J.: Rutgers University Press, 1953), vol. 2: 406.

3. "The President's Colonization Scheme," *Washington National Republican,* August 15, 1862, and "Interview between President Lincoln and a Committee of Colored Men," *Washington Evening Star,* August 15, 1862.

4. Lincoln, "Address on Colonization" (August 14, 1862), *CW,* vol. 5: 373.

5. Lincoln, "Last Public Address" (April 11, 1865), *CW,* vol. 8: 403; Harold M. Hyman, "Lincoln and Equal Rights for Negroes: The Irrelevancy of the Wadsworth Letter," *Civil War History* 12 (September 1966), 262; William O. Stoddard, *Inside the White House in War Times: Memoirs and Reports of Lincoln's Secretary,* ed. Michael Burlingame (Lincoln: University of Nebraska Press, 2000), 139.

6. Frederick Douglass, quoted in *Reminiscences of Abraham Lincoln by Distinguished Men of His Time,* ed. A. T. Rice (New York: North American Publishing, 1886), 193.

7. Carleton Mabee, "Sojourner Truth and President Lincoln," *New England Quarterly* 61 (December 1988), 521.

8. Lincoln, "Address on Colonization to a Deputation of Negroes" (August 14, 1862), *CW,* vol. 5: 371–72.

9. Douglass, "Oration in Memory of Abraham Lincoln, Delivered at the Unveiling of the Freedman's Monument in Memory of Abraham Lincoln, in Lincoln Park, Washington, D.C., April 14, 1876," *Frederick Douglass: Selected Speeches and Writings,* ed. P. Foner and Y. Taylor (Chicago: Lawrence Hill Books, 1999), 621, 624.

LINCOLN *Emancipated*

BRIAN R. DIRCK

INTRODUCTION

During a recent visit to Washington, D.C., I stopped for lunch at the Lincoln House Restaurant Bar and Deli, a little establishment tucked away among the shops, snack carts and urban what-not on the corner of 10th and H Street. The name is a not-so-subtle marketing ploy for tourists. Ford's Theater stands directly across 10th Street, and the Petersen House, where Lincoln died, is just a few doors down. A Lincoln souvenir shop hawks its wares nearby.

I had walked by the Lincoln House Restaurant a few times during my sightseeing tours, but it did not look very promising—a nondescript city storefront with a faded red sign, a cartoonish print of Lincoln's face, and not much character. Then again, I once had some pretty good "Lincoln French Toast" at the Lincoln Diner in Gettysburg, Pennsylvania. True devotees of Lincoln kitsch cannot be all that picky, anyway. So, on my last day in Washington, I tried out the Lincoln House Restaurant for a late lunch prior to my airport shuttle ride.

I walked in through the narrow front door and was almost immediately pressed back into the wall, trying to get out of the way as the last of the lunchtime rush left. It was quite a procession: two Indian women dressed in traditional Hindu garb, one older and one younger—a mother and daughter?—an African American man, two white guys dressed like FBI agents, two more African American men.

Finally, a portly white gentleman took mercy on me and stopped long enough for me to squeeze into the restaurant.

Two Asian Americans who looked like a husband and wife team ran twin cash registers tucked away in one corner of the place. I searched for something equivalent to "Lincoln French Toast" (Mary Todd Lincoln souvlaki? Maybe a John Wilkes Booth crab cake?). In the end I ordered a rather un-Lincolnian Italian meatball sandwich from a third Asian American behind the counter, who passed my order along to a sweat-stained Hispanic fry cook. I sat down with my food across from a black man in an expensive suit with a Wall Street look, next to a heavy-set blondish white woman, munching on a sub and rocking a sleeping baby in a stroller. Nearby stood a black teenager, engaged in a mild argument with the man running the register. The teenager pointed to the woman, who was busily ringing up customers on her matching register. "I never have this problem with her, man," he said, not too seriously. The Asian man waved him away.

It was hard to find Lincoln in all of this. The Great Emancipator's face adorned the carry-out menus, but that was about it. The brick and concrete front of Ford's Theater was visible across the street, framed in the grimy window by the Lincoln cartoon on one side and a blown-up copy of the menu, translated into Chinese, on the other. Probably the vast majority of customers took little notice of the restaurant's name. A Gerald Ford House restaurant would have generated about as much interest.

Still, it made me think. Was this little deli, this potpourri of modern urban diversity, what Lincoln had in mind for the Union he saved? Eight months before he was shot in that theater across the street, he told a group of Ohio veterans that the war was fought "in order that each of you may have through this free government which we have enjoyed, an open field and a fair chance for your industry, enterprise, and intelligence; that you may all have equal privileges in the race of life, with all its desirable human aspirations. . . . The nation is worth fighting for, to secure such an inestimable jewel."[1] Was Lincoln's "inestimable jewel" the multifaceted, multihued America of today?

Many Lincoln devotees would answer yes. In fact, they would argue, the racially diverse America of the twenty-first century would have been difficult (if not impossible) to achieve without the Great Emancipator. That one act—the signing of an executive order freeing millions of African Americans—is, according to this point of view, the launching point for a nation that was previously a deeply flawed rendering of the vision of equality and diversity embodied in the Declaration of Independence. Lincoln set things right. He made the crooked racial path of America straight. Historian James M. McPherson, for example, characterized emancipation as a "second American Revolution [that] left a legacy of black educational and social institutions, a tradition of civil rights activism, and constitutional amendments that provided the legal framework for the second Reconstruction of the 1960s."[2]

Lincoln's modern admirers are generally not mindless hagiographers. They acknowledge that he was a white male in a country dominated by white males and that he probably had little inkling of the tremendous ethnic and cultural variety that characterizes modern America. "But during the Civil War he came to recognize African Americans as active and vital participants in the cause of democracy," wrote Lincoln scholar Frank J. Williams, and this realization led him to a broader moral vision of the American community, one that had room for racial and ethnic differences. Moreover, in his commitment to freedom and equality he showed an unusual ability to rise above his times, to transcend the muck of American bigotry and show the nation—indeed, the world—the path to a better future. He was "a man who learned from his mistakes and made a difference," observed Lincoln biographer Stephen Oates. "[H]e had an acute sense of history—an ability to identify himself with a historical turning point in his time and to articulate the promise that it held for the liberation of oppressed humanity the world over . . . he made momentous *moral* decisions that affected the course of mankind." Even if he did not exactly predict the Lincoln House Restaurant Bar and Deli, the argument goes, he made its existence possible, and he probably would have been comfortable eating there himself.[3]

Others argue, however, that Lincoln wanted nothing at all like a diverse America, that he, in fact, possessed no vision of an America in which blacks and whites could live in peace and equality. Serious scholars have questioned aspects of Lincoln's racial legacy. In 1975, for example, historian George M. Frederickson wrote an article on Lincoln's racial views that criticized the Civil War president's embrace of various colonization schemes as indicative of a less-than-perfect record on racial equality. He was a "functional opponent of extreme racism," Frederickson pointed out, but he also "continued to his dying day to deny the possibility of racial harmony and equality in the United States."[4]

Two prominent recent critics of Lincoln have been Lerone Bennett and Thomas DiLorenzo. Bennett's *Forced into Glory: Abraham Lincoln and the White Dream* argues (as the title suggests) that Lincoln was at best an unwitting and largely unwilling passenger on African Americans' journey to freedom. "The myth of [Lincoln] the great emancipator has become a part of the mental landscape of America," Bennett wrote, but "no other American story is so false." Arguing that Lincoln embraced emancipation only with the greatest reluctance as a war measure to make black soldiers fodder for Confederate cannon, Bennett cites with disdain Lincoln's dalliances with colonization schemes, plans to compensate white slaveholders for the loss of their "property," and statements Lincoln made that seemed to indicate a belief in black inferiority. "Lincoln must be seen as the embodiment, not the transcendence, of the American tradition, which is, as we all know, a racist tradition," he argues. The Union's president "grew during the war—but he didn't grow much. On every issue vital to Blacks—on emancipation, suffrage, and the use of Black soldiers—he was the essence of the White supremacist with good intentions."[5]

DiLorenzo makes much the same argument, albeit from an entirely different political perspective. Whereas Bennett is more a spokesman for some segments of the African American community, DiLorenzo is a hero to modern-day devotees of Southern Lost Cause mythology. For Bennett, race relations lay at the heart of the war's meaning; DiLorenzo is more interested in moving race and emancipation issues to one side so that he may discuss what he terms the "real" Lincoln agenda: expanding the power of his presidency and the federal government in a bid to enact what DiLorenzo sees as a radical Hamiltonian economic agenda. Lincoln wanted the war to lay the foundation "for the kind of government we have today: consolidated and absolute, based on the unrestrained will of the majority, with force, threats, and intimidation being the order of the day." Race had little to do with this, DiLorenzo argues, and the Emancipation Proclamation—"immediately excoriated throughout the North (and much of the world) as a political gimmick"—was nothing more than a smokescreen to hide Lincoln's economic agenda. "He viewed [emancipation] only as a tool to be used in achieving his real objective," DiLorenzo wrote, "the consolidation of state power, something many Americans had dreaded since the time of the founding."[6]

So who has the "right" Lincoln? Taking into account the full range of intellectual, psychological, political, and cultural factors that animated this extraordinarily complicated man, he was neither the Lincoln Memorial's hallowed perfection of greatness nor his critics' unalloyed bigot. Yet the conversation about Lincoln's legacy seems often to swing back and forth wildly between these two extremes, allowing little room for nuance, ambivalence, or complexity—in other words, little room for truth. This sad state of affairs is equally the fault of those Lincoln enthusiasts who brook no criticism of their hero and some Lincoln critics who seem determined to place everyone in the position of acting either as a teller-of-truth or defender-of-racism.

The following collection of essays tries to offer not a single, unified theory for Lincoln's legacy, but rather a variety of angles from which we may approach this challenging and complex subject. Readers who approach this collection seeking an answer to the question "Was Lincoln a racist?" will likely be disappointed. Several of the chapters openly question the usefulness of the term "racist" in general terms, and we all agree that matters are not so simple where Lincoln is concerned.

Although the authors have approached their subjects with varying degrees of sympathy or disapproval of Lincoln's policies, I think we would all agree that snap judgments and political posturing are distortive and worse than useless. We also agree that what we are providing here are not conclusive answers, but rather starting points for new conversations about Abraham Lincoln, emancipation, and race in American history, for whether he was the White Man's President or the Great Emancipator (or something in between), Lincoln continues to be, on all sides of the troubled legacy of race relations in America, vitally relevant.

1

KENNETH J. WINKLE

"PARADOX THOUGH IT MAY SEEM"

Lincoln on Antislavery, Race, and Union,
1837–1860

In 1837, in response to the emerging antislavery movement, the Illinois legislature adopted resolutions supporting slavery in the South while simultaneously condemning the formation of abolition societies in the North. These resolutions provided Abraham Lincoln, then twenty-eight and in his second term in the Illinois legislature, his first opportunity to take a strong public stand against slavery. Only six legislators opposed the resolutions. Along with a colleague, Lincoln filed a protest stating that "the institution of slavery is founded on both injustice and bad policy; but that the promulgation of abolition doctrines tends rather to increase than to abate its evils." A quarter-century later, as the Republican nominee for president, Lincoln pointed to this declaration with pride and concluded that it "defined his position on the slavery question; and so far as it goes, it was then the same that it is now."[1]

From that point on, throughout his life, his political career, and his presidency, Lincoln argued with increasing vigor that slavery was wrong, labeling it a "moral, social and political evil," even to the point of declaring that "I hate slavery." He also argued, just as forcefully, that a direct attack on slavery—any attempt to end it immediately where it already existed—was not only unconstitutional, but also unwise. As much as he abhorred slavery, Lincoln considered abolitionism counterproductive and insisted that it would provoke sectionalism, even secession, before it would end slavery. Abolitionism would endanger the Union, which Lincoln revered as essential to everyone's freedom—the "last best, hope of earth." He therefore preferred the free soil doctrine of containing slavery in the South, which he was certain would someday end the institution, putting it "in the course of ultimate extinction." Running for Congress in 1845, Lincoln summed up what he recognized as an apparent paradox: "I hold it to be a paramount duty of us in the free states, due to the Union of the states, and perhaps to liberty itself (paradox though it may seem) to let the slavery of the other states alone."[2]

Only the containment of slavery, Lincoln maintained, would deal it a "natural death" that would not disrupt the Union. He spent his political career, including his presidency, trying to balance these two interests—extending human freedom as far as he considered possible within the limits of the Constitution, while trying to hold an increasingly precarious Union together. He wrote to a Southern friend, privately and with unmistakable anguish, "I also acknowledge your rights and my obligations, under the constitution, in regard to your slaves. I confess I hate to see the poor creatures hunted down, and caught, and carried back to their stripes, and unrewarded toils; but I bite my lip and keep quiet." He reiterated the same principle publicly in 1854 at the height of the Nebraska crisis, counseling that, "much as I hate slavery, I would consent to the extension of it rather than see the Union dissolved, just as I would consent to any GREAT evil, to avoid a GREATER one."[3]

Lincoln based his beliefs on what he considered fundamental, if not eternal, principles that he felt should not be altered capriciously and only then for the sake of national survival. Once he developed these principles, he maintained them with remarkable consistency for decades, through a wide range of shifting political currents. During his life, abolitionists faulted Lincoln for moving too slowly toward emancipation and equality, even denouncing his hesitation to risk disunion in so imperative an effort. One of Lincoln's greatest strengths as a politician and later as a statesman, however, was his forthright enunciation of his beliefs and his steadfast refusal to compromise those convictions out of temporary political expediency. After all, Southern slaveowners also implored Lincoln to compromise his principles to save the Union, and of course he refused. Lincoln himself recognized his steadfastness on this issue as one of his greatest strengths. Responding to Frederick Douglass's characterization of him as "slow and vacillating," for example, Lincoln admitted that he was slow but never vacillating. "I think it cannot be shown," he countered, "that when I have once taken a position, I have ever retreated from it."[4]

Lincoln imbibed his earliest attitudes toward slavery and race growing up in the slave state of Kentucky and the free states of Indiana and Illinois. He rose above the deepest prejudices he encountered there but never managed to overcome them all. He rejected slavery, the conception of slaves as property rather than people, and the denial of their natural rights. Still, he never accepted the social and political equality of African Americans. He believed, pessimistically, that racial prejudices were so central to American society that they would be difficult, if not impossible, for most people to overcome in a single lifetime. "Free them, and make them politically and socially, our equals?" he asked. "My own feelings will not admit of this; and if mine would we well know that those of the great mass of white people will not."[5]

One-fifth of the residents of Kentucky, where Lincoln was born, were slaves. Despite this Southern heritage, Lincoln was relatively isolated from slavery and African Americans in his youth. Hardin County was a society of mostly free, white family farmers rather than large slave plantations, and about one-eighth of its people were slaves. As a boy, Lincoln had even less interaction with free African Americans. As he grew up, only 3 percent of Hardin County's black residents, twenty-eight of them, were free. By comparison, slaves comprised fully one-third of the population of elite plantation districts, such as Mary Todd's childhood home of Fayette County. Still, the Cumberland Road, which ran past the Lincolns' cabin, presented the constant spectacle of slaves herded like cattle between Nashville and Louisville.[6]

Moving northward to the free territory of Indiana at age seven isolated Lincoln even further from African Americans, both slave and free, but introduced him to the racism of the antebellum North. Only 1 percent of Indiana's residents were African American, and almost all of them were free. Like many Northern states, Indiana denied basic rights to African Americans. The state's constitution prohibited the immigration of free blacks. State law banned interracial marriages, prevented African Americans from testifying in court, and kept black children out of public schools. Spencer County, where, as Lincoln put it, he "grew up," hosted no slaves and only fourteen African Americans while he lived there. Lincoln's first memorable glimpses of slavery occurred on several voyages down the Mississippi River to New Orleans that he made as a young man. His earliest recorded racial memory originated when he was nineteen during a trip down the river with a boyhood friend. Lincoln remembered thirty years later that "one night they were attacked by seven negroes with intent to kill and rob them." During a later trip southward as a young adult, Lincoln caught a glimpse of a slave market in New Orleans. His cousin John Hanks, who accompanied him during part of the journey, argued that this experience made an indelible impression and moved Lincoln to sympathize with African American slaves. "There it was we Saw Negroes Chained—maltreated—whipt & scourged," Hanks recalled in 1865. "I can say Knowingly that it was on this trip that he formed his opinions of Slavery: it ran its iron in him then & there." These poignant experiences as a youth helped to shape the racial views of the man. "I am naturally anti-slavery," Lincoln reflected as president. "If slavery is not wrong, nothing is wrong. I can not remember when I did not so think and feel."[7]

When he moved to Illinois in 1831, the twenty-two-year-old Lincoln entered a society that was already long divided over questions of slavery and race. French settlers introduced African American slavery to the Illinois Country in the eighteenth century. After the United States acquired the region, the Northwest Ordinance of 1787 prohibited slavery there. Placating Southern settlers, however, the first governor of the Northwest Territory, Arthur St. Clair, ruled that the ordinance was not retroactive. Any slaves who were in the region before the ordinance took effect would remain enslaved. In 1803, William Henry Harrison, governor of Indiana Territory, which included Illinois, set up a system of involuntary servitude, allowing terms to run as long as ninety-nine years. In 1809, Illinois became a separate territory and adopted the system of "registered servants." Illinois residents could "import" slaves who were younger than fifteen and register them at the county seat. Such registered servants could be sold and resold in an underground slave market. Children born to registered servants belonged to their masters until they turned thirty-five, in the case of male slaves, or thirty for females.

Another law allowed the employment of slaves for one-year terms that were renewable indefinitely.[8]

On achieving statehood in 1818, Illinois retained this system and imposed other restrictions on the rights of free African Americans. The state's "Black Code" denied basic legal and political rights, including the right to testify in court against whites and to vote or hold office. Reflecting popular fears of "amalgamation," African Americans were denied the right to marry whites. In 1824, settlers from the South launched a campaign for a constitutional convention to reestablish slavery in Illinois. The measure was popular in the southern third of the state, known as Little Egypt, but failed by a wide margin. In short, most whites in early Illinois were willing to tolerate a modified form of slavery for African Americans, along with severely restricted rights, but not complete, hereditary enslavement.[9]

In 1831, when Lincoln arrived in Illinois, free blacks accounted for 3 percent of the population, and the state still had 747 slaves. Sangamon County had thirty-eight African Americans, a third of whom were slaves when Lincoln arrived. John Todd, the patriarch of the Todd family in Springfield, owned four slaves, making him the largest slaveowner in the county. Local government accommodated slavery through the registration of servants and apprenticing of African American children. In 1835, for example, Todd took on an eight-year-old African American girl "to learn the art and mystery of domestic housewifery" until she turned eighteen—in other words, to be an unpaid servant. The county commissioners followed Southern tradition in recognizing slaves not as people but as property, imposing a tax of 1/2 of 1 percent on "slaves and indentured or registered negro or mulatto servants." On the other hand, the county commissioners were also responsible for issuing certificates of freedom, which they did on request, albeit infrequently.[10]

In 1837, Lincoln moved to Springfield. Despite the legality of involuntary servitude and the discrimination inherent in the Black Code, an African American community was beginning to take root in the new state capital. Eighty-six African Americans lived in the town, comprising almost 5 percent of the population. Two-thirds of them lived in free African American families, and the other third lived as servants in white families. Black servants were fashionable among the town's elite families, including quite a few of Lincoln's future in-laws, friends, and political allies and opponents. The number of slaves fell between 1830 and 1840, from eleven to five. These five remaining slaveowners included Mary Todd's sister, Elizabeth Edwards, which meant that Lincoln's future wife had an African American slave in her home while Lincoln was courting her.[11]

The presence of African Americans, both slave and free, provoked a range of responses in Lincoln's Springfield. At one extreme, whites sometimes set their own slaves free. In 1831, for example, the county commissioners freed a slave after a white man posted a bond on his behalf. "Henry Yates came into court and gave bond as this law requires," they reported, "in setting free a negro man named Nelson aged fifty five years." At the other extreme, the demand for labor spawned an underground market for slaves. In 1830, Pascal Enos received a letter asking him, "Will you please have the goodness to ascertain if Mr. Wm Kirkpatrick has a coloured boy for sale & what he would take for him, what is his character, if sober, honest and a good hand with horses."[12]

Between these two extremes, most whites neither owned slaves nor freed them, but cooperated actively or passively in the enforcement of Southern slavery. Runaway notices peppered local newspapers, promising rewards ranging from $100 to $250, about half a year's wages for a skilled craftsman. One notice offered $250 for an entire family—husband, wife, and four-year-old daughter—who "left my farm in my absence, and without cause." Sometimes local residents were seized as runaway slaves and forced back into slavery. In 1842, an Arkansas man claimed James Foster, who had lived in Springfield for two years, as a runaway slave. Judge Samuel Treat, who kept an African American servant of his own, demanded proof of ownership and then surrendered Foster to his master and his fate in Arkansas. Beyond the courts, mobs sometimes ran down suspected fugitives voluntarily. Several residents of a nearby town spotted two African Americans traveling to Chicago in 1845 and, on the strength of a runaway notice in a Springfield newspaper, gave chase. They drove the two into the woods and caught one of them in a thicket. Despite his protests of freedom, he was relegated to the upper floor of the courthouse until his captors' letter to Missouri received a reply.[13]

The most systematic response to racial tensions in Springfield was the formation of a local colonization society. The American

Colonization Society formed in Washington, D.C., in 1816, mounting a campaign to create an overseas colony for African Americans. Some colonizationists were racists, who strove to eliminate all African Americans, both slave and free, from American soil. Others hoped to undermine slavery by creating a viable alternative for slaveowners who might free their slaves if they knew that they would leave America. Still others genuinely believed that African Americans would be better off if they left a predominantly white country and created a black society of their own in a tropical climate. The movement produced local colonization societies in every state except South Carolina and culminated in the creation of Liberia in 1822.[14]

Springfielders were quick to embrace colonization. "We have in this State many colored people, living in degradation and poverty, who, under a government like that of Liberia, would become useful and valuable members of society," the Whig editor of the Springfield *Journal* reasoned, "and would thus be able to give to their descendants blessings and privileges which they can never hope for in this country." In 1833, a local chapter formed in the Methodist Church. John Todd Stuart, Lincoln's future law partner, was the society's secretary. This colonization society soon lapsed, but a new Sangamon Colonization Society appeared and attracted 150 members. The president was Charles Dresser, the Episcopal minister who later married the Lincolns. Like the Todd and Edwards families, the Dressers employed an African American apprentice as a servant. Both John Todd and John Todd Stuart were vice presidents of the colonization society. The Ladies of the Methodist Congregation donated $52 to send two African Americans to Liberia, returning "two of the wandering children of bereaved Africa in the bosom of their mother land," as they put it, "in the enjoyment of all the blessings of civil and religious liberty."[15]

By 1845, the colonization movement was strong enough to support a statewide organization, the Illinois State Colonization Society, founded in Springfield. Its purpose was to establish a colony of free African Americans on the west coast of Africa, as envisioned by the national society. Colonization was a bipartisan effort but generally attracted more Whigs than Democrats, and four-fifths of Springfield's colonization leaders were Whigs. Some colonizationists may have viewed the movement as a stepping-stone to abolition. Most of them probably viewed colonization as entirely consistent with Southern slavery. The editor of the *Illinois Journal* labeled the local chapter "an institution antagonistical to abolitionism."[16]

The growth of abolition societies across the North produced a counterreaction, antiabolitionism, aimed at suppressing antislavery activity as injurious to public order as well as the true interests of the nation. The most notorious antiabolitionist riot in American history occurred in nearby Alton, Illinois, in 1837, where abolitionist editor Elijah Lovejoy was killed by a mob attempting to destroy his printing press. In Springfield, antiabolitionists responded to the Lovejoy murder by holding a public meeting to head off any calls for the emancipation of slaves and the mob violence that might result. They resolved that "the efforts of abolitionists in this community, are neither necessary nor useful," arguing that abolition leaders were "designing, ambitious men, and dangerous members of society, and should be shunned by all good citizens." Instead of promoting equality, they concluded, abolitionism would only "breed contention, broils and mobs." For the moment, they were right. A few years later, an abolitionist attempted to deliver a lecture in Springfield. A group of 150 boys disrupted the talk by making noise with sticks, boards, and horns. They drowned out the speech and threw eggs at the speaker's head. Refusing to intervene, the city police watched the spectacle and just laughed. Democrats seized on this opportunity to condemn the growing influence of "mobocracy" and to warn that abolitionism would lead inevitably to disunion and civil war.[17]

During his four terms in the Illinois legislature, Lincoln's positions generally harmonized with the views of most of his constituents, who avoided any connection with Southern slavery, on the one hand, or Northern abolitionism, on the other. Lincoln took his first, public stands against slavery by asserting that the residents of the District of Columbia had the right to end slavery there and protesting against slavery as an injustice. Lincoln also reflected general opinion on African American rights in Illinois. In his first term as an Illinois legislator, he voted for a resolution "that the elective franchise should be kept pure from contamination by the admission of colored votes." Running for a second term, he announced that "I go for admitting all whites to the right of suffrage, who pay taxes and bear arms." He did not challenge the state's Black Laws, acquiescing in the exclusion of black children from public schools. Overall, Lincoln's legislative experience laid the groundwork for an increasingly vocal attack on the morality of slavery without moving him appreciably forward on questions of racial equality.[18]

During his final term in the legislature, Lincoln once again encountered Southern slavery. In 1841, he visited his old friend Joshua Speed near Louisville, Kentucky. Speed had recently inherited an opulent plantation, Farmington, on which his father had gathered more than seventy slaves. After two months, Lincoln and Speed returned together to Illinois, taking a riverboat down the Ohio to St. Louis. On the river, Lincoln witnessed the eerie spectacle of a dozen slaves coffered together, as he put it, "like so many fish upon a trot-line." He felt genuinely moved. "In this condition they were being separated forever from the scenes of their childhood, their friends, their fathers and mothers, and brothers and sisters, and many of them, from their wives and children," he mused with an eloquence on the subject that would soon become second nature, "and going into perpetual slavery where the lash of the master is proverbially more ruthless and unrelenting than any other where." The scene stayed with Lincoln, and fourteen years later he called its very memory "a continual torment to me." Significantly, Lincoln condemned the slave trade that destroyed families and sent slaves westward but not the slavery on a plantation like Farmington. Just as tellingly, he sympathized with the slaves but felt powerless to ameliorate their plight.[19]

Like his political moderation, Lincoln's legal training and law practice encouraged ambivalence toward slavery. During the 1840s, he argued two "slave cases" that put him on opposite sides of the issue. The first involved a young African American woman named Nance, who was sold as an indentured servant to David Bailey in Tazewell County. Nance, who still had seven years left on her contract, told Bailey that she would not work without pay. Bailey sued Nance's previous master to recover the $432 he spent to buy the servant. Lincoln represented Bailey and argued that Nance had always been free by virtue of the Northwest Ordinance and the Illinois Constitution. Nance's original owner, therefore, had no legal right to sell her to Bailey. The court agreed on the grounds that "the presumption of the law in Illinois is that every person is free without regard to color." Accordingly, "the sale of a free person is illegal."[20]

The second case, which Lincoln argued six years later, put him on the other side of the issue. Robert Matson was a Kentuckian who brought his slaves into Illinois every year to work his farm from planting until harvest. In 1847, his slaves ran away and sued for their freedom, arguing—as Lincoln had done six years earlier—that the Northwest Ordinance prohibited slavery in Illinois. Matson hired Lincoln to get his slaves back. Now Lincoln worked to circumscribe the Ordinance, arguing that it applied only to slaves and slaveowners who were permanent residents of the state. A resident of Kentucky, Matson had a "right of transit," allowing him to transport his slaves into or through free territory for any temporary purpose. Lincoln lost the case when the court granted freedom to Matson's slaves.[21]

Taken together, the two slave cases say little about Lincoln's attitude toward slavery and race but everything about his reverence for the law. Throughout Lincoln's rhetoric and later his policy on both slavery and antislavery ran a profound commitment to do everything possible to enforce the law. As a lawyer, he felt a sacred obligation to defend the interests of his clients, whatever they might be. Further, only the rule of law could preserve the republic that promised freedom, eventually, for everyone. Lincoln revered law as the foundation of self-government, and upholding the law meant tolerating enslavement wherever it was legal while defending freedom wherever it was legal. He refused to challenge the rule of law even to advance a compelling moral reform such as antislavery. He just as consistently rejected any notion of a "higher law," a form of justice of divine rather than human creation, that many abolitionists espoused in the campaign they waged against slavery.

That same attitude informed his stance on slavery while in Congress, where he first had the opportunity to confront slavery as a national problem. As a moderate, he maintained the position that he had taken while in the Illinois legislature—that slavery was wrong, indeed evil, but that Congress had no power to interfere with it in Southern states. Instead, he concentrated on attacking slavery where Congress had undisputed authority to end it, in the western territories and the District of Columbia. Already a nonextensionist in private, Lincoln opposed the Mexican War, which strengthened his views and made them public. He supported the Wilmot Proviso, which sought to exclude slavery from any new territory acquired from Mexico, and he voted for it at least forty times. He also introduced an amendment abolishing slavery in the nation's capital. Neither measure won passage, but both made clear that Lincoln would oppose slavery wherever he felt that he had the legal power to do so.[22]

While Lincoln was in Washington, Illinois adopted a new constitution that explicitly banned slavery. During the constitutional debates, a delegate from southern Illinois offered a provision prohibiting the immigration of free blacks, calling them "a great annoyance, if not a nuisance, to the people of Illinois." The constitutional convention put the exclusionary clause to a popular vote. In April 1848, voters who ratified the new constitution voted on a separate clause restricting African American immigration. The resulting election was literally a referendum on racism, focusing on the single issue of affording African Americans an equal right to move to Illinois. Statewide, the restrictive clause won approval by an overwhelming 70 percent. Illinois joined Indiana and Oregon as the only free states that restricted African American immigration in their constitutions.[23]

Voters in Lincoln's Springfield supported the restriction by an even greater margin, 84 percent. The restrictive clause won bipartisan support from Whigs and Democrats. In keeping with their sympathetic stance toward Southern slavery and their aggressive racism, Democrats provided the mainstay of support, voting for restriction at the rate of 92 percent. Eighty percent of Whigs supported the measure, whereas two-thirds of the small Free Soil contingent in the city opposed it. Somewhat surprisingly, one-third of Free Soilers supported restriction of African American settlement in Illinois, which suggests that even a minority of Free Soilers were motivated more by racism than by humanitarian concern for blacks. Colonization leaders played a conspicuous role in opposing the clause, casting 60 percent of their votes against it, which suggests that by and large colonization represented an attempt to help rather than hurt African Americans.[24]

Despite this onslaught, Springfield's African American community was beginning to solidify by 1850. In conformity with the newly adopted state constitution, there were no more slaves in Springfield. Twenty-seven black families lived in the city, all but one of them headed by men. Nine-tenths of Springfield's African Americans lived in independent families, with only one-tenth living in white households as servants. Nevertheless, there were conspicuous signs of discrimination and poverty. Black families were considerably smaller than white families. Supporting an average of only 1.6 children, African American families were not yet self-sustaining. Economically, African American men were relegated exclusively to the ranks of manual workers. Almost half of them were unskilled laborers, and only three African Americans practiced skilled crafts. Men, like women, specialized in domestic service, and almost one-fourth of them were barbers. In fact, there was not a single white barber in Springfield in 1850. Amid this kind of occupational segregation, African American families owned only about one-seventh as much property as the typical white family in Springfield. Overall, the African American community had dwindled to just 3 percent of Springfield's population and commanded a mere 2 percent of the city's real wealth, and African American men were five times as likely as whites to be unemployed.[25]

Lincoln had extensive interaction with African Americans in Springfield. In 1850, for example, more than twenty African Americans lived within three blocks of the Lincoln family. In keeping with their predominant role within the community, however, Lincoln knew them almost exclusively as servants. At least four African Americans provided domestic help for the Lincolns. Ruth Burns, known as "Aunt Ruth," Jane Jenkins, who lived a block away, and Mariah Vance, who served as cook and nursemaid for the Lincolns' sons, helped Mary Lincoln. William H. Johnson accompanied the family to Washington as Lincoln's personal servant, tending to the president-elect during the two-week railway journey. Lincoln planned to employ Johnson as a servant and messenger, but the African American staff in the White House objected to him as too dark-skinned. Lincoln put Johnson to work keeping the fire in the furnace room until finding him a position as a laborer in the Treasury Department. During his trip to Gettysburg in 1863, Lincoln contracted a mild case of smallpox and probably passed it on to Johnson. Johnson developed a severe case of the disease and died.[26]

Among all the African Americans in Springfield, Lincoln developed his closest relationship with his barber, William Florville. A native Haitian of French ancestry, Florville was the only foreign-born African American in Springfield. Such creoles, as they were known, tended to act as community leaders, and Florville was no exception. His barber shop thrived, and he opened other businesses, including the first laundry in the city. Florville began buying property on Lincoln's advice and grew rich, becoming the community's most prosperous African American. In 1850, he owned five times as much property as the average black household head, almost 50 percent more than the average white man. During the 1850s, he doubled his wealth. He was known as an active leader in the African American community, contributing to charities and the city's black churches and heading the movement to found an African American school.[27]

The 1850s, however, brought severe setbacks for free blacks living in the North, including Illinois. In an attempt to prevent—or at least postpone—civil war, Congress enacted the Compromise of 1850. Engineered by the Whig Henry Clay of Kentucky and the Democrat Stephen Douglas of Illinois, the compromise included the Fugitive Slave Law, which required federal officials to facilitate the return of runaway slaves back to their owners in the South. Free African Americans now faced a heightened threat of capture and reenslavement. The Fugitive Slave Law drew a horde of Southern "slavecatchers" pouring northward in search of runaways. The Underground Railroad developed to help fugitive slaves escape from the South and reach freedom farther north. Rumors circulated that an Underground Railroad was operating in Springfield. The presumed "conductor" was Jameson Jenkins, a forty-year-old drayman with a wife and daughter. In 1850, three slavecatchers ran down a band of fourteen fugitives from Missouri and Kentucky who were hiding in Springfield. Rumor held that Jenkins had been leading the slaves northward to freedom. "A general fight ensued," according to news reports, "in which there were some bloody heads and noses exhibited." The spectacle became known ever after as the "slave stampede." The slavecatchers consigned a "lame negro" to the Springfield city jail and took the rest back to St. Louis. Ten of the runaways managed to escape during a "severe fight" that left one fugitive and one slavecatcher badly wounded. When they returned to Missouri, all that the slavecatchers had to show for their trouble was one African American woman and her two children.[28]

Even when permitted to remain in Springfield, African Americans suffered harassment. In 1851, a gang of white boys mounted a campaign of intimidation against a black woman in the city. "The house occupied by 'Violet,' a colored woman,—who minds her own business and interferes with no one,—has been assailed night after night, by a parcel of half-grown boys, for the mere purpose of distressing her, until she is now nearly a maniac," a witness reported. "On Friday night last some of these persons actually entered her house, while she, frantic, made the neighborhood ring with the cry of 'murder! murder!'" The police did nothing. Rather than condemning the episode as an instance of racist violence, the local newspaper simply cautioned that Violet's impending insanity would add another pauper to the city's welfare rolls. "If the corporation do not want the support of another individual," ran the warning, "they had better see to this thing in time, if it is not now too late." Instead of prompting sympathy for free blacks, the Fugitive Slave Law and its resulting campaign of reenslavement ironically renewed calls for colonization. The increased threat of violence against blacks led the Whig newspaper to conclude that "they never can enjoy equal rights with white citizens, either in a social or political view. All efforts tending to produce such results, are an injury to the race, and destructive to the harmony and peace of the community."[29]

Henry Clay's death in 1852 gave Lincoln his first opportunity to summarize his views on slavery in the wake of the Compromise of 1850. In his eulogy Lincoln hailed Clay as both a defender of liberty and a champion of moderation. To Lincoln, as for Clay, the two were not contradictory but were complementary. Lincoln excused Clay's ownership of slaves as an inherited condition and his rejection of abolitionism as the reasoned judgment of a statesman who loved his country. Speaking for Clay—and perhaps for himself—Lincoln argued that "cast into life where slavery was already widely spread and deeply seated, he did not perceive, as I think no wise man has perceived, how it could be at *once* eradicated, without producing a greater evil, even to the cause of human liberty itself." Slavery was wrong, but abolitionism was not the best remedy, threatening to destroy the very nation that was the best guarantee of freedom for all. "His feeling and his judgment, therefore, ever led him to oppose both extremes of opinion on the subject," Lincoln reasoned. "Those who would shiver into fragments the Union of these States; tear to tatters its now venerated constitution; and even burn the last copy of the Bible, rather than slavery should continue a single hour, together with all their more halting sympathisers, have received, and are receiving their just execration."[30]

Like Clay before him, Lincoln opposed the abolition of slavery
"at *once*," all the while hoping for its eventual extinction. He strove
to avoid the emerging opposite extremes—of slavery's extension,
among Southerners, and abolitionism, among Northerners. Lincoln
concluded his eulogy by embracing colonization, which he viewed
as the best way to undermine slavery indirectly by making eventual
abolitionism more acceptable to whites. Colonization might lead to
the ultimate extinction of slavery, improve the immediate lot of
African Americans, and even redeem Africa itself, without threatening the bonds of Union. Lincoln labeled such a result "a glorious
consummation" for all.[31]

For Lincoln, colonization represented a middle ground between the extension of slavery, on one hand, and abolitionism,
on the other. Colonization might head off the other two movements. The next year, Lincoln spoke before the local colonization
society at the Presbyterian Church and addressed the annual
meeting of the Illinois State Colonization Society in Springfield
in 1855. Two years later, the society elected him one of its eleven
managers. He continued to dream of an overseas colony of
African Americans until late in his presidency, when the severity
of the Civil War convinced him at last that emancipation represented the only just and practical solution to the moral dilemma
of slavery. In 1852, however, the most that he could countenance
was nonextension and colonization to achieve what he held out
as "the possible ultimate redemption of the African race."[32]

In May 1854 Congress passed the Nebraska Bill, which repealed
the Missouri Compromise and allowed popular sovereignty to decide the question of slavery in the Kansas and Nebraska territories.
Northerners of all political persuasions were appalled at the possibility of Southerners reintroducing slavery into a region where freedom
had been guaranteed since 1820. Senator Douglas sponsored the bill,
which heightened the outrage that ensued in Illinois. Lincoln hoped
that "this Nebraska measure shall be rebuked and condemned every
where." Literally overnight, the volatile Nebraska issue produced a
political revolution—"a hell of a storm," Douglas called it—that
swept the North. As Lincoln sized it up, "The country was at once in
a blaze." Whigs and Free Soilers castigated the bill as new evidence
that a conspiracy of Southern slaveowners—the "slaveholding
power," Lincoln labeled it—was subverting the republic to extend
the evil institution westward.[33]

The Nebraska Act lent a renewed moral dimension to Lincoln's outrage against slavery. The act, as Lincoln later confided, "aroused him as he had never been before." An early and vocal opponent of slavery, Lincoln was the perfect spokesman for the Republican Party's new emphasis on the immorality of slavery. Addressing a meeting of Republicans in Peoria, Lincoln labeled the institution a "monstrous injustice," declared that "I hate it," and reiterated his determination to prevent its spread. Lincoln also distinguished himself from Democrats through his refusal "to deny the humanity of the negro." Yet he lamented that Northerners could do nothing about slavery where it already existed, in the South. "If all earthly power were given me," he conceded, "I should not know what to do, as to the existing institution." Lincoln now made a public commitment that he maintained until he issued the Emancipation Proclamation eight years later—not to interfere with Southern slavery. Simply put, Lincoln was "arguing against the EXTENSION of a bad thing, which where it already exists, we must of necessity, manage as we best can."[34.]

After electing a senator in 1855 and a governor in 1856, Lincoln and other Illinois Republicans set out to unseat the state's leading Democrat, Senator Stephen Douglas. That effort received a boost in March 1857 when the U.S. Supreme Court's *Dred Scott* decision threw the Democratic Party into disarray. In their infamous ruling, the court denied the right of African Americans, both slave and free, to sue in federal courts, overturned the Missouri Compromise as unconstitutional, and denied the power of Congress to ban slavery in western territories. *Dred Scott* undercut the viability of free soil as a method of achieving the nonextension of slavery, which was the fundamental goal of the Republican Party. The decision also angered many Northern Democrats, who hoped that the West would remain free through the action not of Congress but actual settlers exercising their rights under popular sovereignty. Douglas faced the dilemma of standing by President Buchanan and endorsing the decision or breaking with the Democratic administration to pursue popular sovereignty as a compromise approach to settling the West.[35]

In June 1857, Lincoln responded forcefully to *Dred Scott,* which he decried as subversive of the very foundation of the American republic. Dismissing the constitutional validity of the court's argument, Lincoln now insisted that the spirit of American freedom lay not in the Constitution itself, but in the Declaration of Independence. The statement that "all men are created equal" was a fundamental goal of the founders that everyone had the responsibility to pursue and bring to fruition. "This they said, and this meant," Lincoln argued with elegant simplicity. "They did not mean to assert the obvious untruth, that all were then actually enjoying that equality, nor yet, that they were about to confer it immediately upon them." Lincoln's experience among slaves and free African Americans had taught him that racial equality remained an unrealized dream. "They meant simply to declare the *right,* so that the *enforcement* of it might follow as fast as circumstances should permit." Lincoln's reading of the Declaration convinced him that all Americans, both black and white, had the right to enjoy freedom. The nation's present struggle was an effort to *enforce* that right, which the founders had pursued as a national ideal.[36]

Lincoln viewed freedom as far more than a right conferred by government in a document, even one as fundamental as the Declaration. Freedom was an inalienable right in its fullest sense, a "natural right" belonging to all by virtue of their humanity. Denying equality to African Americans and denying them their freedom were two different things. Lincoln was willing to do the one but not the other. "I protest against that counterfeit logic which concludes that, because I do not want a black woman for a *slave* I must necessarily want her for a *wife,*" he argued. "I need not have her for either, I can just leave her alone." He acknowledged practical barriers to equality that arose from the dissimilarity of races. "In some respects she certainly is not my equal," he continued, "but in her natural right to eat the bread she earns with her own hands without asking leave of any one else, she is my equal, and the equal of all others." In this single sentence, Lincoln reaffirmed his opposition to racial equality in America while reiterating his commitment to human freedom. His reasoning also held out promise for the *eventual* equality of the races. Through diligence, education, frugality, self-discipline, and a host of other personal virtues, African Americans could improve themselves, as Lincoln had done, and someday achieve an equality of their own making. The equality that the founders envisioned was not absolute and immediate, but rather a potential for improvement that might find its fulfillment only if unencumbered by artificial restraints, above all slavery. Lincoln had benefited immensely from the unfettered right to improve himself, and now he hoped to share those benefits with everyone else, regardless of race.[37]

Imbibing much the same hope, Illinois Republicans sought to remove Douglas from the Senate, and they selected Lincoln to unseat and succeed him. The election of 1858 would determine the composition of the state legislature, which would then choose a senator. In an unprecedented move, Illinois Republicans nominated Lincoln as their candidate for the seat, acknowledging his personal and moral leadership of the party and designating him as the chief advocate for the Republican cause. Lincoln and Douglas agreed to a series of seven debates, one in each congressional district, between August and October 1858. In one sense, Lincoln and Douglas pursued a similar strategy to try to win the Senate seat. Both of them sought to avoid the extremes within their parties and move toward the middle of the political spectrum. For Douglas, this meant finding a way to dissociate himself from the Buchanan administration and the *Dred Scott* decision. In late 1857, Douglas engineered a dramatic break with Buchanan, opposing the admission of Kansas as a slave state. Across the North, and especially in Illinois, the Democratic Party split in two. In the wake of Douglas's rebellion, many Republicans hoped to win him over to their cause. Lincoln countered Douglas's move toward the middle and rejected any notion of a Republican Party that included Douglas and popular sovereignty. Lincoln himself attempted to occupy the middle of the spectrum by continuing to advocate the nonextension of slavery while disavowing any interest in either abolitionism or immediate equality for African Americans.[38]

During the debates, each man struggled to push his opponent out of the center and into the extremes. Lincoln launched an opening salvo by delivering his famous "House Divided" speech in Springfield even before the debates began. He attempted to keep Douglas out of the Republican fold by lumping him together with other administration Democrats. Reviewing the spread of slavery from the beginning of the nation, Lincoln argued that Douglas was part of a conspiracy to overturn American freedoms. President Buchanan, Chief Justice Roger Taney, former President Franklin Pierce, and Douglas were a "dynasty" that devised a *"dark* and *mysterious"* plan to extend slavery not only westward but also northward. Lincoln predicted yet another Supreme Court decision that would make slavery legal in Northern states as well as western territories. Soon enough, Northerners would discover that "the *Supreme* Court has made *Illinois* a *slave* State." Lincoln predicted that a crisis would soon envelop the nation. Like a house divided against itself, "I believe this government cannot endure, permanently half *slave* and half *free*. I do not expect the Union to be *dissolved*—I do not expect the house to *fall*—but I *do* expect it will cease to be divided. It will become *all* one thing, or *all* the other." And Lincoln predicted that the Southern dynasty of slaveowners would do all in their power to make the nation all slave.[39]

Many of Lincoln's own supporters considered the House Divided speech too radical, because it denied any middle ground for compromise between slavery and freedom. Political supporters told Lincoln that "nothing could have been more unfortunate, or unappropriate" and that "had I seen that Speech I would have made you Strike out that house divided part." Lincoln's in-laws, the Edwardses and Stuarts, "got mad at Mr L because he made the house-divided-against-itself Speech," one of them reminisced. Privately, Lincoln assured his friends that "you may think that Speech was a mistake, but I never have believed it was, and you will see the day when you will consider it was the wisest thing I ever said." The biblical allusion signaled Lincoln's refusal to compromise on the subject of slavery, and he vowed that he was "willing to perish with it, if necessary." Lincoln's speech escalated the Republicans' antislavery campaign by warning that slavery was not only spreading westward, but also ultimately threatened to engulf the North.[40]

In response, Douglas mounted a two-pronged challenge to Lincoln's charges. First, he accused Lincoln of fomenting an unnecessary "war of sections" between free states and slave states through his prediction that slavery would soon become national. Second, he argued that Lincoln not only opposed slavery—that he was an abolitionist—but also advocated legal, social, and political equality for African Americans. Lincoln decided that he had to counter both charges as his only chance of winning election to the Senate and moving the Republican cause forward. This strategy put Lincoln squarely in the middle of the political spectrum, where he so often situated himself during his long political career. He vehemently opposed the spread of slavery both westward and northward, but he just as vehemently opposed the abolition of slavery in the South and complete equality for African Americans in the North.[41]

Most political candidates prefer to highlight what they *intend* to do if elected. Douglas's charges forced Lincoln to declare definitively and repeatedly what he would *not* do if elected. Lincoln's critics were so effective that he proved most forceful when describing not what he stood for but what he stood *against*. Douglas's ploy required Lincoln to expound upon his racial views, which he considered irrelevant to the debate over slavery and consented to do only when Douglas's campaign of race baiting promised to bear fruit. Lincoln set the tone for the debates during his first meeting with Douglas, at Ottawa, Illinois. He denied Douglas's charge of abolitionism but repeated his commitment to restrict slavery to the South, declaring, "I have no purpose directly or indirectly to interfere with the institution of slavery in the States where it exists." In keeping with the sentiments of most Illinois voters, he stated bluntly, "I have no purpose to introduce political and social equality between the white and the black races." And Lincoln echoed popular assumptions about racial distinctions by endorsing the idea that "there is a physical difference between the two, which in my judgment will probably forever forbid their living together upon the footing of perfect equality, and inasmuch as it becomes a necessity that there must be a difference, I, as well as Judge Douglas, am in favor of the race to which I belong, having the superior position." He drew a sharp distinction between opposing slavery and supporting amalgamation.[42]

Throughout the debates, however, Lincoln reiterated that slavery was wrong, a "moral, social, and political evil," and a "monstrous injustice." Lincoln's greatest weapon against Douglas was simply to acknowledge the humanity of African Americans. According to Lincoln, Douglas "has no very vivid impression that the negro is human; and consequently has no idea that there can be any moral question in legislating about him." Endowed with equal human rights by the Declaration of Independence and the nation's founding principles, African Americans had above all the right to be free. "It does not follow by any means," Lincoln reasoned, "that because a negro is not your equal or mine that hence he must necessarily be a slave." Northerners could not end slavery immediately, but they could restrict its spread. They could not grant equality to African Americans immediately, but they could remove the barrier of slavery that prevented them from achieving equality eventually. Government could not and should not grant equality. Only self-improvement achieved through free labor could do that. With both candidates struggling to hold the political center, the election was close. Republicans won the popular vote for state legislators, but an apportionment system that favored the Democrats gave Douglas a 54–46 margin in the legislature and ensured his reelection.[43]

When Lincoln stood in the state capitol and called America a "House Divided," he drew on personal experience. He had seen the slave trade of the Deep South, in New Orleans, and experienced the plantation slavery of the Upper South, in Kentucky. He saw slavecatchers descending on his own state of Illinois, the African American community losing rather than gaining rights, and their situation deteriorating rather than improving over time. He knew from experience that the voters of Illinois would never countenance the formal reintroduction of slavery into their state, yet he saw many of them acquiesce in the running down of fugitive slaves. He also understood that most white Northerners of his generation could never imagine African Americans as their social and political equals.

Lincoln, at times, asked those who doubted his policies to judge them by their ultimate results, the "fruit" that they were likely to bear. "By the *fruit* the tree is to be known," Lincoln reasoned. Lincoln genuinely expected his policy of nonextension to administer an eventual deathblow to slavery. Right or wrong, Lincoln considered his approach more likely to "bring forth *good* fruit," in the long run, than abolitionism. As he began his campaign for president in 1860, Lincoln felt powerless to do two things—end slavery where it already existed in the South and grant equality to African Americans in the North. Between those extremes, however, Lincoln was determined, first, to contain slavery, to keep it from spreading to the West or to the North, and second, to guarantee to African Americans basic if not equal rights, what he termed "the natural rights enumerated in the Declaration of Independence." In these fundamental respects, he differed from Douglas and other Democrats. He was confident that achieving those two goals would put slavery "in the course of ultimate extinction." And that *was* within Lincoln's power to achieve.[44]

PHILLIP S. PALUDAN

GREELEY, COLONIZATION, AND A "DEPUTATION OF NEGROES"

Three Considerations on Lincoln and Race

Any writing that engages the question of Lincoln and Race walks a perilous path. It has to be careful what form the questions about the subject take. The most dangerous of these questions will be "Was Lincoln a Racist?" The danger lies in what that question assumes and the response likely to be provoked. The question assumes that Lincoln can be equated with racism, or that anyone can be. It reveals a form of essentializing that describes a person by one of the qualities they reveal. What makes a racist? A range of situations and incidents might evoke the charge: a foul comment, a stupid joke, an insensitive remark. Would it be legitimate to call someone a racist who used the "N" word ten times? Over what period? How vehemently? To whom?

Furthermore, such essentializing feels dishonest. Most people would legitimately bristle at a picture of themselves that denies their complexity as human beings. Complexity is a fundamental quality of being human. A single label denies my humanity. D. David Bourland has made the point that I struggle to make: "Everything in the 'real world' changes: sometimes . . . [r]apidly . . . sometimes . . . slowly. Every person, as well as every 'thing' undergoes such changes. One particular verb in English—'to be'—carries with it archaic associations and implications of permanence and static existence that we do not find in the 'real world.'"[1]

The use of "is" to describe me and/or you raises my suspicions about the intent of the speaker. I fear that she or he is using me as a means to her or his ends and not as an end in myself. Although there are moral reasons to give up using the verb "to be" when describing anything more complex than an amoeba, such an approach may be a bit strong. We may need to essentialize to think. Our minds seem to work by linking things together, making connections through a series of metaphors concerning what is bundled with what. In addition, there is a certain linguistic convenience in saying that someone "is" a Republican, a Democrat, or something else. We ought to beware, however, as historians especially, of what we are doing. We should be alert to the cost of the convenience. George Santayana says it this way: "The little word *is* has its tragedies; it names and identifies different things with the greatest innocence; and yet no two are ever identical, and if therein lies the charm of wedding them and calling them one; therein too lies the danger. Whenever I use the word *is* except in sheer tautology, I deeply misuse it; and when I discover my error, the world seems to fall asunder, and the members of my family no longer know each other."[2]

Besides misrepresenting Lincoln by asking, "Was he a racist?" there comes another danger to the analytical process. This danger stands on the other side of the main one. The problem we face then is likely to be to answer the question by saying, "No he was not a racist." The discussion becomes binary, we reflect what David Hackett Fisher referred to as the "fallacy of the counter position." We define a historical event within the narrow boundaries of a single quality that the event or person has or does not have. Doing this misses the complex nature of the issue. A third, fourth, fifth, or *n*th quality may actually be a more significant part of the subject; the whole of the qualities may be greater than the sum of its parts. This chapter rests on the premise that Lincoln shared the complexity of other human beings. At times, his behavior reveals racist tendencies; at other times it shows the opposite. When we describe human beings, "and" must replace "or" to prevent us from lying about the past and the present.[3]

Lincoln used the "N" word, told stories that ridiculed black people, and enjoyed minstrel shows, which were based on black inferiority.[4] But Lincoln never used the word with malice. One can claim that any use of the word implies malice. To do so, however, would fly in the face of legal decisions that provide a range of penalties for use of the word and, at times, provide no penalties at all. Randall Kennedy—an African American, if that matters— speaks of the legitimate "ambiguity" surrounding the use of the term when different people use the word in different contexts. Lincoln seems have been surprised and apologetic when reprimanded by a black visitor for using the word "Cuffee" to signify blacks. Lincoln asked a group of petitioners for equal pay for black soldiers, "Well, gentlemen, you wish the pay of Cuffee raised?" The protestor said, "Excuse me Mr. Lincoln, the term 'Cuffee' is not in our vernacular." Lincoln replied, "I stand corrected, young man, but you know I am a southerner by birth and in our section that term is applied without any idea of an offensive nature."[5]

Lincoln did use racist language in jokes and in private and public conversations. Does that brand him as a racist? It does so to some degree. But the essentializing in that assertion seems to ignore question of degree. Was Lincoln as racist as George Fitzhugh, as James Hammond, as Jefferson Davis, as Stephen Douglas, even as racist as many members of his own party? Among the range of politicians active in the nation in 1850s and 1860s, where would you place Lincoln? In light of what he gradually did, in the face of a political and social environment where racism was rampant, in a world where white people had to be persuaded to accept black rights in their own interest, more than in black people's interest, we would be hard-pressed to be satisfied with the term unless the accuser abandoned the words "was" or "is" and spoke of degrees in a historical context of where and when. An important consideration in that discussion relates to motive—Lincoln and true racists of the time used the "N" word. Surely, however, it makes some difference whether it is used thoughtlessly or in malice. There is a difference between being kicked and being tripped over.

I seek to supply such historical context by focusing on three major documents used to discover the nature of Lincoln's behavior in matters of race: his letter to Horace Greeley of August 18,

1862; his colonization proposals; and his August 14, 1862, meeting with "a deputation of Negroes." The question demands a thorough investigation for both contemporary and historical reasons. As the nation's most prominent icon, Lincoln stands for what we want to think about ourselves. Politicians and private citizens wrap themselves in Lincoln's persona—unless they are so hostile to everything he stands for that they reject him out of hand, but the Lincoln haters are small in number—they do not even include the Ku Klux Klan.[6] Almost everyone else, worldwide, wants to get right with Lincoln, so it is very important to get Lincoln right.

There may also be an ethical imperative. Immanuel Kant argues that we should treat each other as ends in themselves and not as means to our ends. Far too often, as most of the Lincoln discussion reveals, writers and speakers line up Lincoln to march in their parade, to substantiate their arguments, treating him as the same kind of partisan that they are. It seems a close question, but I believe we owe the dead a different fate: to try to reveal them as they would reveal themselves in moments of complete honesty and as they, and we, would have our stories told, as molders and victims of a time and place. Make no mistake, the dead have almost certainly lied about themselves from time to time; the historian's job includes catching those prevarications, putting them in full context. There are few (if any) circumstances whereby our duty becomes the creation of a story about the past that hides a complex world behind a slogan.

The famous letter Lincoln wrote to Horace Greeley in August 1862 provides a useful baseline, revealing Lincoln's views on emancipation. This letter is perhaps the most frequently cited document to attack Lincoln's reputation as the Great Emancipator. Emancipation is the lowest rung on the ladder to equal justice. It does not depend on commitment to racial equality, although it is, of course, indispensable to achieving that end. To deny Lincoln's commitment to the first step truly rejects Lincoln's egalitarian credentials. If one can minimize or refute Lincoln's commitment to emancipation, the whole case for his egalitarian ideals falls.

Two major attacks form the basis for challenging Lincoln's commitment to equal justice at step one. At one side of this accusation is the claim that he wanted to keep blacks as slaves; at the other is the insistence that his motive in freeing slaves was not the good of the slaves, but protection of the white people's

Union. For good measure, critics throw in the smear that Lincoln really freed very few, if any, slaves. A variation on this theme is the argument that it was really the slaves, not the president, who brought freedom.[7] In whole or in part, all these accusations fail.

Lincoln's letter to Greeley was a response to an editorial of August 19, 1862, that appeared in the most widely read newspaper in the nation, the *New York Tribune*. In essence, Greeley told the president that he should immediately free the slaves. Lincoln answered this point by saying,

> "As to the policy I 'seem to be pursuing' . . . I have not meant to leave anyone in doubt. I would save the Union. I would save it the shortest way under the Constitution. . . . If there be those who would not save the Union unless they could at the same time save slavery I do not agree with them. If there be those who would not save the Union unless they could at the same time destroy slavery, I do not agree with them. My paramount object in this struggle is to save the Union, and is not either to save or destroy slavery. If I could save the Union without freeing *any* slave I would do it, and if I could save the Union by freeing *all* the slaves I would do that and if I could do it by freeing some and leaving others alone I would also do that. I have here stated my purpose according to my view of *official* duty; and I intend no modification of my oft expressed *personal* wish that all men every where could be free.[8] [emphases original]

What have we here? A declaration that Lincoln chooses the Union over freeing the slaves? An assertion that freeing slaves and saving the Union are options in a zero sum game? Looking closely at the letter, how do these charges fare?

First, note the timing—August 22. Lincoln had already decided, at least a month before, that he would free the slaves. He told two cabinet secretaries of his decision on July 21 and the full cabinet July 22. He was withholding a public announcement until some Union army won a victory. Lincoln was preparing public opinion for an event that was going to happen. In service of this goal, he was also holding public discussions with a religious delegation, debating with them the possible consequences of emancipation, showing the public that he had considered conservative, as well as liberal, views. He also engaged a delegation of African Americans in a discussion about colonization—a meeting soon to be discussed.[9]

The environment of the Greeley letter exuded propagandizing—a task that Lincoln knew very well how to do, and had to do to lead the nation. The letter expressed Lincoln's views but in a context where the largest possible audience would hear things it wanted to hear: the Union is the reason that emancipation will happen; black freedmen will not swarm north to take white jobs or challenge the social order. That was a significant point in a society heavily tinged with racism, passionate for saving the white man's Union. Lincoln knew that emancipating because slavery hurt black people inspired few followers unless they could also see that ending slavery helped white people. He did not have to persuade blacks or abolitionists of emancipation's benefits. He did need to attract moderate and conservative whites to the cause. He might easily have called antebellum history to his side here. Antislavery feelings grew hardly at all when abolitionists described the suffering of slaves. When the "Slave Power" challenged Northern liberties and institutions, a Republican Congress and president came to office.

The Greeley letter has often been used to contrast saving the Union with freeing the slaves. However, as the secessionists would have stated in 1860–1861 the Union that Lincoln wanted to preserve was a Union where slavery was in danger. That is why they left that union. Secessionists imagined that, with Republicans in charge of the government, Congress would foreclose expansion into the Caribbean. "Black Republicans" would forbid slavery from the territories in the west; those territories would become free states; those states would elect to Congress antislavery representatives and senators. A Republican-dominated congress would create an environment that would draw border states into the Northern economy—as deep Southerners feared was already happening in Kentucky. Seeing the handwriting on the wall, border slaveholders would sell their slaves to deep Dixie, further expanding Free Soil's domain and power. In short, the Union that Lincoln said was the foundation of his policies was a Union where slavery was imperiled. Even without a direct attack on the peculiar institution, Republicans would place slavery in the course of ultimate extinction.[10]

Another way of undermining the Lincoln image is to diminish the impact of the Emancipation Proclamation itself, arguing in essence that his Greeley letter revealed his limited view of emancipation's reach. Lerone Bennett quotes approvingly a Missouri antislavery man saying that the proclamation "did not . . . whatever it may otherwise accomplished at the time it was issued, liberate a single slave." Bennett himself says that the alleged charter of freedom "was not a real emancipation proclamation at all, and did not liberate African American slaves." As recently as 2000, a collection of scholarly articles asserted that the proclamation "freed only those slaves over whom the proclamation could have no immediate influence."[11]

These views seem to rest on a feeling that Lincoln should simply have done "the right thing." He should have awakened one morning and said, "Darn it, I'm going to free the slaves today." It seems to have been the president's wish that he could do just that. But he could not. He had taken what he called "the most solemn oath" to protect and defend the constitution. He could not do the right thing unless it was also the constitutional and lawful thing. As he told Greeley, his personal feelings had to yield to his constitutional duties.

Lincoln's commitment to the rule of law had deep foundations. It arose from a personal experience, gained strength from his faith that reason must triumph over passion as the source of democratic government and personal growth, found nurturance in his vocation as a lawyer, and was cemented in an environment where political rhetoric found its roots in constitutional debate.

The personal experience occurred when Lincoln was sixteen. One day in his presence, a bright and promising nineteen-year-old friend (a person very much like Lincoln himself), named Matthew Gentry, went insane. Lincoln never forgot Gentry. In 1844, he wrote a long poem about revisiting his childhood home. The poem begins as a melancholy reflection on the people who have died and abandoned the place, but then Lincoln changes directions: "But there is an object more of dread / Than ought the grave contains— / A human form with reason fled / While wretched life remains." Several stanzas follow as Lincoln muses on the horrors (the fascinating horrors?) of madness.[12]

Lincoln embraced reason also as a means of escaping the almost antiintellectual world of his parents. He taught himself geometry to learn to reason and calculate more carefully, and he entered the profession of the time most associated with reasoning and analysis. He did not drink alcohol, because it made him feel "flabby," as he put it. Two early speeches—one in 1839 and another in 1844, the year of the visit back home—attacked uncontrolled passion and celebrated the triumph of reason. He practiced law for a quarter of a century and was fully devoted to that work. Most of his political speeches rested on constitutional issues and argument, the debates with Douglas most notably. Presidential speeches emphasized constitutional issues.

Even if he wanted to, Lincoln was not free to leave constitutional moorings. The only legitimate reason for waging war was that the South had violated the Constitution by abandoning a lawfully created union and repudiating the results of a constitutional election. War necessities, which required Lincoln to suspend habeas corpus, call for a draft, raise money, and a host of other duties demanded constitutional justification. Emancipation fit perfectly onto the list of actions that the fundamental law had to validate. The president wanted slavery to die, but he was President, not private citizen, Lincoln. When Secretary of Treasury Salmon Chase asked that Lincoln expand the coverage of the Emancipation Proclamation, Lincoln replied,

> Knowing your great anxiety that the emancipation proclamation shall now be applied to certain parts of Virginia and Louisiana, which were exempted from it, last January, I state briefly what appear to me to be difficulties in the way of such a step. The original proclamation has no Constitutional or legal justification, except as a military measure. The exemptions were made because the military necessity did not apply to the exempted localities. Nor does that necessity apply to them now any more than it did then— If I take the step must I not do so, without the argument of military necessity, and so, without any argument, except the one that I think the measure politically expedient, and morally right? Would I not thus give up all footing upon Constitution or law? Would I not thus be in the boundless field of absolutism? Could this pass unnoticed, or unresisted? Could it fail to be perceived that without any further stretch, I might do the same in Delaware, Maryland, Kentucky, Tennessee, and Missouri; and even change any law in any state? Would not many of our own friends shrink away appalled? Would it not lose us the elections, and with them, the very cause we seek to advance?[13]

Lincoln took seriously his commitment to acting constitutionally—not only because he was personally committed to doing so, but also because there was a large constituency out there who would punish him if he did not.

Lincoln was limited by the Constitution in emancipating the slaves, but how far did that limitation restrict the number of slaves the proclamation reached? On January 1, 1863, it freed approximately 2.9 million of the nearly 4 million slaves in the South. That represents 74 percent of the slaves in the nation and 82 percent of the slaves in the Confederacy. Did the proclamation free them right away? No more than the Declaration of Independence made the colonies independent. But from the moment of declaring and proclaiming, both documents established the baseline of victory in war. No one would retreat from this line. The colonists pledged their lives, their fortunes, and their sacred honor—Lincoln pledged that slaves would be "henceforth and forever, free." The army that had been called on to save the Union instantly became an army of liberation. Saving the Union had become officially linked to freeing the slave, as Lincoln had forecast to Greeley.

As soon as the ink was dry on the proclamation, Lincoln began to diminish greatly his support for a controversial plan: the colonization of freed African Americans to Africa. Nothing so clearly demarks Lincoln's racial vision, at least according to his critics, as colonization. Bennett's *Forced into Glory: Abraham Lincoln's White Dream* builds its major case on the president's "plan" for a nation of white, not black, people. Bennett calls this "ethnic cleansing." From a polemicist like Bennett, this phase shocks but does not surprise. It is nevertheless surprising that one of the most respected historians of the Civil War era, Eric Foner, also uses the phrase, "ethnic cleansing" to characterize Lincoln's colonization proposals.[14] In a *New York Times* review of William Miller's *Lincoln's Virtues,* Foner writes, "Lincoln's support of a policy that might be called the ethnic cleansing of America was no transitory fancy." A case might be made that the Indian policy of the United States resembles the Bosnian horror, but applying it to colonization is, in a moral sense as well as a question of fact, staggeringly out of place. It demeans the experience of Bosnian and other people of Yugoslavia, trivializing what they went through. It is much like calling a gangland murder a "holocaust." Whatever the possible costs of a colonization program might have been, it did not involve corpses, and, in a voluntary process, there were not likely to be any in the future.

Historians still must take some of the blame for obscuring colonization's extent and meaning. The first reason is that writers on the subject have never clearly asked the simple question "How many people did Lincoln want to colonize?" Surely to call colonization "ethnic cleansing" requires that at least thousands of people (probably a substantial portion of the targeted population) be sent, or terrorized, away.

But, because we have not tried to discover how many African Americans were involved, it has been impossible to know whether Lincoln's policy approaches, even in numbers—laying aside "atrocity"—what most people understand as "ethnic cleansing." Of course, what was deep in the president's mind can never be extracted. We can, however, look to see how many times he spoke of colonizing and how many African Americans he actually helped to colonize to get some idea.

This seems sensible, but another problem arises. It is not always clear what people in Lincoln's world meant when they said colonize the blacks or how many were to go. Some people used the ominous word "deportation." Thomas Jefferson, whom Lincoln quoted on this point without comment, used that word. In his Cooper Union address, Lincoln quoted the third president as saying, "It is still within our power to direct the process of emancipation, and deportation, peaceably, and in such slow degrees, as that evil will wear off insensibly."[15] Henry Clay favored forced colonization, and Lincoln praised Clay for his support of colonization.[16] As to Lincoln, though, the evidence is very strong that he never advocated force in connection with colonization. Every time he said the "C" word, he was silent about its dimensions. In the Collected Works he mentioned "colonization" twenty-seven times. In only one case did Lincoln even imply that coercion might be part of his view of colonization.

In his First Annual Message, Lincoln considered what would happen to slaves who might become free in two circumstances: (1) under the First Confiscation Act or (2) under state action. In the following densely phrased paragraph, the president said,

> I recommend that Congress provide for accepting such persons from such States, according to some mode of valuation, in lieu, *pro tanto,* of direct taxes, or upon some other plan to be agreed on with such States respectively; that *such persons, on such acceptance by the general government, be at once deemed free; and that, in any event, steps be taken for colonizing both classes, (or the one first mentioned, if the other shall not be brought into existence,) at some place, or places, in a climate congenial to them. It might be well*

to consider, too,—whether the free colored people already in the United States
could not, so far as individuals may desire, be included in such colonization.[17]

This seems to suggest that people freed by the chances of war
might face "steps be[ing] taken" for their colonization and that free
blacks could be colonized if they wanted to. But if the persons freed
by the First Confiscation Act (slaves of disloyal masters being used to
help the rebellion directly) were free, did that not mean that they
were free to choose to be, or not to be, colonized or deported? What
were the steps that would be taken? Faced with these vagaries, it
seems very unlikely that Lincoln favored forced deportation.

Lincoln himself, after his quotation from Jefferson, used "deportation" one more time. That was in his Second Annual Message.
Here, by December 1, 1862, however, Lincoln's commitment to voluntary colonization was fixed. He used the word "deportation," but
only in the context of using "voluntary" specifically several times.
Furthermore, in a cabinet meeting on September 24, 1862, when
Attorney General Bates spoke in favor of compulsory deportation,
Lincoln "objected emphatically." He said, "Their emigration must
be voluntary and without expense to themselves."[18]

As to the question of how many were to engage in colonization, matters are much clearer. Despite the fact that few people of
the time defined how many they foresaw being colonized, or
what they meant about by the term or its synonym, it is clear
that, by its very nature Lincoln's colonization would be small. It
was voluntary, a sure sign of limited numbers. Furthermore Lincoln spent only $38,000 of the $600,000 that Congress funded
for colonization; the reason for spending so little was that few
blacks were inspired to leave the United States. The president
knew that, if he had been listening to the political discourse of
the time—a highly probable course of action. He knew also that
their abolitionist supporters in the main rejected colonization.
Any effort to force blacks from the country would have required
far more effort than Lincoln could afford in the midst of war. The
logistical problems in moving roughly 4 million people across the
ocean were at least formidable.[19] Finally, it is very hard for another
reason to see Lincoln or anyone else forcibly colonizing blacks. The
numbers of black soldiers had been growing, openly, and quietly,
since the summer of 1862. The recruiting process began informally

when escaping slaves jumped into Ben Butler's lines at Fortress Monroe. Butler called them "contraband" and used them for hard or dirty labor around the camp. Some were returned to loyal masters by conservative commanders; more liberal ones took them in. As Union forces moved south, however, there were fewer owners who could persuasively claim to be loyal. The first sable soldiers we know of appeared in the fall of 1861, as Jim Lane in Kansas acquired them to help in the border wars. The number kept growing and became more "official." On April 3, 1862, General Hunter wrote to Secretary of War Stanton, asking for 50,000 rifles and 50,000 pairs of "scarlet pantaloons." Hunter quickly followed with his proclamation freeing the slaves in the Sea Island areas. Lincoln rejected that emancipation but said nothing about Hunter's recruiting. The general went on recruiting the "First South Carolina Colored Regiment." Reporters heard about this and raised the issue in their newspapers. Worried border state congressman Charles Wycliffe of Kentucky asked for an inquiry. Stanton denied that he was involved but asked Hunter to provide an explanation about the alleged arming of fugitive slaves. Hunter answered in early July 1862. He denied that there were any fugitive slaves in his department. There was, however, a regiment of loyal men whose former masters were "fugitive rebels." Hunter lamented that there was no fugitive master law. The deserted men of the regiment were, however, going to rely on a part of the treason law that allowed them to "pursue, capture and bring back those persons of whose protection they have been thus suddenly bereft."[20]

As Lincoln increased his commitment to emancipation, he kept the possibility of black soldiers in mind. At first, he restricted the use of blacks to being laborers. In the preliminary Emancipation Proclamation, he asked that freed blacks think in terms of colonization. One hundred days later, in the final proclamation, he asked that blacks be "received into the armed service of the United States to garrison forts, positions, stations and other places, and to man vessels of all sorts in said service." This document has received most of the spotlights. As far back as July 17, 1862, however, Congress approved and the president signed two similar laws. The Militia Act said that "the President. . . . Is hereby authorized to receive into the service of the United States, [African Americans] for the purpose of constructing entrenchments, or performing camp service or any other labor, or *any military service or naval service for which they may be found competent.*" Furthermore, on that day the Second Confiscation Act echoed, "the President is authorized to employ as many persons of African descent as he may deem necessary and proper for the suppression of this rebellion . . . for this purpose *he may organize and use them in such manner as he may judge best for the public welfare"* [my emphases]. As the war proceeded, approximately 200,000 African Americans served in Union forces.[21] Even while Lincoln was pleading for emancipation with colonization he was allowing blacks an alternative path to take away from slavery, and from colonization itself.

Lincoln did not publicly advocate colonization after January 1, 1863—the day the Emancipation Proclamation went into effect—but he did advocate it by helping to organize two colonization efforts, the Chirique project, led by Senator Samuel Pomeroy, and the Ile de Vache project. The first of these failed because Nicaragua and Haiti—the two countries targeted to receive the five thousand–plus colonists that Senator Pomeroy said he had assembled—changed their minds. The second came a cropper when the president was persuaded that the white men who undertook the lead in these projects were enriching themselves at the expense of the blacks and the government. It was then, in July 1864, that his secretary John Hay said, "I am glad the President has sloughed off that idea of colonization. I have always thought it a hideous and barbarous humbug." The entire project of government-supported colonization fell apart by September 1864, when Congress repealed the laws funding the project.[22]

There is no doubt that Lincoln was devoted to colonization for a long time. One has only to read the speeches in which he advocated gradual compensated emancipation with colonization to feel that devotion. In May 1862, the president asked the border states, "Will you not embrace it? So much good has not been done, by one effort in all past time, as, in the providence of God, it is now your high privilege to do. May the vast future not have to lament that you have neglected it."[23] In June Lincoln pleaded, "Our common country is in great peril, demanding the loftiest views, and boldest action to bring its speedy relief. Once relieved, its form of government is saved to the world; it's beloved history, and cherished memories, are vindicated; and its happy future fully assured, and others, the privilege [*sic*] is given, to assure that happiness, and swell that grandeur, and to link your own names therewith forever."[24] Despite this passion, at no time, with one

possible and ambiguous exception, did he propose to force anyone who did not want to leave the country to do so.

In his widely condemned meeting with the "Negro Deputies"
in August 1862, Lincoln certainly did try to persuade blacks to
go. He used about every rhetorical trick he knew: guilt, a nation's
gratitude, a chance to emulate the nation's founders, the opportunity to change racial prejudices in America, to improve conditions in the outside world, and to benefit themselves as well.

Historians who at least find this meeting distasteful lay the
general charge against it of being "patronizing," but I think we
should try to look dispassionately, quieting for a while the outrage about past national failings that springs from living in the
early twenty-first century.[25] Lincoln did not treat these delegates
with contempt, and he did not reveal the "soft racism" of addressing them in a tone different from one he would use to a white
delegation. He did not act as though they should be treated with
kid gloves. Finally, almost everything he said was true. The conditions he described may have been lamentable, but they were in fact
the conditions of racism in the United States on August 14, 1862.
Lincoln did not endorse them; he sought to change them.

It is important to note who the delegates were. They were representatives of the "Anglo-American Institute for the Improvement of Industry and Art" visiting the White House to discuss
with Lincoln the subject of colonization. They seem to have
come to the meeting to oppose Lincoln's colonization projects. In
light of this opportunity, Lincoln presented his strongest brief in
favor. The delegates do not seem to have been upset at all by
what they heard. In fact, their leader, Edward Thomas, wrote to
Lincoln forty-eight hours later that, when they arrived at the
meeting, "We were entirely hostile to the movement until all the
advantages were so ably brought to our view by you and we believe that our friends and co-laborers for our race [in Boston, New
York, and Philadelphia] will when the movement is explained by
us to them join heartily in sustaining such a movement."[26] Soon,
however, opposition flared up. The American Colonization Society opposed Lincoln's proposal as offering only menial jobs as
miners in the Caribbean colonies while going to Africa gave
greater autonomy. Most other black Americans, Frederick Douglass leading, opposed the meeting and its ideals, though it might
be noted that Martin Dulany, Henry Highland Garnett, and even

one of Douglass's sons favored colonization. After hearing Lincoln's argument, this group did not. That switch in views may have persuaded the president to believe that he was on the right track on colonization. After the protests quieted, however, the deputation changed their minds again, rejecting Lincoln's plan.[27]

What exactly did Lincoln say to these delegates? He told them that money had been set aside by Congress ($100,000 for District of Columbia blacks and $500,000 for blacks freed by the army) to aid in colonizing them. He then posed the question "Why should they leave this country?" and answered it: "You and we are different races. We have between us a broader difference than exists between almost any other two races. Whether it is right or wrong I need not discuss, but this physical difference is a great disadvantage to us both, as I think your race suffer very greatly, many of them by living among us, while ours suffer from your presence." As a picture of race relations in the mid-nineteenth century this is quite accurate. It does not state Lincoln's opinions of right or wrong. It does not seem to reflect the way he treated black people that he personally met. Douglass and Harriett Tubman both testified to the president's absence of race prejudice when he met them. Don Fehrenbacher has argued that Lincoln had little personal race prejudice.[28] Lincoln was simply stating the situation as he saw it. It was "a fact with which we have to deal. I cannot alter it if I would." That has a suspicious tone about it, but then he showed his connection to these black men by saying, "It is a fact about which we feel alike, you and I."

He knew blacks had suffered from slavery—"perhaps the greatest wrong inflicted on any people"—but the injustices of slavery abided in freedom. "[E]ven when you cease to be slaves, you are yet far removed from being placed on an equality with the white race . . . on this broad continent, not a single man of your race is made the equal of a single man of ours. Go where you are treated the best, and the ban is still upon you." That was the America in which all the people there knew they lived.[29]

Lincoln knew, as did almost every person at least in the North, that many of the founders of the nation had been right when they lamented the impact of slavery on white masters. Jefferson referred to it in *Notes on the State of Virginia:* "There must doubtless be an unhappy influence on the manners of our people produced by the existence of slavery among us." For at least a generation before war broke out, it had been the impact of slavery on white people that built Northern anger against expansion into a great war. Northerners were also persuaded that it was the influence of slavery on Southern whites that led them to secede and to fire on the flag. Opinion was almost unanimous that without slavery, and hence the presence of slaves in the nation, there would have been no war. Slavery had been the "witch at the christening" in 1787, and her influence had grown to deadly, bloody proportions.[30]

So again Lincoln was stating the obvious when he told the delegation that the "evil" impact of the institution on white men had led to "white men cutting one another's throats, none knowing how far it will extend. . . . But for your race among us there could not be war, although many men engaged on either side do not care for you one way or the other." To emphasize his point Lincoln repeated, "Without the institution of Slavery and the colored race as a basis, the war could not have an existence."[31] Douglass blasted Lincoln's argument that blaming the black people for civil war was like a horse thief blaming his thievery on the existence of horses. The true culprits were the masters of slaves, but Douglass was mistaking immediate causes for root causes. No one could responsibly have said that slaves directly caused the war, but it remains undeniable that their presence, as slaves, unleashed the irrepressible conflict.[32]

Yet Lincoln suggested that some African Americans could lead others to greater freedom. He made a distinction, as before, between free blacks and slaves, but this time there was nothing ominous in the distinction. There were free blacks who did not see what they might gain by colonization, but slaves who would be freed if they were colonists would be more willing to go. Lincoln understood that free blacks were more inclined to stay in this country than were their enslaved colleagues. But, Lincoln told them, "This is (I speak in no unkind sense) an extremely selfish view of the case."

What he asked the free blacks to do was to help the enslaved blacks to freedom by showing white people that blacks would colonize outside the boundaries of the nation. Furthermore, the free blacks were better people to rely on, for, "if we deal with those who are not free at the beginning and whose intellects are clouded by slavery, we have very poor materials to start with. . . . It is exceedingly important that we have men at the beginning capable of thinking as white men, and not those who have been systematically oppressed."

Therefore, Lincoln was urging these free blacks to take on two roles as exemplars. They were to show recently emancipated slaves that colonization was a proper choice for them and their families. Free black colonizers would also serve another purpose. Their commitment and their presumed success as colonizers would "give a start to white people" by letting them believe that, just like free blacks, emancipated blacks would seek their future in foreign lands. There was also implicit in Lincoln's policy another vision of perhaps greater significance that would impress whites and serve blacks. In new lands, colonizers would demonstrate the benefits of free labor, building not only the fortunes but also the character that free labor was seen to inspire.[33]

In doing all this, blacks would make sacrifices, but they would be helping their enslaved brothers and sisters; that would compensate for the discomforts of colonizing. George Washington, for example, had endured sacrifices because "he was engaged in benefiting his race—something for the children of his neighbors, having none of his own." In making this appeal Lincoln seems to have lapsed, as he rarely did, into condescension: "For the sake of your race," he said, "you should sacrifice something of your present comfort for the purpose of being as grand in that respect as the white people." This statement does grate on modern sensibilities, but we need to read that last line with an earlier discussion in mind, for, when Lincoln told free blacks that they should lead the colonization enterprise, he had explained that "[i]t is exceedingly important that we have men at the beginning *capable of thinking as white men,* and not those who have been systematically oppressed." It seems quite clear here that Lincoln thought free blacks were "capable of thinking as white men." His view of black abilities was environmental and not the frozen view of racial difference adopted by true racists. Free blacks could think as free white men thought; slave blacks could not. When slavery ended, ex-slaves could prove and expand their abilities to act as whites acted.

The president then tried to sell them on the place they would go. He first mentioned Liberia and spoke of the success gained there where, despite troubles and the deaths of some settlers, "their offspring outnumber those deceased." Nevertheless, he understood that many objected to moving as far as Africa and so proposed a colony in Central America. The place had advantages: it was on a "great line of travel" and had many natural resources, among them the climate "with your native land–thus being suited to your physical condition." There were harbors there and "rich coal mines" that would "afford an opportunity to the inhabitants for immediate employment till they get ready to settle permanently in their homes."

It was true that land speculators would make a profit on this emigration, but that was inescapable—whites, like blacks "look to their own self interests." And the immigrants could turn the speculators gains into a gain of their own. "You are intelligent, and know that success does not as much depend upon external help as on self-reliance." In any event Lincoln's appeal failed. Colonization died as Congress cut off funds even as Lincoln lost interest in a project that he had once so warmly embraced. War accelerated the timetable of emancipation, but the war was won as much because of Lincoln's leadership as any other factor. It ultimately did not matter that few African Americans chose to leave their country.

This meeting with the "deputation of Negroes" saw Lincoln state that whites and blacks were equally capable of rational thought, assert the wide and deep racism of whites, and urge the advantages of a colonizing experience that would allow blacks to relive the experience most critical to the thought of the age—people moving to new lands, exercising their energy and ingenuity to create the character and the prosperity on which ordered liberty thrived.

Each of these three documents, used to affirm Lincoln's antiblack bias, turns out in the end to be more complex. Lincoln was not a one-dimensional man: his occasional "racist" remarks revealed everything from the instinctual bias of a childhood in proslavery territory to the careful efforts of a subtle politician to achieve a radical goal by wrapping it in conservative bunting. As a result of Abraham Lincoln's efforts, slavery—the foundation of war and American racism—began its death march. It was a march that began with the debates with Douglas and was followed by Lincoln's election, his request to the border states to end slavery, his signing every act of Congress hostile to slavery, his first Emancipation Proclamation, the second Emancipation Proclamation, the use of African American troops, the move to get reconstructing states to adopt black voting, the demand for the Thirteenth Amendment, not to mention being the first American president to invite blacks to the White House, and publicly calling Douglass "my friend." Worse things have come from "racists."

KEVIN R. C. GUTZMAN

ABRAHAM LINCOLN, JEFFERSONIAN

The Colonization Chimera

Since his own day, Abraham Lincoln, the sixteenth president of the United States, has been known as a follower of
Thomas Jefferson.[1] In one sense, this is ironic: Lincoln's devotion to the Whig Party of Henry Clay set him squarely in
opposition to all of the basic elements of Jefferson's political
legacy.[2] Well, not quite all of them. The second sentence of
the Declaration of Independence was Lincoln's guiding principle. As he put it, the Declaration "set up a standard maxim
for free society, which should be familiar to all, and revered
by all," in America and elsewhere.[3] *To that extent,* Lincoln is
properly understood as a devoted acolyte of the third president, the Master of Monticello.[4] This, however, is not the sole
element of Lincoln's debt to Jefferson.

Jefferson's conception of American nationhood and Lincoln's had much in common. One of the elements their vi-
sions of America shared was a desire to see the population
of European stock occupy the bulk of North America without African intermixture. The means for achieving this end
was to be colonization of the enslaved Africans—who, in
the minds of both Jefferson and Lincoln, remained essentially African despite their long residence in America.

For Jefferson, the facts of the Africans' essential for-
eignness and their irreducible humanity caused no end of

consternation. He hoped finally to be rid of the problem by deporting them, sending them somewhere, anywhere, outside Virginia (or outside the United States, depending on the context in which the matter came to mind). For Lincoln, as William Lee Miller puts it, the political environment of Illinois required (even if it would have come from him anyway—a question to which we cannot know the answer) concession of the nearly universally accepted points concerning the "necessity" of racial hierarchy and the proper superordination of the white race—the voters' race. Miller concludes that what Lincoln should be noted for is his insistence on the basic humanity of the enslaved race.[5] The concessions and the insistence could be reconciled, however, through the Jeffersonian mechanism: colonization of blacks abroad.

Neither Jefferson nor Lincoln understood colonization to be a hateful policy.[6] Rather, Lincoln seems to have followed his predecessor (at least until 1862) in holding colonization the best that could be done for blacks and whites alike. According to Lincoln scholar Harry V. Jaffa, advocacy of colonization was a glowing tribute in a day when blacks' capacities were routinely downplayed; as Jaffa notes, the idea that blacks were capable of establishing a free society implied a type of equality with whites that most Americans rejected. Yet Lincoln, like Jefferson, was certain that this equality could only be exercised in separation from whites.[7] In holding to this Jeffersonian view, Lincoln was unlike many of his black contemporaries, who certainly did understand the desire for a Lly-white America as a racist urge. As Jefferson and Lincoln understood matters, however, their compatriots' hostility to blacks was a given; the statesman's task was to operate within a set of political constraints to reach the optimal outcome practicable. Thus, while Frederick Douglass and others may have decried his having done it,[8] Lincoln took steps to implement this program while he was president.

Jefferson and Lincoln have been the objects of extraordinary attention. Lincoln, it is said, has been the subject of more books than anyone save Christ and Napoleon I, and Jefferson scholarship is also quite voluminous. In recent decades, much of the scholarship on the two great American symbol-statesmen has focused on their racial attitudes and race-related policies; as George

M. Fredrickson notes, the Lincoln scholarship has been divided roughly between those who describe Lincoln as a nineteenth-century precursor to the civil rights movement and those who find much in his career that is marked by racism.[9] Although Fredrickson endeavors to deduce Lincoln's authentic attitudes and goals from his lengthy written record and the recorded observations of those who came into contact with him, it is perhaps fair to note that division concerning Lincoln's true views has in no sense attenuated in the years since Fredrickson's description. At root, the problem is one of falsifiability: how does one disprove the thesis that Lincoln all along acted as a master wire-puller, keeping his own counsel and calculatedly saying things he did not really believe for political effect? Jefferson, similarly, is the subject of a prize-winning volume with a title that neatly sums up the difficulty of divining his own actual racial views: *American Sphinx*.[10]

Does it really matter what these two men thought or what their confidential motives were? Far more significant, it seems to me, is what they did, wrote, and said as political actors. Of those, we have extensive evidence. This chapter examines the outward men, leaving it to a greater authority to pry into their hearts.

Jefferson's political principles were undergirded by an insistence on eliminating vested privilege and legal distinctions—among white Americans. Thus, most notably, Jefferson insisted that primogeniture and entail, the feudal land tenures governing inheritance of about two-thirds of the land in Virginia and an unknown proportion of the Old Dominion's slaves, be abolished.[11] He was also primarily responsible for a change in Virginia law governing intestate estates that put female heirs on an equal footing with male.

In this way, Jefferson hoped and helped both to make Virginia's families more equal and to make Virginia's sexes more equal. Through his Virginia Statute for Religious Freedom, which his associate James Madison pushed to adoption in the General Assembly, Jefferson also helped to abolish the hoary distinction between devotees of the established religion and religious dissenters; so proud was he of this statute, in fact, that Jefferson asked for it to be memorialized on his gravestone.

Jefferson's insistence on self-government for Virginians was based on his, and the rest of the Virginia elite's, peculiar understanding of

Virginia's history. First laid out systematically in Richard Bland's 1766 pamphlet "An Inquiry into the Rights of the British Colonies, Intended as an Answer to the Regulations Lately Made Concerning the Colonies," this version of Virginia's past held that Virginia's first settlers had established their society with their own money and through their own efforts.[12] Because man had a natural right to emigrate, Bland asserted, members of the new society in eastern North America found themselves completely free to establish whatever type of government they preferred.

As it happened, Bland went on, Virginia's first English settlers chose to ask the kings of England also to serve as kings of America. From that point, Virginians had a contractual relationship with the English—then British—crown, and the monarch was obliged to defend their rights as necessary. This history had much to recommend it in the context of the Imperial Crisis of the 1760s and 1770s, and Bland seems to have been persuaded by his own argument. Jefferson certainly was, too: Bland's account became the basis of Jefferson's "A Summary View of the Rights of British America," his account of Virginia's constitution in *Notes on the State of Virginia,* and his draft Declaration of Independence.[13]

In Jefferson's hands, the common-law account of Virginians' rights and of the Old Dominion's place in the world took on a distinctly racial cast. It was particular families who inherited the rights that were at issue between the crown and the colony; it was particular families who had inherited the rights to the defense of which English kings had pledged themselves and their heirs; it was a particular people that staked these claims. Throughout his career, Jefferson would continue to hold to the notion that the Virginians were a specific race of people; blacks who happened to live in Virginia, whether free or enslaved, were not part of that conception.

It comes as no surprise, then, that the most notable area in which Jefferson did not take significant action to equalize the favored and the disfavored in Virginia society was the one in which the inequality was most flagrant: the subjugation of slaves to their masters.[14] Yet, as old people are prone to do, Jefferson tried in retirement to put his record in the best light. In a letter written to Edward Coles, a young Albemarle County neighbor, in 1814, Jefferson claimed that, in his early days as a member of the colonial House of Burgesses, he had supported an initiative intended to reduce the severity of Virginia's laws regarding slavery.[15] As he told it, young man Jefferson had joined in planning this initiative with Bland, one of the most eminent burgesses, and then had seconded the older man's motion. In Jefferson's account, the house treated Bland very roughly in response to their foray; Jefferson told Coles that, despite his hopes for an amelioration of slaves' condition, the public silence on the matter had led him to assume that the public was generally apathetic on the issue. Prolonged absence from the commonwealth during the 1780s had left Jefferson unable to gauge the public sentiment in this regard, and Coles's letter was the first indication he had received that perhaps his hopes concerning the younger generation's sentiments would be fulfilled.

What Jefferson omitted from this account was the story of his writings and private musings on the racial question. Jefferson's record on the question of whites and blacks joining in an equal citizenship in the United States of America was clear: for more than four decades, he consistently held, with varying degrees of certainty, that it was impossible. His reasons never changed, and his favored remedy never varied. Jefferson was the first notable scientific racist in American history, and he was strongly committed to the idea that Africans and their descendants were inferior to whites in body and mind.[16] For that reason, and because he was certain that their freedom would lead to a race war bound to result in one race's destruction, Jefferson favored the deportation of blacks.

The *locus classicus* of Jefferson's thinking concerning the place of blacks in American society is his sole book, *Notes on the State of Virginia.*[17] Completed in 1781, while Jefferson was the governor of Virginia, this work originally served as a group of responses to queries posed by the secretary of the French legation at Philadelphia. Nevertheless, Jefferson's book must have far exceeded the expectations of that foreign functionary.[18] Rather than simply some disconnected jottings in response to a list of matter-of-fact questions concerning the physical attributes and arrangement of Virginia, Jefferson offered up a philosophical treatise on his native state; he catalogued its abundant natural resources, described its constitutional history and law, and guided readers on a journey into the labyrinthine psyche of his slaveholding republican society.

The most notorious passage of *Notes on the State of Virginia,* in which Jefferson dealt with the matter of slaves' place in Virginia society, came in response to the question of "the particular customs and manners that may happen to be received in that state."[19] He began with the commonsense observation that it is difficult for a resident of a state to know which of his nation's manners are idiosyncratic and which are merely manifestations of the ubiquitous. However, he said, "There must doubtless be an unhappy influence on the manners of our people produced by the existence of slavery among us.' Note here that it is not true, as many hostile commentators have insisted, that Jefferson was saying that the only notable thing about slavery in Virginia was the effect it had upon white Virginians. Rather, he was concerned to say what manners were peculiar to Virginia, and those that were concomitants of slavery in his state seemed likely to strike a Frenchman as peculiar.

In referring to slavery's effects "among us," Jefferson implied that the slaves were not to be numbered among "us"—that is, Virginians. That was precisely what he meant, for in Bland's account of Virginia, as understood by Jefferson, the slaves were not "African Americans" or "enslaved Americans," but a captive nation found among the white Virginians.[20] They were a separate race in both our sense (that is, they were not of European ancestry) and an older sense (pertaining to a given people, not necessarily coextensive with what we usually signify by the word "race," with a common heritage). This perception of the blacks as exotic was an essential predicate to Jefferson's ultimate prescription for Virginia's (and the United States') racial ills.

The effects of slavery upon the manners of the master race, in Jefferson's telling, were entirely negative:

> The whole commerce between master and slave is a perpetual exercise of the most boisterous passions, the most unremitting despotism on the one part, and degrading submissions on the other. Our children see this, and learn to imitate it. . . . The parent storms, the child looks on, catches the lineaments of wrath, puts on the same airs in the circle of smaller slaves, gives a loose to his worst passions, and thus nursed, educated, and daily exercised in tyranny, cannot but be stamped by it with odious peculiarities. The man must be a prodigy who can retain his manners and morals undepraved by such circumstances.

Jefferson, then, was certain—from his own experience, he *knew*—that owning slaves affected whites' fitness for republican citizenship. It acculturated the youngest of the masters for command and thus gave them "odious peculiarities." Rather than calm, thoughtful statesmen characterized by self-control, it made them into subjects of "boisterous passions."

Turning to slavery's effects upon the enslaved race, Jefferson continued:

> And with what execration should the statesman be loaded, who permitting one half the citizens thus to trample on the rights of the other, transforms those into despots, and these into enemies, destroys the morals of one part, and the amor patriae of the other. For if a slave can have a country in this world, it must be any other in preference to that in which he is born to live and labour for another: in which he must lock up the faculties of his nature, contribute as far as depends on his individual endeavours to the evanishment of the human race, or entail his own miserable condition on the endless generations proceeding from him.

In other words, one of the great evils attendant upon slavery was its tendency to alienate the slaves from the country they might otherwise be expected to grow to love: the country of their birth. Jefferson, substituting his train of reasoning for the slaves' actual sentiments, concluded that slaves could not possibly have the love of country natural to mankind; lacking this affection, the basis of social virtue, the blacks of Jefferson's experience/imagination lacked others, too. Here we encounter a characteristically Jeffersonian refusal to take responsibility: just as he shunted off moral responsibility for American slavery in his draft of the Declaration of Independence, declaring its existence in Virginia to be George III's fault, so here the slaves' incapacity for entering into Virginian citizenship, their lack of amor patriae, flowed naturally from their enslavement.[21]

What would Jefferson do about this state of affairs? Once more into the breach for the author of "A Summary View of the Rights of British America" and the first draft of the Declaration of Independence? No. Instead, Jefferson counseled that his countrymen and interested foreign observers "must be contented to hope" reforms would "force their way into every one's mind. I think a change already perceptible, since the origin of the present revolution." He hoped for "a total emancipation . . . with the consent of the masters, rather than by their extirpation."

What should follow that hoped-for emancipation? Supposing this large population of denizens of Virginia devoid of amor patriae were freed, what did Jefferson believe should become of them? One of the questions Jefferson answered in *Notes on the State of Virginia* concerned the administration of justice and the form of the laws. In responding to that question, he provided a selective description of the Revision of the Laws undertaken by the General Assembly in 1776, of which he had been one of the main authors.[22] Jefferson s description omitted the provision defining eligibility for citizenship, which expressly extended that status to "white" people.[23] Among the things Jefferson did say, however, was that the revision was intended to include a proposal "to emancipate all slaves born after passing the act." According to Paul Finkelman, if that bill ever actually was prepared, it has not survived; Finkelman says that the text first appeared in the *Notes*.[24] Yet, in light of the notoriety of the effort in question and the fact that the other members of the committee charged with drafting the revision were still alive when Jefferson published his *Notes*, it seems likely that Jefferson's account was true.

More interesting than the question of whether Jefferson's account is accurate is his description of the revisers' plan for the freedmen. After being left with their parents until they attained a certain age, he said, the freedmen were to be instructed in "tillage, arts or sciences, according to their geniuses," then colonized at the age of majority (eighteen for females and twenty-one for males) to "such place as the circumstances of the time should render most proper." Virginia would at that point "declare them a free and independant people" and grant them a defensive alliance.

To make up for the blacks' absence, Jefferson said, Virginia would have to scour the world for white workers willing to come take the places Virginia's former subjugated group had only recently vacated. Why was all this necessary? Jefferson imagined his reader wondering. Why eject the slaves, only to replace them with free whites, instead of simply learning to live and work alongside the slaves? There followed a remarkable passage in which Jefferson projected his own likely resentment onto his chattels, then pondered at length the reasons behind the disgust he felt at the presence of people of African descent in the Old Dominion:

> Deep rooted prejudices entertained by the whites; ten thousand recollections, by the blacks, of the injuries they have sustained; new provocations; the real distinctions which nature has made; and many other circumstances, will divide us into parties, and produce convulsions which will probably never end but in the extermination of the one or the other race.

Thus, Jefferson struck a pose of neutrality between the white Virginians and their black slaves. Although it was only the fruit of his imagination when he wrote it, Jefferson's prediction that emancipation would bring race war in its train soon would seem to receive awful validation from events in the French colony of St. Domingue.[25] Still, he left this idea aside as quickly as he raised it, because the reasons why blacks were unfit for society with whites, in his estimation, spurred him to more intensive, heartfelt ponderings:

> To these objections, which are political, may be added others, which are physical and moral. The first difference which strikes us is that of colour. Whether the black of the negro resides in the reticular membrane between the skin and scarf-skin, or in the scarf-skin itself; whether it proceeds from the colour of the blood, the colour of the bile, or from that of some other secretion, the difference is fixed in nature, and is as real as if its seat and cause were better known to us. And is this difference of no importance? Is it not the foundation of a greater or less share of beauty in the two races? Are not the fine mixtures of red and white, the expressions of every passion by greater or less suffusions of colour in the one, preferable to that eternal monotony, which reigns in the countenances, that immoveable veil of black which covers all the emotions of the other race? Add to these, flowing hair, a more elegant symmetry of form, their own judgment in favour of the whites, declared by their preference of them, as uniformly as is the preference of the Oran-ootan for the black women over those of his own species. The circumstance of superior beauty, is thought worthy attention in the propagation of our horses, dogs, and other domestic animals; why not in that of man?

Unsuspecting admirers of Jefferson are hard-pressed not to be dumbfounded at these ruminations, marked as they are at turns by the dilettante's careful flaunting of his scientific knowledge and by the master's honed revulsion toward, and subscription to absurd rumors about, his slaves. He leaps from implicit reliance upon the aesthetic theories of Edmund Burke—who taught, among other things, that the light was more beautiful than the dark—and the scientific teachings of his time to the question of the impression made by blacks' forms and faces, hair and odor.[26] Soon enough, he is launched into waters only the most extreme racists have seen fit to navigate since his day, and he does not spare the observation that orangutans prefer black women.[27] From this to Josiah Nott, not to say Thomas Dixon and Theodore Bilbo, is not very far at all—at least, not when it comes to content.[28] Jefferson's detached pose, however, is markedly at variance with the fiery partisanship of Dixon or the demagogic race-baiting of Bilbo. In that sense, just as Jefferson the amateur scientist paved the path for later scientific racists, the patrician Jefferson may be said to have set the stage for later demagogues' low-toned racial appeals.[29]

Yet, he did not stop there. Blacks, in his estimation, tended to have a stronger odor than whites because while whites tended to secrete more than blacks "by the kidneys," blacks tended to secrete more "by the glands of the skin." Then again, he said, perhaps the difference between whites' and blacks' pulmonary structures accounted for this difference. (One wonders whether the idea ever occurred to Jefferson that perhaps the hard labor to which he and his cousins drove them accounted for the tendency of black Virginia slaves to perspire more than whites.) Slaves were better able to stay up late after a hard day's labor and more prone to brave military and other hazards than whites, Jefferson said, which led him to hazard that blacks lacked the foresight necessary to recognize the drawbacks of bravery and carousing.

The next item in this recitation of antiblack myths is that blacks were more ardent after women, yet less loving of them; Jefferson followed this with the observation that blacks' "griefs [were] transient." ' In general," he concluded, "their existence appears to participate more of sensation than reflection," which explained why they tended to sleep "when abstracted from their diversions, and unemployed in labor."

After noting his slaves' "lack of forethought," Jefferson reflected on their lack of intellectual achievement. He would respect them for their intellectual gifts, he said, if he could find one "capable of tracing and comprehending the investigations of Euclid." Alas, "in imagination they [were] dull, tasteless, and anomalous." Although his essay frequently had veered into the area of natural aptitude, Jefferson at this point declared that, for some reason, "[i]t would be unfair to follow them to Africa for this investigation. We will consider them here, on the same stage with the whites, and where the facts are not apocryphal on which a judgment is to be formed." (Did Jefferson intend the reader to infer that the facts thus far adduced, such as that the "Oran-ootan" was attracted to black women, were not apocryphal?)

Only the most isolated of slave masters could even momentarily have overlooked the discrepancy between his own daily routine, and thus his opportunity for self-education, and that of his slaves. Jefferson admitted that, although "millions" of Africans had been transported to or born in America, the preponderance "ha[d] been confined to tillage." Yet, he added, a number of them had been exposed to the conversation of their masters and intercourse with the white population generally, so they might have improved themselves. Still, while the Indians had mastered certain types of art and oratory without these advantages, Jefferson had never encountered a single black who had painted, sculpted, or thought on a level above "plain narration." In simple language, Jefferson was saying that blacks were naturally doltish. When blacks interbred with whites, the minds and bodies of their offspring were the better for it.

Among the Romans, Jefferson averred, slavery was far harsher than African slavery in the United States. Despite this, he mused, the Romans' slaves made notable contributions to Latin and Greek science and letters. "But they were of the race of whites. It is not their condition, but nature, which has produced the distinction.—Whether further observation will or will not verify the conjecture, that nature has been less bountiful to them in the endowments of the head, I believe that in those of the heart she will be found to have done them justice. That disposition to theft with which they have been branded, must be ascribed to their situation." After making this concession, Jefferson noted that the slaves in Homer's Hellenic epics, being white, were able to maintain the strictest respect for the property rights of their owners. "The opinion, that [Africans] are inferior in the faculties of reason and imagination, must be hazarded with great diffidence," Jefferson then noted, for a faculty is very difficult to weigh, and what was at stake was a conclusion that could "degrade a whole race of men from the rank in the scale of beings which their Creator may perhaps have given them." With this caution at his back, he admitted, "I advance it therefore as a suspicion only, that the blacks, whether originally a distinct race, or made distinct by time and circumstances, are inferior to the whites in the endowments both of body and mind." "This unfortunate difference of colour," Jefferson continued, "and perhaps of faculty, is a powerful obstacle to the emancipation of these people." After all, he asked, what could be done with them if they were freed? The problem was not susceptible of so easy a solution as the one the Romans applied, for a Roman slave, "when made free, might mix with, without staining the blood of his master." In America, on the contrary, "he is to be removed beyond the reach of mixture."

These ideas were not those of a moment but remained in Jefferson's mind, as we have seen, for the balance of his life. Thus, for example, Secretary of State Jefferson wrote to the noted freeman Benjamin Banneker in 1791 to say, "No body wishes more than I do to see such proofs as you exhibit, that nature has given to our black brethren, talents equal to those of the other colors of men, and that the appearance of a want of them is owing merely to the degraded condition of their existence, both in Africa & America. I can add with truth, that no body wishes more ardently to see a good system commenced for raising the condition both of their body & mind to what it ought to be, as fast as the imbecility of their present existence, and other circumstances which cannot be neglected, will admit."[30] (Whether the noted statesman's assertions impressed his correspondent is unknown.) Similarly, President Jefferson wrote to the eminent Frenchman, the Abbé Grégoire, on February 25, 1809, with thanks for a collection of blacks' writings. "Be assured," the world's most eminent slaveholder wrote,

[N]o person living wishes more sincerely than I do, to see a complete refutation of the doubts I have myself entertained and expressed on the grade of understanding allotted to them by nature, and to find that in this respect they are on a par with ourselves. My doubts were the result of personal observation on the limited sphere of my own State, where the opportunities for the development of their genius were not favorable, and those of exercising it still less so. I expressed them therefore with great hesitation; but whatever be their degree of talent it is no measure of their rights.

He concluded by noting, "On this subject they are gaining daily in the opinions of nations, and hopeful advances are making towards their re-establishment on an equal footing with the other colors of the human family." Seemingly, Jefferson here wanted the Frenchman to understand both that slavery's existence—embarrassing to both the United States and republicanism as it was—could be traced at least in part to the whites' estimation of blacks' natural capacities and that he personally hoped to see it brought to an end. In passing, he also implicitly discountenanced the notion, floated in his *Notes on the State of Virginia,* of blacks' separate place in the animal kingdom.[31]

The ideas expressed in the *Notes* repeatedly affected Jefferson's conduct in high office, as well, both as regarded domestic affairs and as it related to foreign policy. Thus, for example, President Jefferson was responsible for instituting the United States' long-held posture of hostile nonrecognition toward the Republic of Haiti, and he even went so far as to offer Napoleon aid in reconquering that former French colony; a freedmen's republic near the United States' coast was simply too much for Jefferson to bear.[32] A second notable illustration may be found in Jefferson's response to Gabriel's Rebellion. In 1800, as the country lurched toward its ultimate transition from Federalist to Republican governance, president-to-be Jefferson was confronted by a horrible turn of events in his own home state. As Governor James Monroe, a Jefferson lieutenant, informed him, slaves in the vicinity of Richmond had been discovered to have been plotting, and actually trying to implement, the overthrow of the commonwealth.[33] Several of them were identified, tried, and hanged; as Monroe reported, quite a number yet awaited execution, and the notion of the state most associated in the public mind with the Jeffersonian party hanging scores of slaves just as the Republicans assumed power in Washington struck Monroe as dreadful—at least, from a public relations point of view. He wanted to show leniency to those only peripherally involved in the conspiracy.[34]

Jefferson wrote Governor Monroe to say, "Surely the legislature would pass a law for their exportation, the proper measure on this & all similar occasions?"[35] Eventually, legislators begged Monroe to acquire an appropriate place to resettle conspirators and traitors in Africa or Latin America.[36] They also finally resolved that Monroe should correspond with President Jefferson about locating a foreign receptacle for free blacks who might voluntarily relocate from the Old Dominion. Monroe dutifully communicated this idea to Jefferson.[37] In response, Jefferson first asked rhetorically whether Virginia might not purchase appropriate lands in the United States' western territories.[38] No, he decided, that was probably "a more expensive provision than the H of Representatives contemplated." In addition, he noted, both Virginia and its sister states might doubt the desirability of the elevation of a state thus populated to equality in the Union.

Then, he turned to his and the Virginia officials' preferred option: colonization abroad. "Could we procure lands beyond the limits of the U S to form a receptacle for these people?" he asked. It seemed unlikely that the neighboring British and Indians would display "so disinterested a regard for us, as to be willing to relieve us, by receiving such a colony themselves; and as much to be doubted whether that race of men could long exist in so rigorous a climate." The Spaniards to the south and west of the United States also would be unwilling to provide a refuge for free blacks from the United States, he prognosticated.

Thus, Jefferson returned to the issue of a black state within the United States' unsettled western territory. Soon enough, the Americans would become so numerous as to cover the entire extent of their territory "with a people speaking the same language, governed in similar forms, & by similar laws; nor can we contemplate with satisfaction either blot or mixture on that surface." Blacks, free or slave, would be a "blot," so their presence in Jefferson's imagined all-white America could not be tolerated; a racial "mixture" would be even worse. The president would be willing to sound out Britain, Spain, and France on the question of an asylum for freed blacks from the Empire for Liberty, if the General Assembly asked him to do so, but he expressed little doubt that any such effort would fail.

Jefferson next turned his attention to "St. Domingo." "The West Indies," he said, "offer a more probable & practicable retreat for them. Inhabited already by a people of their own race & color; climates congenial with their natural constitution; insulated from the other descriptions of men; nature seems to have formed these islands to become the receptacle of the blacks transplanted into this hemisphere." He guessed that the Europeans affected by his policy would be less ill-disposed to see the American blacks transported thither, because those islands' population already was overwhelmingly black. Haiti was an especially likely destination, because the former slaves already had established self-government there. Jefferson also noted, "I should conjecture that their present ruler might be willing, on many considerations, to receive even that description which would be exiled for acts deemed criminal by us, but meritorious, perhaps, by him." If all else failed, "Africa would offer a last & undoubted resort." Whatever Virginia decided, Jefferson vowed, he would act upon its wishes expeditiously.

Jefferson believed that the British West African colony of Sierra Leone presented a promising option; at the same time, in response to the condition presented by that official, Jefferson promised the British chargé d'affaires that any blacks sent from America would be free.[39] In the end, however, Minister Rufus King's feelers in England proved unavailing, and the attempt to send American blacks to the British territory failed.[40]

Jefferson's devotion to the idea of colonizing as many American blacks as possible died only when he did. Thus, in the context of the Missouri Crisis of 1819–1821, he was found on the side of those who insisted upon the right of Missourians to decide for themselves, without congressional interference, the question of whether they would have slavery in their state.[41] As Jefferson claimed to understand the matter, extension of the South's peculiar institution would not increase the number of people held in slavery by even one, so the supposed moral issue involved in the campaign to keep slavery out of Missouri must be a mask for some other motive. He had no difficulty arriving at the conclusion that what lay at the root of anti-Missouri agitation was an attempt by Northern crypto-Federalists to resuscitate their moribund party. This they could achieve, Jefferson argued, by drawing a geographic line between the (minority) slaveholding section and the (majority) free section of the country. The Missouri Crisis was all about Federalist electoral machinations!

One can barely read through Jefferson's correspondence on Missouri without gasping at the evident insouciance of it. Surely he recognized that the balance of power in the Senate was at issue. Surely he knew that the change of attitudes concerning slavery he claimed to have hoped for had not yet eventuated in the South, while it had made great headway in the North, and that the division over Missouri's application for statehood reflected this uneven progress of antislavery opinion. If so, there is absolutely no evidence in Jefferson's own writings that he ever came to these conclusions, which seem so obvious to us. In fact, it was in the context of the Missouri debates that Jefferson proposed "diffusion," or the spread of slave population concentrated in the southeast up to then through the new territories of the West. If he could not have colonization *tout court,* he might have the next best thing: the removal of part of Virginia's slave population to Missouri, and from Missouri to points north and west. That something along this line would eventuate seems to have been Jefferson's wish to his dying day.[42]

Jefferson's thirteenth successor as president had similar hopes—and for similar reasons. Lincoln's pursuit of the goal of colonization, however, is less easily explained than Jefferson's. In 1831, five years after Jefferson's death, Virginia was rocked by Nat Turner's Rebellion. Among the fruits of that greatest of American slave revolts was an extensive debate in the Virginia General Assembly over the future of slavery in the Old Dominion. Watching the debate from afar, Thomas Roderick Dew was prompted to write a pamphlet detailing the reasons why colonization of the slave population was flatly unfeasible. By all accounts, Dew's work disabused all but the most fervent advocates of their belief in any colonization scheme's practicability.[43] Nevertheless, Lincoln followed his hero Henry Clay in working energetically and determinedly for colonization.[44]

Lincoln did not write a philosophical work such as Jefferson's *Notes on the State of Virginia,* so his views must be gleaned from his public speeches and policy proposals, along with others' recollections of private conversations. Fortunately, however, all of these classes of evidence provide considerable documentation of his support for colonization and the reasons for that support.[45] Most important, perhaps, is a group of amendments President Lincoln proposed on December 1, 1862, in his annual message to Congress. With the Civil War in full swing and Union armies' success to that point limited, Lincoln proposed that Congress recommend three constitutional amendments to the states for their enactment.[46] That suite of proposals highlights the sixteenth president's vision of the American future.

Lincoln's first proposed amendment began, "Every State, wherein slavery now exists, which shall abolish the same therein, at any time, or times, before the first day of January, in the year of our Lord one thousand and nine hundred, shall receive compensation from the United States." In other words, President Lincoln proposed that the states be encouraged to adopt compensated emancipation plans sometime before 1900. (In setting this deadline, Lincoln must have intended to allow time for implementation of gradual emancipation—or postnativity emancipation—plans, which typically provided freedom at the age of maturity for any slave born after a certain date. Such expedients had been adopted in several of the states, and this had been the favored scheme of Clay.)[47] Next, Lincoln proposed a second amendment saying, "All slaves who shall have enjoyed actual freedom by the chances of the war, at any time before the end of the rebellion, shall be forever free; but all owners of such, who shall not have been disloyal, shall be compensated for them, at the same rates as is provided for States adopting abolishment of slavery, but in such way, that no slave shall be twice accounted for." Finally, his third proposed amendment, which was intended to be adopted in tandem with the others, read, "Congress may appropriate money, and otherwise provide, for colonizing free colored persons, with their own consent, at any place or places without the United States."

This set of amendments had three purposes, which were entirely consistent with both Lincoln's conduct of the Union war effort specifically and his political stance throughout his career generally. Those purposes were to coax the Confederate states back into the Union keep the slave states that had remained in the Union from leaving it, and smooth the path of free blacks (eventually including all American blacks) out of America. In Lincoln's conception, the Confederate states must be brought back into the Union, the slaves must be freed, and the freedmen must be colonized abroad. Lincoln concluded his discussion of this topic by noting, "Liberia and Hayti [sic] are, as yet, the only countries to which colonists of African descent from here, could go with certainty of being received and adopted as citizens; and I regret to say such persons, contemplating colonization, do not seem so willing to migrate to those countries, as to some others, nor so willing as I think their interest demands. I believe, however, opinion among them, in this respect, is improving; and that, ere long, there will be an augmented, and considerable migration to both these countries, from the United States."[48]

These proposals may seem to be particularly revealing because they came in the aftermath of the preliminary Emancipation Proclamation of September 22, 1862, which reputedly put the United States government on the path to "a new birth of freedom," a new understanding of blacks' place in American society. In reality, the preliminary Emancipation Proclamation had included an often unnoticed section in which the president pledged that "the effort to colonize persons of African descent, with their consent, upon this continent, or elsewhere, with the previously obtained consent of the Governments existing there, will be continued." Emancipation, Lincoln hoped, would be a preliminary to colonization.[49]

As Lincoln's foremost biographer, David Donald, explained these proposals, they came in response to Lincoln's quandary. As the war progressed, a growing number of Southern slaves emulated those who had made their way to the British lines in response to Lord Dunmore's proclamation of 1775: they fled to the Union army. What could the federal forces do with them? In Donald's pithy summary, these "fugitives could not be returned to their masters; they could not live in idleness near Union army camps; and they must not be turned loose in the negrophobic border states. The Northern states did not want them."[50] Therefore, Lincoln proposed sending them out of the country.

How did Lincoln himself understand this program for removal of blacks from the United States? How did he justify it to himself? Perhaps more correctly, what course of reasoning led him to the conclusion that colonization of freedmen was a necessary or desirable expedient?

A clue can be found in the eulogy Lincoln had delivered on the death of his "beau ideal of a statesman," the Kentucky Whig Henry Clay, in 1852. After lauding Clay for his patriotism, magnetism, gravitas as a speaker, and overriding fidelity to the Union, Lincoln averred that Clay always had been primarily concerned with the elevation of the downtrodden. As Lincoln put it, "Mr. Clay's predominant sentiment, from first to last, was a deep devotion to the cause of human liberty—a strong sympathy with the oppressed every where, and an ardent wish for their elevation. With him, this was a primary and all controlling passion."[51]

Two points must be noted here: first, that Clay was for many years the president of the American Colonization Society, the foremost colonization advocacy organization; and second, that Clay was the chief sponsor of the Missouri Compromise and of the Compromise of 1850. This latter point is not incidental; indeed, Lincoln lauded him for it repeatedly in the course of his eulogy.[52] In fact, in describing Clay's role in resolving the dispute over Missouri's application to join the Union as a slaveholding state, Lincoln took care to quote extensively from Jefferson's famous "firebell in the night" epistle. Among other things, the Illinoisan repeated Jefferson's statement that he would favor any "practicable" means of eliminating slavery from the American landscape, including Jefferson's statement of hope that "a general emancipation, and *expatriation* could be effected; and, gradually, and with due sacrifices I think it might be."[53]

Clay, Lincoln said, had been a slaveowner; in fact, like Jefferson, he had been a significant slaveowner. Yet, Lincoln noted that Clay had never defended slavery as a "positive good" but had called for its ultimate elimination. Clay's description of the American Colonization Society's aims, as recounted by Lincoln, clearly did not put Clay in the camp of those who argued for blacks' equality, let alone citizenship. In fact, Clay seems in Lincoln's account to be intent on persuading slaveholders that colonization is a potential buttress to the "peculiar institution." "We are reproached with doing mischief by the agitation of this question," Lincoln quoted Clay as saying. "The society goes into no household to disturb its domestic tranquility; it addresses itself to no slaves to weaken their obligations of obedience. It seeks to affect no man's property. It neither has the power nor the will to affect the property of any one [sic] contrary to his consent. The execution of its scheme would augment instead of diminishing the value of the property left behind. The society, composed of free men, concerns itself only with the free. Collateral consequences we are not responsible for." (Clay's scheme resembled Jefferson's notion of diffusion in these projected effects.)

Having noted Clay's argument that the society's aims could be squared with the continued health of the institution of slavery, Lincoln lionized Clay for being among its earliest members and for "many . . . years" its president. His name had been one of the society's main supports, and the society "one of the most cherished objects of his direct care and consideration." What was it, precisely, that Lincoln considered so estimable about Clay's activity on behalf of the American Colonization Society? Clay's "suggestion of the possible ultimate redemption of the African race and African continent, was made twenty-five years ago. Every succeeding year has added strength to the hope of its realization. May it indeed be realized! If as the friends of colonization hope, the present and coming generations of our countrymen shall by any means, succeed in freeing our land from the dangerous presence of slavery; and, at the same time, in restoring a captive people to their long-lost father-land, with bright prospects for the future; and this too, so gradually, that neither races nor individuals shall have suffered by the change, it will indeed be a glorious consummation. And if, to such a consummation, the efforts of Mr. Clay shall have contributed, it will be what he most ardently wished, and none of his labors will have been more valuable to his country and his kind." Freeing "his country [America] and his kind [?]" of the presence of the African race were results ardently to be desired, and Lincoln admired Clay for his contributions to that cause. He would further the cause, too, given the chance.

Lest it be thought that Lincoln merely adopted this stance in the context of a rhetorical imperative to validate the notorious positions of his fallen hero, here is what aspiring senator Lincoln said six years later, in the full flush of his 1858 campaign against Senator Stephen A. Douglas: "As long ago as the adoption of the old [Kentucky state] Constitution, Mr. Clay had been the earnest advocate of a system of gradual emancipation and colonization of the state of Kentucky. And again in his old age, in the maturity of his great mind, we find the same wise project still uppermost in his thoughts." For Lincoln the senate candidate, colonization of American blacks was a "wise project." It seems that he agreed with Clay, too, when he said, "I believe it better that Slaves should remain Slaves than be set loose as free men among us."[54] (Here again, he agreed with Jefferson, who had developed his reasoning on this score in *Notes on the State of Virginia*.)[55]

One might argue, as some have, that Lincoln's reasoning in speaking of colonizing blacks was that, to root slavery out root and branch, he had first to be elected to office, and before he could do that he had to ingratiate himself with a racist constituency. There is, however, no direct evidence to that effect. On the contrary, Lincoln's public ruminations on slavery, and on the place of free blacks in American society, took him further than tactical necessity (so-called) would have required.[56] Lincoln, a devotee of the degrading minstrel shows that mocked blacks for their lack of education and their non-European phenotype, gave voice to most of the classic themes of nineteenth-century racial demagoguery.[57] Thus, for example, in his September 18, 1858, debate with Douglas, Lincoln said,

> I am not, nor ever have been in favor of bringing about in any way the social and political equality of the white and black races, [applause]— . . . I am not nor ever have been in favor of making voters or jurors of negroes, nor of qualifying them to hold office, nor to intermarry with white people; and I will say in addition to this that *there is a physical difference between the white and black races which I believe will for ever forbid the two races living together on terms of social and political equality*. And inasmuch as *they cannot so live*, while they do remain together there must be the position of superior and inferior, and *I as much as any other man am in favor of having the superior position assigned to the white race* [emphases added]. I say upon this occasion I do not perceive that because the white man is to have the superior

position the negro should be denied everything. I do not understand that because I do not want a negro woman for a slave I must necessarily want her for a wife. [Cheers and laughter.] My understanding is that I can just let her alone. I am now in my fiftieth year, and I certainly never have had a black woman for either a slave or a wife. So it seems to me quite possible for us to get along without making either slaves or wives of negroes. I will add to this that I have never seen to my knowledge a man, woman or child who was in favor of producing a perfect equality, social and political, between negroes and white men. I recollect of but one distinguished instance that I ever heard of so frequently as to be entirely satisfied of its correctness—and that is the case of Judge Douglas' old friend Col. Richard M. Johnson. [Laughter.] . . . I have never had the least apprehension that I or my friends would marry negroes if there was no law to keep them from it, [laughter] but as Judge Douglas and his friends seem to be in great apprehension that they might, if there were no law to keep them from it, [roars of laughter] I give him the most solemn pledge that I will to the very last stand by the law of this State, which forbids the marrying of white people with negroes. [Continued laughter and applause.][58]

This passage is notable on several scores. In it, Lincoln assumes that blacks' and his primary identity is racial. Race is immutable ("there is a physical difference between the white and black races which I believe will for ever forbid the two races living together on terms of social and political equality," he says, in language very similar to Jefferson's), and Lincoln opts for his race's superordination instead of what he casts as the only alternative: its subordination.[59] He clearly and repeatedly vows that he has no intention of ever conceding the equality of black citizens but assumes that they must always be subordinated. Lincoln then engages in the most vociferous form of race-baiting: his opponent likely wants to marry a black woman; Lincoln would never consider marrying a black woman; and former vice president Johnson is worthy of contempt and derision because of his notorious relationship (including racial intermixture) with a black woman. This type of humor, the reporter noted, elicited laughter from Lincoln's audience.

Lincoln knew how to gauge an audience on the question of slavery —and on the place of black people in Illinois, and Midwestern, society. In a speech delivered at Springfield on June 26, 1857, for example, he considered the relative strengths of the two parties' positions on colonization. His assumption was that his audience would approve of the idea and reward the party that supported it more strongly. To ensure that they got the message, he insisted that only colonization could eliminate racial intermixture. It was true, he conceded, that the Republican Party's platform said nothing to the point, "But I can say a very large proportion of its members are for it, and that the chief plank in their platform—opposition to the spread of slavery—is most favorable to that separation."[60]

What was the most direct route to separation? Colonization. Neither party had a stated policy on colonization at the time, he noted; the parties only acted in ways that bore, positively or negatively, on colonization. What was needed to project the issue to the fore was a change of the public's heart. This could be expected when the public became convinced that moral right and self-interest coincided. (Although Lincoln did not directly say that they did, that was certainly his implication.) He lauded his party as the one whose policies tended to the advancement of the colonization cause, and he did so in a way that seems oddly surprising to us now: "The Republicans inculcate," he said, "with whatever of ability they can, that the negro is a man; that his bondage is cruelly wrong, and that the field of his oppression ought not to be enlarged. The Democrats deny his manhood; deny, or dwarf to insignificance, the wrong of his bondage; so far as possible, crush all sympathy for him, and cultivate and excite hatred and disgust against him; compliment themselves as Union-savers for doing so; and call the indefinite outspreading of his bondage 'a sacred right of self-government.'" In other words, to assert that a slave was a man and had a man's rights was to lend support to the cause of colonization, in Lincoln's reasoning. Lincoln concluded by claiming, contrary to Jefferson's evaluation, that opening Kansas to slavery tended only to raise the value of slaves, and thus to weaken any impetus toward colonization. Voters must support exclusion of slavery from Kansas and the advocate of that exclusion, Lincoln. One reason that they must do so was to facilitate colonization, and thus limit the incidence of racial intermixture.

Public hostility to blacks has often been relied upon by Lincoln historians in explanation of the famous White House meeting with a group of blacks held by Lincoln on August 14, 1862.

Through this meeting, Lincoln is supposed to have hoped to steer inveterate white supremacists to accept the liberation of the slaves.[61] According to a contemporary newspaper account, Lincoln opened the meeting by noting that Congress's recent appropriation for the purpose had made it "his duty, as it had for a long time been his inclination, to favor" colonization.

Why, the president asked, should black Americans agree to leave their native land—or, as he put it, "this country"? "You and we are different races. We have between us a broader difference than exists between almost any other two races. Whether it is right or wrong I need not discuss, but this physical difference is a great disadvantage to us both, as I think your race suffer very greatly, many of them by living among us, while ours suffer from your presence. In a word we suffer on each side." (This passage is oddly evocative of the "Manners" chapter of Jefferson's *Notes on the State of Virginia,* with its fulsome account of slavery's ill effects upon the master class.) He called their attention to the universal inequality between blacks and whites in America, which pressed heavily on the blacks; their presence in America had caused the war, according to the president's sage appraisal. Thus, "It is better for us both, therefore, to be separated." How? He urged the four to take the lead in establishing a federally financed colony of expatriate African Americans in Central America "for the good of mankind."

Lincoln anticipated that his visitors might conclude that they could more easily remain in the United States than leave it. "This is (I speak in no unkind sense) an extremely selfish view of the case," he lectured them. Free blacks such as those four needed to recognize, in Lincoln's conception, that freedmen would be unable, both by education and by temperament, to lead a newly colonized community. What were needed were black colonists whose experience of freedom left them "capable of thinking as white men."[62]

In the traditional telling, this was all a matter of posturing. Lincoln, the story goes, was preparing the electorate of the Union for an emancipation proclamation. One historian speculates that among Lincoln's intentions in pressing for establishment of a flourishing colony of freedmen was to demonstrate that black Americans were fit for freedom.[63] How does one know this? The educated opinion on the subject is almost unanimously supportive of the idea that Lincoln did not really want colonization, and scholars typically come down hard upon writers who take Lincoln at his word.[64] Defending Lincoln against the charge that in the middle of the nineteenth century he forthrightly favored a policy not consonant with twenty-first-century sensibilities, one scholar summarized his analysis of Lincoln's various calls for colonization of African Americans by saying, "This is the way honest people lie."[65] He added that, because Lincoln's Machiavellian deployment of the colonization ruse succeeded in lulling the generally racist North into acceptance of Lincoln's real goal, emancipation, this encouragement of the fantasy of an all-white America was, "at least during Lincoln's presidency, a mostly beneficial feature of the mental landscape of America." "All in all, Lincoln's record suggests that he employed the idea of colonization to allay his own uncertainties, and more importantly the fears of the vast majority of whites, concerning the eventual place of the free black people in the United States."[66] After 1862, as has been noted, the president never mentioned colonization in public. This observation recalls Jefferson's response to criticism of his record concerning slavery, only a few months before his death, that, "My sentiments have been forty years before the public. Had I repeated them forty times, they would only have become the more stale and threadbare."[67] After proposing a colonization amendment to the U.S. Constitution in 1862, what more did Lincoln need to say about his views concerning colonization?

The Emancipation Proclamation was adopted, Lincoln always insisted, as a war measure. It was an essential ingredient of Union victory, as quickly became clear to him.[68] As he explained in August 1864—that is, more than a year after the proclamation took effect—Lincoln had meant what he had said in his famous 1862 letter to Horace Greeley: "If I could save the Union without freeing any slaves I would do it; and if I could save it by freeing all the slaves I would do it; and if I could save it by freeing some, and leaving others alone I would also do that."[69] He also still adhered, he continued, to his other assertion in the Greeley letter, to the effect that "[w]hat I do about slavery and the colored race, I do because I believe it helps to save the Union; and what I forbear I forbear because I do not believe it would help to save the Union. I shall do less whenever I shall believe what I am doing hurts the cause; and I shall do more whenever I shall believe doing more will help the cause. All this I said in the utmost sincerety [*sic*]; and I am as true to the whole of it now, as when I first said it.

When I afterwards proclaimed emancipation, and employed colored soldiers, I only followed the declaration just quoted. . . . The way these measures were to help the cause, was not to be by magic, or miracles, but by inducing the colored people to come bodily over from the rebel side to ours." As Wendell Phillips put it, the Emancipation Proclamation of January 1863 meant that freedmen were now to be "colonized" into the United States Army.[70]

Thus, historian Kenneth J. Winkle was partly correct in saying, "He continued to dream of an overseas colony of African Americans until late in his presidency, when the severity of the Civil War convinced him at last that emancipation represented the only just and practical solution to the moral dilemma of slavery."[71] Lincoln did decide during the war that emancipation must be his war policy. The war made the colonization issue moot, for the moment, and we cannot know precisely whether Lincoln contemplated taking up the question again after the war. We do know, however, that he suggested in his last public speech (April 11, 1865) the enfranchisement of "the very intelligent" and "those who serve our cause as soldiers," which seems to suggest that, if Lincoln had begun to contemplate converting slaves into citizens, he had done so only in the most grudging way.[72] Such a parsimonious parceling out of the suffrage seems at least consistent with, if not actually demonstrative of, a continued wish to colonize: after all, how could Union soldiers and "the very intelligent" be denied the vote by April 11, 1865? Could any less have been done? (Andrew Johnson's experience as Lincoln's successor points to a negative answer.) It seems entirely likely that Lincoln continued to hold to the Jeffersonian view he had expressed in 1858: that blacks were entitled to the self-government the Declaration of Independence denominated a natural right, but that, for their good and whites', they could exercise it only "upon [their] own soil."[73]

Whatever Lincoln thought of colonization in his dying hours, the project certainly was not dead yet.[74] Despite the Lincoln assassination, the Jeffersonian colonization chimera continued to exert its odd appeal on American politicians and other prominent figures, from President Ulysses S. Grant to black nationalist Marcus Garvey, for decades to come.[75] Only gradually did the idea of incorporating the descendants of former slaves into the American polity win widespread acceptance. Jefferson and Lincoln surely would have been shocked by this development. To that extent, at least, Lincoln was a thorough Jeffersonian.

JAMES N. LEIKER

THE DIFFICULTIES OF UNDERSTANDING ABE

Lincoln's Reconciliation of Racial Inequality and Natural Rights

The historical conception of Lincoln's views on race has run quite a gamut of interpretation over the past one hundred thirty–odd years. Most recently, Lerone Bennett's polemical *Forced into Glory* has thrown a gauntlet into the face of traditional scholars for its assertion of Lincoln's white supremacist notions and his weak commitment to the ending of slavery. Bennett's work emanates from the New Left tradition that coemerged with the 1950s and 1960s civil rights movements, which attacked the assumptions of American history as a continual advance toward progress and democracy and in which men such as Lincoln—who valued the preservation of constitutional union more than that of black freedom—were depicted as bigots. The image of Lincoln as racist, however, did not begin with Bennett; oddly, white segregationists in the early twentieth century, ranging from Thomas Dixon to D. W. Griffith, also saw Lincoln as a champion of an all-white United States, committed to the principle of the separation of races. The demagogic politician James K. Vardaman of Mississippi, in a visit to Springfield in 1909 after a horrific lynching and riot, declared that, when it came to the subject of black inferiority, "my views and his [Lincoln's] on the race question are substantially identical." Stephen Oates's words are significant here: "That angry blacks and white segregationists should embrace the same Lincoln myth is one of the great ironies of modern race relations."[1]

That a person who appears as the Great Emancipator to some should appear as the Great Racist to others should not be surprising. During a time of intense moral and regional divides over the question of slavery, Lincoln's political success stemmed from his ability to offer different images to different audiences, representing himself as a compromise candidate amid a breadth of extreme factions. The very ambiguity and discrepancies that propelled him into the presidency—and hence, into historical fame—have made it possible for a variety of groups to appropriate his image and present his legacy in seemingly opposite ways.[2]

During the past half-century, the national debate over race in the United States has moved us further from an understanding of Lincoln and his time. In many ways, contemporary scholars and activists lack the necessary apparatus for explaining his contradictions, illustrating the salience of David Lowenthal's phrase "the past is another country."[3] In denouncing Lincoln as a "racist," Bennett employs the term in its current pejorative meaning, a meaning it did not acquire until the mid-1900s, when changes in the social sciences and the atrocities of Nazi Germany permanently linked the belief in racial inequality with genocide and barbarism. Bennett further contends that "there are no degrees of racism; there are only racists who express their racism in different degrees," a broad application of a loaded term that places Lincoln on the same par with Hitler—useful perhaps as political invective but clearly a distortion of historical realities.[4] As Lincoln was a product of his time, so is Bennett—so are we all—a product of this one. A pragmatic politician, Lincoln lived in an era when white supremacy represented more of a potential asset to him than a liability. Despite constant efforts to use his myth to justify present purposes, Lincoln would likely find the values of our day as distasteful as we find his views on race; however, a deeper exploration of that very difference offers an opportunity to bridge some of the gap that separates us from this enigmatic figure.

Over the past generation, racial discussion in the United States has been conducted through the discourse of "civil rights," tentatively defined here as the rights that people (whether as individuals or as members of specific groups is a matter of some recent contention) enjoy through their membership in a democratic republic that values equality and liberty. The contribution of contemporary liberalism to this discourse is the premise that, if racial equality (as well as other kinds) is to occur, racism must be eliminated. Building on the earlier teachings of the Boas school, multicultural education sets the goal of shattering the belief that some people and cultures are superior to others and that those holding racist views to the contrary need to be converted, or at least have their voices rendered impotent. Remembering, of course, that Lincoln was an adaptable politician who might well have accommodated himself to this set of values depending on his constituency, it seems plausible he would have rejected our current "civil rights" agenda in at least three ways. Lincoln's definition of "equality" did not include the possibility of an egalitarian society where hierarchies based on race, class, gender, and other variables did not exist. Nor did he believe it possible, or even for that matter desirable, that personal prejudice could be eliminated from the minds of citizens. Most important, the understanding of Lincoln and other nineteenth-century Americans about the meaning of "civil rights" remained limited and guarded as compared to now. "Civil rights" were reserved for those persons deemed able to meet the corresponding responsibilities of citizenship in a democratic community, which—it was believed—blacks, Indians, women, and others regarded as inferior could not. Lincoln was certainly no champion of "civil rights" in the contemporary sense; rather, his progressivism lay in his understanding of "natural rights," those that lay outside the realm of the state simply by virtue of being born human. Not generally considered a deep thinker, Lincoln's many speeches, debates, and writings nonetheless reveal an ongoing intellectual effort to address some of the major philosophical questions of the modern age—namely, what is a human being, what rights do human beings enjoy, and what type of equality is possible among them in light of their diversity of cultures and capabilities?

David Herbert Donald has warned that it is a mistake to apologize for Lincoln's racial views simply as "a man of his time," but certainly placing those views within the context of mid-nineteenth-century racism is important for an understanding of him.⁵ Prejudice based on skin color has likely always existed in some form or another, but racism as a systematic ideology that justified oppression grew and crystallized during the antebellum decades. In contrast to earlier ideas that saw slavery as a temporary condition that helped elevate blacks to Western standards, Southern spokesmen by the 1830s offered new, unambiguous assertions of blacks' permanent inferiority. Much of this was a conscience-easing attempt to rationalize the enormous profits generated by the expansion of cotton over the backs of slave labor and also as an answer to abolitionist tracts condemning slavery as immoral and un-Christian. Proponents defended slavery as a civilizing institution that tamed Africans' "bestial nature" and rendered them into passive "Sambos"—childlike, loyal, reliant on their masters' guidance and protection. Because blacks were not considered "human" to the same extent as whites, they could be worked to extremes and even be separated from their families, with no moral guilt attaching to the slaveowner. Others described slavery as a "natural" condition that stretched even to some whites, part of a larger human hierarchy with multiple layers of superiority and inferiority.⁶ This latter notion may have stimulated a deep fear in Lincoln that slavery's rationale would eventually spread to the erosion of equality and establishment of subjugation for fellow Caucasians.

Most scholars agree that Lincoln uncritically accepted the dominant racial prejudices of his day; indeed, as an aspiring statesman who required the votes of other whites, he would have done well to conceal any doubts about black inferiority if he ever held them. Accused by Stephen Douglas of advocating black equality, he issued his famous quote at the Charleston, Illinois, debate in 1858:

> I am not, nor have ever been, in favor of bringing about in any way the social and political equality of the white and black races. I am not nor have ever been in favor of making voters or jurors of negroes, nor of qualifying them to hold office, nor to intermarry with white people ⁷

Four years later, he reiterated his belief in black-white separation before a delegation of African Americans, whose aid he tried to enlist on behalf of colonization to Central America:

> You and we are different races. We have between us a broader difference than exists between almost any other two races. Whether it is right or wrong I need not discuss, but this physical difference is a great disadvantage to us both, as I think your race suffer very greatly, many of them by living among us, while ours suffer from your presence. In a word we suffer on each side. If this is admitted, it affords a reason why we should be separated.

In addressing this delegation, mostly well-educated black elites from the Washington, D.C., area, Lincoln attempted to congratulate the group for "being as smart as white people" to elicit their support for his colonization schemes:

> But you ought to do something to help those who are not as fortunate as yourselves. . . . If intelligent colored men, such as are before me, would move in this manner, much might be accomplished. It is exceedingly important that we have men at the beginning capable of thinking as white men. . . . For the sake of your race you should sacrifice something of your present comfort for the purpose of being as grand in that respect as the white people.[8]

Such back-handed compliments did not endear Lincoln to this particular group and may have been an example of what Frederick Douglass had in mind in 1876 when he said, "In his interests, in his associations, in his habits of thought, and in his prejudices, he was a white man. He was preeminently the white man's President, entirely devoted to the welfare of white men."[9]

Lincoln clearly believed in black inferiority, but whether he attributed that inferiority to some innate deficiency in blacks or to their continued degradation by whites is difficult to say. Nor does the question seem ever to have occurred to him. Beginning with Gunnar Myrdal's 1944 *An American Dilemma*, twentieth-century social scientists would locate the causes of black inequality in the systematic discrimination they suffered from white rule, but such an approach lay far off in the future.[10] Evidenced by his statement "whether it is right or wrong, I need not discuss," Lincoln considered himself a realist, less concerned with the causes of black inequality than with its implications. His was a racism born of ignorance, for as a child of the northwestern frontier he had few opportunities to interact with nonwhites and seldom considered the possibility that their cultures and perspectives had something valuable to teach him. As the issue of black-white relations became paramount in his political rise, Lincoln developed more occasions to think about the morality of slavery and seemed most at ease and at his most original when discussing that subject. With other people of color—Native Americans, Hispanics, Asians—Lincoln was content to rely on dominant cultural stereotypes as a substitute for his own judgment.

Little record exists of Lincoln's attitude toward Native Americans. A common story told in his household while growing up was how his grandfather had been killed in ambush by an Indian in 1784, leaving his father, Tom, an orphan at age six. During Abraham's brief military service in the Black Hawk War in 1832, he saw no action and joked years later that his primary combatants had been mosquitos.[11] The best available evidence of his views about indigenous people comes from his remarks to a visiting Indian delegation to the White House in March 1863. Although it is difficult to tell from the written record, Lincoln's words here seem couched and hesitant, lacking the confidence he normally displayed when addressing whites, as if he felt ill at ease in the presence of people he perceived as different. After explaining with some condescension that "we pale-faced people think that this world is a great, round ball," he had a professor explain basic geography to the Indians, then went on to explain the main difference between the white and red races:

> The pale-faced people are numerous and prosperous because they cultivate the earth, produce bread, and depend upon the products of the earth rather than wild game for a subsistence. This is the chief reason of the difference; but there is another. Although we are now engaged in a great war between one another, we are not, as a race, so much disposed to fight and kill one another as our red brethren. You have asked for my advice. . . . I can only say that I can see no way in which your race is to become as numerous and prosperous as the white race except by living as they do, by the cultivation of the earth.[12]

The irony of Lincoln's assertion of moral superiority about whites "not killing each other," during the middle of a bloody civil war, is rich.

As black inferiority justified slavery, the myth of the Indian as "hunter-savage" delivered a convenient rationale for whites' westward expansion. By 1860, the Republican Party had formulated its economic platform to dispose of government land by encouraging poor Easterners and prospective European immigrants to enter the West and establish homesteads—all of which provoked inevitable conflict with Native Americans.[13] Indian policy received scant attention from the Lincoln administration, which is not surprising in view of its distractions. Native Americans were encouraged to abandon hunting and gathering as means of subsistence and become peaceful settled farmers, part of a long-term assimilation plan advocated by Eastern reformers. Such efforts would not reach fruition until the Grant administration, though Lincoln did endorse the goals of reformers while giving little priority to implementing their ideas. Yet as president, Lincoln also pursued policies that relocated Indians to inferior land, far from where their presence might offend white settlers. Herein lay an interesting consistency between Lincoln's plans for black colonization and Indian removal: in both cases, the separation of races offered in his mind a practical political solution to avoid racial conflict.[14] Lincoln admitted his own unwillingness to confront white Westerners' prejudice to the Indian delegation in 1863:

> It is the object of this Government to be on terms of peace with you, and with all our red brethren. We constantly endeavor to do so. We make treaties with you, and will try to observe them; and if our children should sometimes behave badly, and violate these treaties, it is against our wish. You know it is not always possible for any father to have his children do precisely as he wishes them to do.[15]

If Lincoln had any serious thoughts about native cultures, which is doubtful, he kept them well to himself. On the basis of his few public utterances and the overall thrust of his party's policies, however, it is improbable that, had he lived into the Indian Wars of the late 1860s and 1870s, he would have been any more of a strong advocate for Indians' "civil rights" than he was for those of African Americans.

Lincoln's public opposition to the U.S.-Mexican War stands as one of the few positions he took on his government's policies toward Hispanics and Latin America. As a Whig member of the Illinois delegation to the House of Representatives, he introduced in December 1847 a series of resolutions denouncing President James K. Polk's handling of the war. The following month, Lincoln delivered a meticulously argued speech in Congress exposing what he saw as the vagueness of jurisdiction along the Texas-Mexico border, where both countries, Lincoln felt, had a legitimate claim to ownership, thus rendering Polk's declaration of war unconstitutional and contrary to international law. Lincoln apparently had high hopes for this speech but was soon disappointed when the Democrats ignored his remarks and his fellow Whigs gave him only weak support. In principle Lincoln did not oppose territorial expansion, as seen by his willingness as president to stimulate homesteading on Western lands. Even the annexation of Texas had not offended his sensitivity about expanding slavery, because in that case Texas already had existed as a slaveholding polity and annexation did not therefore entail a spreading of human bondage to new areas. Rather, Lincoln's opposition rested more on a fear that slavery might expand into Mexico itself, a free nation, and that Polk's handling of the border crisis that precipitated the war represented a usurpation of war-making powers that the Constitution left exclusively to Congress. Lincoln wrote in a letter to his law partner, William Herndon, that Polk's actions placed the president where kings had always stood—one of many analogies to "divine right" theory that he would make in subsequent years. Like the lawyer he was, Lincoln's concern rested more with the legalities of the process by which land was acquired from Mexico than with the consequences of acquisition for the Mexican people.[16]

Lincoln frequently used racial slurs when describing Mexicans or other Latinos, though such remarks should always be placed in their proper context. In his debate with Douglas at Galesburg, Illinois, Lincoln attacked the concept of popular sovereignty—Douglas's notion that the people of a territory should determine the slavery issue for themselves—by asking a hypothetical question as to whether Douglas would apply the doctrine in an acquisition like Mexico where the inhabitants were "nonwhite":

When we shall get Mexico, I don't know whether the Judge [Douglas] will be in favor the Mexican people that we get with it settling that question for themselves and all others; because we know the Judge has a great horror for mongrels, and I understand that the people of Mexico are most decidedly a race of mongrels. I understand that there is not more than one person there out of eight who is pure white, and I suppose from the Judge's previous declaration that when we get Mexico or any considerable part of it, that he will be in favor of these mongrels settling the question, which would bring somewhat into collision with his horror of an inferior race.[17]

These comments appeared in a period of intense "race-baiting" during the debates when Douglas accused Lincoln of advocating miscegenation, and here Lincoln seems to have used popular (though vulgar) language to expose the contradictions in Douglas's thought. Even when the debates had ended, however, he occasionally used derogatory terms in speeches with no direct political motive. In a patriotic address on discoveries and inventions in February 1859, Lincoln contrasted the innovation and brilliance of "Young America" with the "Old Fogy" countries, crediting Americans' technological success to their powers of observation, reflection, and experiment: "But for the difference in habit of observation, why did yankees, almost instantly, discover gold in California, which had been trodden upon, and over-looked by [I]ndians and Mexican greasers, for centuries?"[18]

It was in this same speech that Lincoln made one of his few remarks about the peoples of Asia, the "nonwhite" group with whom he had the least acquaintance and least opportunity to think about. For one who had never been to Asia or, for that matter, even out of the United States, Lincoln unreservedly claimed curiosity and scientific progress as the exclusive domain of the Western world. Within this paradigm, he recognized Asia as the birthplace of "the human family," meaning that he saw Asians, like blacks, as human beings, but that theirs was an ancient, crumbling civilization whose time had long passed:

> The human family originated, as is now thought, somewhere in Asia, and have worked their way principally Westward. Just now, in civilization, and the arts, the people of Asia are entirely behind those of Europe; those of the East of Europe behind those of the West of it; while we, here in America, think we discover, and invent, and improve, faster than any of them. They may think this is arrogance; but they can not deny that Russia has called on us to show her how to build steam-boats and railroads—while in the other parts of Asia, they scarcely know that such things as S.Bs & RR.s exist. In anciently inhabited countries, the dust of ages—a real downright old-fogyism—seems to settle upon, and smother the intellect and energies of man.[19]

Lincoln's intent here may have been to praise the labor theory of value that had become an important part of the Republican Party's ideology, but the historical framework that he employed was common to historians and philosophers influenced by *folk* romanticism. The "East to West" concept of history owed its articulation to the German scholar Georg W. F. Hegel, who saw the zeitgeist beginning in the Orient and moving westward to the Egyptians, Greeks, and Romans in a gradual realization of liberty through constitutional governments. Nineteenth-century nationalists were quick to use Hegel's theories to convince the masses that their particular countries would be next on "the great stage of history," a ploy that Lincoln apparently used in this speech to flatter voters during his ascent into national prominence.[20]

It has been said of the sixteenth president that his gift lay in ascertaining the moods and prejudices of his constituencies and acting in accordance with what he thought their political will would support. If this is so, then Lincoln was a pessimist on the possibility of whites' acceptance of nonwhites. Often, he spoke publicly in flattering praise of white Americans' technological and moral superiority while denigrating various peoples of color, peoples with whom he had little actual contact. How much of this represents the inner heart and mind of the private Lincoln may be a different matter. Able to enjoy a raucous laugh at the expense of people he did not know, he was capable of kindness toward individual persons of color at a personal level. Carl Sandburg told a famous story about Lincoln during the Black Hawk War when an elderly Indian rambled into camp, causing the whites to rush upon him with intent to kill. Lincoln reportedly jumped to the man's side and faced his comrades down, saying, "This must not be done." When one of his fellows called him a coward, he replied, "If any man thinks I am a coward let him test it," and the tempers cooled with no violence.[21] Much has been written about Lincoln's enjoyment of minstrel shows and his habit of telling racist jokes. Although his sense of humor definitely remains out of step with modern sensitivities, his use of minorities in anecdotes was often done to illustrate some common-sense point that exposed the pretentiousness or revealed the flaws in some supposedly more refined person's thinking. One of Lincoln's favorite stories concerned an Englishman who met an American Indian. Anxious to impress him, John Bull asked, "The sun never sets on the English dominion. Do you understand how that is?" "Oh yes," replied the native, "that is because God is afraid to trust them in the dark."[22] While understandably seen as demeaning today, Lincoln's humor did seem to acknowledge that blacks and Indians—both seen by his culture as primitive—nonetheless possessed some basic insights into human nature, insights that his own unsophisticated rural upbringing may have prepared him to appreciate.

Assuming that his public record reflects his private sentiments, Abraham Lincoln believed the nations of Asia and Latin America to be backward, favored expansionist policies onto Indian lands at the expense of tribal sovereignty, and thought African Americans incapable of self-government. In this sense, Bennett's characterization of him as a "racist" is accurate, even though the label has been employed so often and so broadly that its significance has been diluted. More precisely, Lincoln can be described as an ethnocentric nationalist, one who measured other cultures and subcultures through the prism of his own and found them wanting; for him, what was right for white Americans was right for the world. The American system of constitutional government, and its accompanying economic progress, remained his most cherished ideals, ones that other nations and peoples should emulate. To his defense, few politicians have gained power by believing or saying otherwise. Although he was no cultural relativist, Lincoln did construct a worldview that allowed for a limited version of diversity. Whereas he thought very little about the traditions and fates of nonwhites, he gave extensive consideration to the future of white people—or, more specifically, Euro-Americans and European immigrants—and their place in the United States. Paradoxically, Lincoln's understanding of "whiteness" would move him to a broader interpretation of such concepts as "equality," "human," and "natural rights" than it would most of his contemporaries. This may be the most difficult aspect of his thinking for present-day Americans to grasp: that his very concern for the institutions and freedom of the white race would lead to a deeper appreciation for the rights of nonwhites.

In contrast to traditional models that see racial categories such as "white" and "black" as static and fixed, whiteness studies over the past decade have begun to explore the ways by which a single classification came to be applied to the vast diversity of European immigrants who settled in North America.[23] During the colonial era, "white" implied less of an entrenched racial consciousness than a handy adjective that described anyone who was neither a slave nor an Indian. Although the 1790 Naturalization Act limited citizenship to free white persons, the framers' understanding of "white" lacked the essentialist, pan-European meaning that it acquired later. Heightened immigration during the antebellum decades ultimately helped to broaden the word's application. From 1846 to 1855, more than three million immigrants came to the United States, nearly half of them from Ireland alone and almost a million from Germany. With a foreign-born population of nearly four million by 1860, the nation's ethnic character had changed considerably from the Anglo-Saxon society, steeped in English traditions, that the founders had visualized. Although "Old World" prejudices against Irish and Germans continued, generic concepts such as "white" and "Caucasian" proved flexible enough to admit non-English ethnic groups as citizens. Such changes were reflected in the expanded suffrage and egalitarian rhetoric of the Jackson era, as politicians extolled the equality and virtues of "the white race" and elaborate new theories emerged under the banner of Manifest Destiny proclaiming the inevitability of white control of the continent.[24] In essence, Lincoln became politically mature when the meaning of whiteness was expanding and solidifying, ameliorating ancient differences between European peoples even as it intensified their differences with those seen as "nonwhites."

Lincoln's awareness of these changes is reflected in his recorded debates with Douglas, coming on the heels of the 1856 elections in which for the first time the great mass of Irish immigrants voted.[25] Scholars have long acknowledged the expansive interpretation of the Declaration of Independence that Lincoln offered in the debates, but they have not addressed the way that he framed it within the country's growing ethnic pluralism. In his Chicago speech of July 1858, Lincoln reminded his listeners that the majority of them were not, in fact, part of that "race" of Anglo-Saxon Englishmen who wrote the Declaration:

> We have besides these men—descended by blood from our ancestors—among us perhaps half our people who are not descendants at all of these men, they are men who have come from Europe— German, Irish, French and Scandinavian—men that have come from Europe themselves, or whose ancestors have come hither and settled here, finding themselves our equals in all things. If they look back through this history to trace their connection with those days by blood, they find they have none, they cannot carry themselves back into that glorious epoch and make themselves feel they are part of us, but when they look through that old Declaration of Independence they find that those old men say "We hold these truths to be self-evident, that all men are created equal," and then they feel that that moral sentiment taught in that day evidences their relation to those men, that it is the father of all moral principle in them, and that they have a right to claim it as though they were blood of the blood, and flesh of the flesh of the men who wrote the Declaration, and so they are.[26]

Despite his frequent genuflections to white supremacy, Lincoln realized that "whiteness" lay not in blood or in lineal descent— the traditional underpinnings for "race"—for, if it did, many Americans of the 1850s would have been excluded from citizenship. This became apparent in his attack on Douglas's strict interpretation of the Declaration, which said that the founders had intended the document to apply only to themselves and fellow British subjects:

> Douglas says no man can defend it except on the hypothesis that it
> only referred to British white subjects, and that no other white men
> are included—that it does not speak alike to the down trodden of all
> nations—German, French, Spanish, etc., but simply that the English
> were born equal and endowed by their Creator with certain natural
> or equal rights among which are life, liberty and the pursuit of happi-
> ness, and that it meant nobody else. Are Jeffersonian Democrats will-
> ing to have the gem taken from the magna charta of human liberty
> in this shameful way? Or will they maintain that its declaration of
> equality of natural rights among all nations is correct?[27]

Lincoln envisioned the Declaration as a growing ideal that
transcended mere blood and ancestry, thus making it possible
for non-English peoples to enjoy the principles that it proclaimed. To do otherwise, and admit a less inclusive interpretation, would mean in effect the disfranchisement of recent
immigrants who could claim equality within the white race.
Douglas seems to have ignored Lincoln's challenge on this
point while subtly conceding it; in his later speeches, Douglas
quietly replaced his use of "British subjects" when referring to
the Declaration with the words "white men" or "men of European birth."[28]

The intellectual historian John Patrick Diggins has claimed
that Lincoln's continuing relevance lay in his conviction that the
Declaration, in spite of its Anglo-Saxon origins, had come to belong by the mid-nineteenth century to subsequent generations of
immigrants, thereby opening the United States to a multinational
constituency. Diggins argues that Lincoln prophesied the nation's
evolution from Anglo-American to Euro-American to its present
multicultural state.[29] If this is so, his understanding of the fluidity
and expansiveness of racial concepts such as "white" may have
been the precursor to his ideas about the universality of human
rights. Lincoln's personal prejudice did not permit him to accept
nonwhites as social equals, but he understood history well
enough to know that questions of who was "white" or not, and
who was entitled to natural rights or not, was open to change. In
praising the accomplishments of white America, he minimized
the importance of skin color or natural intelligence to a higher
belief in a set of moral principles:

You say A. is white, and B. is black. It is *color*, then, the lighter, having the right to enslave the darker? Take care. By this rule, you are to be slave to the first man you meet, with a fairer skin than your own. You do not mean *color* exactly?—You mean the whites are *intellectually* the superiors of the blacks, and, therefore have the right to enslave them? Take care again. By this rule, you are to be slave to the first man you meet, with an intellect superior to your own. But say you, it is a question of *interest;* and, if you can make it your *interest,* you have the right to enslave another. Very well. And if he can make it his interest, he has the right to enslave you.[30]

It needs to be understood that Lincoln's avocation of such principles did not stem from a particular concern for people of color, whom he may well have regarded as inferior. Rather, he was far-seeing enough to realize that the same justifications for slavery that subjugated blacks could in time be applied to certain whites, thus reversing many of the freedoms that had been extended to new people since the time of the United States' founding. Lincoln believed this reversal had begun already with the nascent nativist movement of the 1850s: "When the know-nothings get control, it [the Declaration] will read, all men are created equal except negroes and foreigners and Catholics. When it comes to this, I shall prefer emigrating to some country where they make no pretense of loving liberty."[31] This became his major objection to the *Dred Scott* decision, for in its reasoning that the Declaration and the Constitution did not apply to blacks, the judiciary set the precedent for even narrower interpretations that could circumscribe the rights of other Americans.[32]

Lincoln's critics, be they his political opponents or his biographers, have criticized his use of the Declaration on at least two major grounds, one charging him with an inaccurate reading of the founders' intent, the other with engaging in esoteric abstraction. States-rights advocates such as John Calhoun and Douglas denied the existence of any common moral foundation outside of local interests and reminded Lincoln that Thomas Jefferson himself had been a slaveowner who never intended his document to apply to anyone other than fellow revolutionaries. Furthermore, the guiding premise of the American Revolution, as articulated by Thomas Paine, was that tradition imposes no authority on subsequent generations, rendering Jefferson's intent meaningless. Lincoln responded to such charges with his own reminder that historical circumstance already had extended liberty and equality to Frenchmen, Irish, and other groups whom the founders probably did not intend to include. For him, the specific context of Jefferson's words mattered less than their spirit; like the Constitution, the Declaration was a living document to be reinterpreted by each generation, well in keeping with Paine's warning about the tyranny of tradition.[33] The other charge has carried more weight among Lincoln's recent critics, especially Bennett, who has accused him of "academic voodoo" by elevating the Declaration to some abstract principle with no regard for the material conditions of the people it purportedly liberates. The accusation merits consideration, for indeed a similar point was raised by Douglas himself when he asked Lincoln how he could favor "natural equality" for blacks without turning them into social and political equals.[34] Lacking his usual eloquence, Lincoln fumbled to reconcile the contradiction; to determine whether he did so satisfactorily requires a deeper examination of his distinction between "natural rights" and other kinds and approaches the heart of why his ideas seem so unfathomable to our own age.

It is possible, as Bennett contends, to overintellectualize Lincoln, who approached social problems pragmatically and called politics "the art of the possible." Neither philosopher nor theologian, Lincoln did possess an exceptionally talented legal mind. In one of his earliest speeches, he denounced anarchy and mob violence as a violation of the country's laws, the reverence of which he regarded as "the political religion" of the nation.[35] Law reflected the design of the founders, and beyond them, of a body of values and principles emanating from the larger Western tradition. To Lincoln, the establishment of the United States constituted a legal contract between slaveowning and nonslaveowning states wherein the latter promised not to interfere with the interests of the former. American citizenship thus required a continual upholding of that contract, putting aside individual moral reservations. Lincoln's indictment of abolitionism rested on its assertion of moral certainty above that of legal reasoning and procedure, a ploy that he equated with vigilantism.[36] Yet respect for the law meant neither agreeing to extend slavery into areas where it did not previously exist nor institutionalizing theories about human inequality even when they might be correct. Lincoln despised the rhetoric of extreme racists who would begin the process of making exceptions to the doctrine of "equal under the law," because no one could predict where such exceptions would end:

> If one man says it [the Declaration] does not mean a Negro why may not another say it does not mean some other man? . . . Let us discard all this quibbling and this man and the other man—this race and that race and the other race being inferior, and therefore they must be placed in an inferior position. . . . Let us discard all these things and unite as one people throughout this land until we shall once more stand up declaring that all men are created equal.[37]

Like a true conservative, Lincoln rested many of his ideas on nostalgia, and what he feared was that his present age was abandoning the tradition of "natural rights" enshrined by the founding generation.

But what exactly did Lincoln mean by "natural rights"? Clearly, these did not include the right to vote, to marry whites, or in some cases, even to self-ownership. Lincoln's usage of the term appears consistent with that of earlier Western thinkers, namely that of the ancient Stoics and Thomas Aquinas, who saw natural rights as an extension of "natural law," that which has a universal source in God and is known to humans through their ability to reason. Medieval theologians such as Aquinas located natural rights in a person's membership within a specific class, but the term's colloquial meaning in the United States owed more to its articulation by the seventeenth-century physician John Locke. Locke saw natural rights as resting in an individual person simply by virtue of his or her birth into a "state of nature," a condition of pure freedom and equality that supersedes any imposition of government or the creation of a political state. For Locke, the rights to be free from harm, robbery, enslavement, or killing and to enjoy the fruits of one's own labor are absolute because they predate civil society, and in fact, civil society's only purpose is to defend such rights. The connection between natural rights and equality was explored further by the French romanticist Jean-Jacques Rousseau, who distinguished two kinds of "inequality": natural inequality, which refers to age, bodily strength, intelligence, or other physical properties; and political inequality, which has no basis in nature and depends on the customs and consent of society.[38]

Locke's influence on the founding generation has been well documented. Jefferson especially used Lockean discourse in the Declaration of Independence, though he substituted the last word of "life, liberty and the pursuit of property" with that of "happiness." Diggins has argued that Lincoln's interpretation of the Declaration was essentially Lockean and that his reading of it may in fact have been closer to Locke's intent than that of Jefferson's.[39] But if Lincoln's appreciation of natural rights stemmed from this direction, then he likewise inherited these earlier thinkers' ambiguities and inconsistencies. Locke also said that land uncultivated was land unclaimed, providing a useful justification for white Americans to disregard Indian tribal claims. By situating natural rights within the human body and defining "human" based on the capacity for reason, Locke opened the door for arguments that pointed to nonwhites' supposed irrationality and emotionalism and thereby claimed them to be not human at all, entitled to none of the freedoms from enslavement accorded to whites. Even by the late eighteenth century, racial theories appeared that rejected environmental assumptions about blacks and Indians being temporarily degraded and asserted their failings to be permanent, a "natural" inequality to use Rousseau's terms rather than some civil injustice imposed by the state.[40] Racial dialogue in Lincoln's time boiled down to a debate as to whether nonwhites met the criteria for natural rights laid out by the Enlightenment. As its chief defender, Lincoln's own answer to that question proved no better and no worse than Enlightenment thought itself.

More imminent than Locke, the Whig Party exerted a powerful influence over Lincoln and the Republican Party platform. During the Mexican War, the majority of Whigs had endorsed the notion of Americans' superiority within the white race, yet they saw the use of that superiority as a form of immoral force against weaker, inferior peoples.[41] Henry Clay especially became Lincoln's ideological and political role model. The two Westerners held many of the same racist ideas; Clay had been a founder of the American Colonization Society pushing for the removal of blacks to Africa, and he appears to have accepted the polygenic theory, which said that God had made the black and white races separately, thus fostering in him a fear of racial mixing. Clay, however, also had been a strong opponent of slavery, even liberating his own slaves and settling them in Liberia at personal expense.[42] In his eulogy to Clay in 1852, Lincoln articulated the moderate position he would take as a compromise candidate eight years later:

> He did not perceive, that on a question of human right, the negroes were to be excepted from the human race. . . . he did not perceive, as I think no wise man has perceived, how it could be at once eradicated, without producing a greater evil, even to the cause of human liberty itself.[43]

In his last debate with Douglas, Lincoln again quoted from Clay in describing slaveowning as a product of civil society, not some indispensable right to be found in the state of nature. Lincoln expressed his willingness to tolerate slavery temporarily within its original bounds, because ending it all at once would be akin to removing a cancer so large that the patient might bleed to death.[44] Lincoln and Clay shared a belief in black inferiority, but in their eyes that belief was irrelevant when weighed against the slave's basic humanity. White supremacy did not justify the unlawful domination of nonwhites.

Characteristic of many moderate Republicans, Lincoln often engaged in "race-baiting" of his own, accusing Douglas and the Democrats of being the true "amalgamationists" whose advocacy of slavery encouraged racial mixing.[45] But as the heir of Lockean and Whig theories about natural rights and property theory, the Republican Party embraced the fundamental premise that blacks held the same rights to economic advancement as whites, which required their eventual employment as free laborers. "Natural" inequalities might inevitably result in vast differences of wealth and social status, but these ought not to be transformed into "artificial" inequalities to be given credence and legitimacy by the state.[46] Lincoln especially equated the denial of economic rights based on race with Europe's aristocratic system of hereditary privilege; in slaveowners' defense of their institution as resting on the absolute discretion of whites, he saw the danger of a return to monarchical rule:

> [T]his argument strikes me as not a little remarkable in another par-
> ticular—in its strong resemblance to the old argument for the "Divine
> right of Kings." By the latter, the King is to do just as he pleases with
> his white subjects, being responsible to God alone. By the former the
> white man is to do just as he pleases with his black slaves, being re-
> sponsible to God alone. The two things are precisely alike; and it is but
> natural that they should find similar arguments to sustain them.[47]

Such attacks were consistent with his broad reading of the Declaration, essentially casting his moral opposition to slavery within
a much longer American tradition of the fight against artificial
systems of civil privilege.

By classifying race within Rousseau's category of natural inequalities, Lincoln reduced it to an equivalent par with age, mental capacity, physical strength, and other biological factors that
might impede individual progress but provided no basis for a
state-sponsored caste system. For he and other Republicans, "natural rights" meant the economic freedom of all humans—no
matter their physical differences—to compete in a fair market-
place, realizing that some natural hierarchy was bound to result
anyway without civil society's intervention. This idea became apparent in his answer to Douglas, where, once again, Lincoln's
point may be best understood through his appreciation of the diversity within whiteness. It did not stand to reason that the Declaration should make the races practically equal, because it did
not do this even for all whites:

> Now this grave argument comes to just nothing at all, by the other
> fact, that they did not at once, or ever afterwards, actually place all
> white people on an equality with one or another. . . . I think the au-
> thors of that notable instrument intended to include all men, but they
> did not intend to declare all men equal in all respects. They did not
> mean to say all were equal in color, size, intellect, moral developments,
> or social capacity. They defined with tolerable distinctness, in what re-
> spects they did consider all men created equal—equal in "certain in-
> alienable rights, among which are life, liberty, and the pursuit of happi-
> ness." This they said, and this meant. They did not mean to assert the
> obvious untruth, that all were then actually enjoying that equality, nor
> yet, that they were about to confer it immediately upon them.

As has been pointed out elsewhere, Lincoln was no egalitarian. For him, the Declaration was no manifesto for social leveling. Rather, just the opposite: it established the principle, not the promise, of equality as "a maxim for free society, . . . though never perfectly attained" and such would augment "the happiness and value of life to all people of all colors everywhere."[48]

Lincoln's reasoning failed him on at least one point, that of his belief in the slave's basic humanity. His understanding of natural rights rested on the assumption that all humans enjoyed basic freedoms. Many extreme racists agreed with this premise, although some such as Douglas and Calhoun would have located the foundation of those rights within the purview of society rather than in nature. Diehard white supremacists, however, attacked his argument by claiming that, because of their supposed infantile and animalistic character, blacks did not fall within the same classification of "human" and thus enjoyed neither the rights nor responsibilities of white men. To this, Lincoln offered no anthropological evidence, no theories about cultural difference, nor any alternative definition of humanity. Unable to "prove" his views, he could only show them as resting within the national mainstream. Lincoln explained the founders' exclusion of slavery from the Northwest Territories and the abolition of the slave trade—which the Southern states themselves had condoned—as a sign of their recognition about the evils of human bondage. He also pointed to the hundreds of thousands of free blacks, all former slaves or the descendants of slaves, who had been liberated by whites on the basis of some implicit acknowledgment of their human right to freedom. Although not religious in a conventional way, Lincoln's sense of moral order allowed him to fill in the gaps where his logic could not tread, thus allowing him to cast his arguments in terms of simple right and wrong. On several occasions, he recognized the folly of arguing with those who saw slaves as having no more rights than livestock. Either blacks were human or they were not, and at the point in his life when he had to answer that question for himself, Lincoln took the same leap of faith as any abolitionist in reaching a conclusion that was more spiritual and instinctual than empirical and philosophical.[49]

Herein lay the contradictions that have left him and his image open to deserving criticism. If the slave is indeed a man and slavery a moral wrong, preventing its extension westward would be morally insufficient; the continued acceptance of slavery where it existed already would thus constitute a violation of natural rights by the state. According to Lincoln's own reasoning, principles of "union" and "constitutional contract"—both existing to serve political ends—are superseded by natural rights to freedom. Secessionists may have understood Lincoln better than he understood himself when they held that the sole difference between him and John Brown was that of method and timetable. Likewise, in upholding the primacy of a social hierarchy based on achievement, Lincoln saw property as the consequence of individual initiative, rather than seeing it—as did Paine, Marx, and Rousseau—as a creation of civil society that perpetuates the very type of "artificial" inequality that the Republican Party claimed to abhor. Despite his ethnocentrism, Lincoln recognized enough human affinity with other races to oppose enslavement and other violations of what he saw as their natural rights. The stark dichotomy he drew between "natural" and "civil" equality, however, stopped him short of advocating the full actualization of those rights. In this sense, he personifies both Myrdal's dilemma and the weaknesses of Western rationalism.

It is likely that, in his more introspective moments, Lincoln recognized these contradictions. Through the 1850s, he played a leading role in the Illinois Colonization Society, and in 1862 he proposed a constitutional amendment to pay for resettling any blacks who wished to emigrate. Following examples set by Clay, Lincoln investigated the possibility of creating United States protectorates in Central America and the Caribbean islands on the assumption that blacks would prosper if returned to their "native" tropical climates. At a time of unprecedented immigration from Europe, the prospect of relocating millions of slaves and former slaves was not entirely far-fetched, and politically it allowed him to avoid the worst Democratic charges of being a "black Republican." But Lincoln frequently admitted the unfeasibility of colonization, knowing that white Northerners would never finance such a scheme and that African American leaders were opposed to the idea. One of his biographers, David Herbert Donald, suggests that Lincoln's advocacy of a plan he knew to be impossible was a way to escape having to think about a problem he found unsolvable. Whether from his own views or his awareness of the views of fellow whites, Lincoln simply could not visualize people of different races pursuing their natural rights side by side, living within the same polity, governed by the same laws and constitution. The hostility of the majority would always intrude on the rights of minorities as long as prejudice remained a staple of human character, and to dream for the elimination of prejudice was to engage in a utopian fantasy that his political pragmatism would not allow.[50]

Some historians have seen in Lincoln's colonization schemes a certain consistency with mid-nineteenth-century ideas about climatic determinism. Notable scientists such as Louis Agassiz posed theories about the ways in which racial differences vary according to the earth's physical geography and that all races flourish best within their own native climatic zones. Lincoln and other Republicans may have been influenced by such theories, believing that all races deserved self-government and natural equality but only in their respective physical environments—a kind of "separate but equal" doctrine elevated to science. Within such a paradigm, Lincoln's ideas appear sound, but only when applied to black-white relations. The contradiction becomes evident when considering his ideas in the context of westward expansion and its effect on other races; after all, Lincoln never said whites should realize their own progress by returning to Europe. Though never passionate about Manifest Destiny, he supported white Americans' imperial expansions far beyond their own "native land." In all his dealings with Native Americans, Lincoln expected them to abandon their indigenous ways and assimilate to whites' cultural values, clearly belying the façade of "race respective to place" that he used to justify black colonization. Blacks' best hope lay in a return to "their own soil," but whites could go where they wished.[51]

Despite the discrepancies in his thinking, Lincoln often took unpopular stands to protect the rights of minority people as he understood them. The Minnesota Sioux uprising, in which bureaucratic delays of food and annuities had caused the Indians to kill more than three hundred fifty whites, became a tense political situation for his administration. In October 1862, Union troops crushed the Sioux rebellion and convened a military commission to try more than fifteen hundred prisoners, some of them captured women and children. During the ensuing trials, Lincoln received detailed letters from white Minnesotans describing the atrocities and demanding revenge. Despite his own opinion of Indians as savages and obstacles to white progress, he requested trial transcripts of each of the 303 Sioux condemned to death. Lincoln and other reviewers were shocked at the illegality of the trials, with their lack of evidence and violations of constitutional rights against self-incrimination. His legal sensibilities offended, he reduced the number awaiting execution to thirty-nine; when thirty-eight of them met the gallows in December (with one pardoned), Minnesota witnessed the largest mass execution in the nation's history. Lincoln's restraining of whites' desire for vengeance damaged his party's political strength in Minnesota in the 1864 elections, to which Lincoln replied, "I could not afford to hang men for votes."[52]

Similar repercussions followed in his limited initiatives for black rights. Lincoln took great care to sell the Emancipation Proclamation as an act designed to save the Union, omitting any mention of his personal distaste for slavery. Even so, the Emancipation's announcement aided the return of a Democratic majority to Congress in fall 1862. LaWanda Cox perhaps has summarized Lincoln best by claiming him as both a mirror of his present and a beacon of the future, holding the dominant prejudiced views of his day but demonstrating a capacity for growth.[53] When a bigoted Pennsylvanian sent him a telegram in 1864, declaring that blacks "must be governed by white men forever," Lincoln drafted this sarcastic reply through his secretary: "I will thank you to inform me, . . . whether you are a white man or black one, because in either case, you can not be regarded as an entirely impartial judge. It may be that you belong to a third or fourth class of yellow or red men, in which case the impartiality of your judgment would be more apparent."[54]

There has been considerable debate over whether the pained experiences of his last four years caused Lincoln to reassess his views on racial inequality. Arguments that he remained an advocate of colonization to the end rest on the autobiography of General Benjamin Butler, who claimed that as late as April 1865 Lincoln was still investigating the deportation of blacks to Africa. Oates has pointed out that Butler is a questionable source on the subject, with no corroborating evidence to support the claim.

Lincoln never favored radical tendencies to expand black suffrage without constitutional mandate, but he did consider extending equal citizenship to those individual African Americans whom he considered worthy. In discussions over the establishment of a Reconstruction government in Louisiana, Lincoln suggested the possibility of allowing well-educated, middle-class blacks to vote. Likewise, black men's military record in the Union Army impressed him sufficiently as to recommend veterans for citizenship status, having "proved" their capacity and loyalty to his satisfaction. Although it is possible that Lincoln glimpsed before his death a vision of a multicultural America where exceptional people of color lived and participated as citizens, side-by-side with whites, it is equally plausible to argue—as George Fredrickson does—that the beliefs and prejudices of a lifetime do not change so abruptly. The spotty historical record allows both his defenders and his critics to find in his last words and actions what they wish.[55]

The nationwide grief that spread with the news of Abraham Lincoln's death in spring 1865 soon gave rise to the myth of the "Great Emancipator," the same myth enshrined in countless memorials and tributes, the same myth that has come under demanding historical scrutiny by a new generation that finds Lincoln's views outdated and abhorrent. According to revisionists, the Lincoln image has obscured the efforts of thousands of slaves, free blacks, and abolitionists who played a collective role in destroying America's disgraceful system of human bondage, men and women who created the volatile context that forced a reluctant president to act. This new scholarship has made an understanding of the "real" Lincoln more difficult, but it also has aided in the search for a more human Lincoln, one that may be more relevant for twenty-first-century Americans. If the advances of social history are to continue, some demystification of icons like Lincoln is necessary. Bennett accurately maintains that Lincoln was no radical, no visionary, that his moderation defined him both as an acceptable political candidate and an acceptable symbol. It is Lincoln, not William Lloyd Garrison or Douglass, whose name is linked with "black freedom," because the freedom he offered was more abstract and rhetorical than real and immediate.[56] A healthy skepticism of the Lincoln myth and "the great man" tradition from which it flows reveals more than the limitations of one man but also those of Americans' commitment to their own cherished ideals.

Demystification, however, does not mean total destruction. Lincoln completed much of the work that the founding generation had left undone: an expansive reading of the Declaration that embraced non-English Europeans under its banner, a conception of humanity and natural rights that he extended unequivocally to people of color, and a commitment not to allow further compromises with slavery to impede Americans' realization of natural equality. Such principles seem weak today, but only because we have exaggerated the stretch of Lincoln's halo by elevating him to impossible standards. As a believer in minorities' civil rights, he was a failure; as one who prepared the groundwork for minorities to later claim their own civil rights, his role was substantial. Just as Lincoln assumed the unfinished tasks of the founders, civil rights activists a century after his death assumed his by attempting to place the meaning of freedom and equality on more material foundations and by shattering the distinction between "civil" and "natural" rights. To hold Lincoln's ideas about racial inequality as his sole defining feature, as though such ideas exclude him from the possibility of idealism or complexity, is to engage in anachronism and oversimplification.

This is not to say that Lincoln's racism should be excused or overlooked. What is most important is that he subordinated his racism to his conviction that all people—whatever their racial, cultural, or mental capacity—are entitled to certain fundamental rights. For him, a just society did not require the elimination of personal prejudice but rather the rendering of such prejudices as irrelevant in the public sphere.[57] Such ideas still hold valuable lessons for a nation that has grown more complicated and diverse since Lincoln's death, with regard to not only color, but also language, national origin, religious belief, sexual orientation, and the like. To conceive of a prejudice-free society in such an environment—where even one American would witness the multiplicity of belief systems and subcultures and judge all of them as equal to his or her own— would seem a naïve, utopian fantasy to a pragmatist like Lincoln. One need not be born in the nineteenth century to wonder whether his reconciliation of race and natural rights lends itself to an alternative definition of "multiculturalism" and whether his tattered image might still prove inspiring to a country that has yet to resolve the questions with which he grappled.

ABRAHAM LINCOLN, EMANCIPATION, AND THE SUPREME COURT

Legend has it that Abraham Lincoln drafted the Emancipation Proclamation in the war department's telegraph office, a place he frequently visited (it was a short walk from the White House) to escape office-seekers and read the latest dispatches from the front. According to the chief of the telegraph operation, Lincoln came to him one day in June 1862 and requested "some paper, as he wanted to write something special. I produced some foolscap and handed it to him. He then sat down and began to write." Lincoln "would look out of the window a while and then put his pen to paper, but he did not write much at once," the telegraph chief observed, and "he would study between times and when he had made up his mind he would put down a line or two, and then sit quiet for a few minutes. . . . I became much interested in the matter and was impressed with the idea that he was engaged upon something of great importance . . . [when] he had finished the document [Lincoln] . . . told me that he had been writing an order giving freedom to the slaves of the South."[1]

The story may or may not be true, but, as historian Mark Neely points out, it "does serve to suggest the way that myths about Lincoln grow."[2] It also suggests that we know little about how Lincoln came to embrace emancipation as a war aim. What was he thinking—perhaps while he was sitting quietly in the war department's telegraph office—as he mulled the pros and cons of formally extending freedom to several million African Americans, a step fraught with both promise and dangerous consequences, and utterly lacking in precedent? No one knows for sure.

The critical period appears to have been the first nine months of 1862. Proemancipation pressure on Lincoln had been building in various quarters: the radical wing of the Republican Party, free African Americans in the North, white abolitionists, and the hundreds of thousands of runaway slaves who caused endless headaches for the Union army. These considerations had been present for some time; indeed, one could argue that emancipation had been in the back of Lincoln's mind ever since he took pains to reject the idea in his first inaugural address. The various factors pushing him in the direction of black freedom, however, reached critical mass sometime in the spring. According to Francis B. Carpenter, an artist who spent a lot of time talking to Lincoln while painting his portrait, the president put the date of his conversion to the emancipation cause at "midsummer 1862," probably some time in June.[3] A month later, during a carriage ride with Secretary of Navy Gideon Welles and Secretary of State William Seward, Lincoln confessed his plans to end slavery. On July 22, he broached the subject with his cabinet, presenting the proclamation as a decision already made and merely awaiting the proper timing and circumstances.[4]

With his cabinet Lincoln seemed resolute and determined, but to the public he appeared to have been all over the map during that spring and early summer of 1862. Even as he quietly began making plans for what would become the Emancipation Proclamation, Lincoln tried to persuade Congress and border state political leaders that they would be better off drafting programs of compensated emancipation. In March he took the unusual step of submitting a special message to Congress calling for the adoption of a joint resolution "that the United States ought to co-operate with any state which may adopt the gradual abolishment of slavery, giving to such state pecuniary aid to be used by the state at its discretion, to compensate for the inconveniences public and private, produced by such change of system." Lincoln defended this idea from a variety of vantage points: it would weaken the Confederacy's hold on its citizens, it would lessen the social and political shock to slaveowners, and if it shortened the war, it would be cost-effective. "In my judgement, gradual, and not sudden, emancipation, is better for all," he argued. To Horace Greeley Lincoln wrote in late March that, as far as he was concerned, the best emancipation plan needed "three main features—gradual—compensation—and vote of the people."[5]

When he did release the Emancipation Proclamation, the results were less than edifying from an abolitionist's point of view. Lincoln committed the deed in careful stages, submitting a preliminary document a few days after the Union victory (of sorts) at Antietam and giving the rebels ninety days to return to the American fold before losing their slaves. When on January 1, 1863, Lincoln formally issued his Emancipation Proclamation, it was a dry, tersely worded document that provided no ringing Lincolnian declarations of freedom and liberty. A century later, historian Richard Hofstadter famously observed that the proclamation possessed all the "moral grandeur of a bill of lading."[6]

To many, the proclamation was more noteworthy for what it did not do. It specifically exempted slaves held in areas then under Union control. This included the forty-eight counties that comprised the new state of West Virginia, as well a few others in Virginia and Louisiana that were occupied by federal troops, which were to be "left precisely as if this proclamation were not issued." Nor did the proclamation include the thousands of African Americans held in bondage in the loyal slave states of Missouri, Kentucky, Maryland, and Delaware.[7]

These exemptions led to the oft-expressed criticism that the Emancipation Proclamation did not really free anyone, ignoring the slaves Lincoln could have freed in the loyal border areas while applying only to those slaves in the Confederacy he could not really reach. "Cold, forbidding, with all the passion and eloquence of a real estate deed, the Proclamation doesn't contain a single quotable sentence and does not enumerate a single principle hostile to slavery," argued Lincoln's chief modern critic, Lerone Bennett, "for the Emancipation Proclamation did not in and of itself, free anybody."[8]

Lincoln's pursuit of compensated emancipation and the proclamation's "bill of lading" quality led many Americans, then and since, to question the level of Lincoln's commitment to his own emancipation policy. William Lloyd Garrison, though happy that the president had finally seen the abolitionists' light, grumbled that the proclamation seemed equivocal and timid; Lincoln "can do nothing for *freedom* in a direct manner, but only by circumlocution and delay."[9] Some modern observers have echoed Garrison's sentiments. His pursuit of various schemes for compensated emancipation made him, in the eyes of Bennett, at best a tainted and reluctant antislavery hero, one who "was tenacious and even devious in supporting *his* plan of gradual emancipation" and who was more energetic "in opposing the idea of an *immediate* emancipation proclamation, which he feared more than slavery." Lincoln's various contradictions and hesitations during the summer of 1862 indicate to Bennett that "the Emancipation Proclamation was *never* Lincoln's plan. The Proclamation was forced on him by events and the pressure of Black and White activists." George M. Fredrickson referred to "Lincoln's quasi-racism" which "simultaneously denied black equality as a practical option for American society while affirming it as a theoretical possibility in another place and under other circumstances." David Brion Davis stated simply that, for Lincoln, emancipation "was a reluctant act, dictated by the grim necessities of war."[10]

Lincoln's defenders argued that his pursuit of compensated emancipation and the proclamation's limitations were motivated by a realistic appraisal of America's political landscape. Despite the desire of congressional radicals such as Thaddeus Stevens and Charles Sumner to pressure the nation toward an embrace of immediate emancipation, Lincoln believed that many Americans were simply not ready for the war to degenerate into a "remorseless revolutionary struggle" involving a racial upheaval. Move too quickly, the president feared, and the political balance of power could shift to the Democrats—who were eager to "play the race card" against the Republicans, and did so mercilessly in the 1864 election—and possibly even shove the border states into the Confederacy's arms. "He was a *politician*," observed William Lee Miller, and as such he was "seeking to shape major party victories, and much of the time seeking office himself, in one of the most racially prejudiced—perhaps most prejudiced—of Northern states [Illinois]."[11]

These arguments are valid, but there is another dimension to Lincoln's thoughts about race and emancipation during the spring and summer of 1862, one that depends upon a fresh appreciation of an often-overlooked facet of Lincoln's life: his status as a lawyer, with a corresponding keen eye for legal procedures and institutions. All of the other perspectives focus on Lincoln the able politician, but he was also the most experienced trial attorney Americans have ever placed in the White House, having litigated thousands of cases during a law career that spanned a quarter-century. It would have been extraordinary if Lincoln had not looked at emancipation from a legal perspective.

Where would such a perspective have led him? As he drafted the Emancipation Proclamation, he knew that Republicans, Democrats, border state politicians, Congress, the army, abolitionists, white Southerners, white Northerners, and African Americans were all looking over his shoulder. His politician's sense told him this was so, but his lawyer's sense surely told him that another point of view was also present—the United States Supreme Court.

Few historians have noted the possible role of the Supreme Court in Lincoln's deliberations.[12] Lincoln himself did not openly discuss the Court's influence on his thinking. Throughout the spring and summer of 1862 he offered a variety of observations on emancipation to audiences black and white, conservative and liberal, yet he never discussed what he thought the Supreme Court would do if emancipation ended up on its docket. Scholars have also overlooked the possible role of the Supreme Court because we tend to read backward to the spring of 1862 the pro-Lincoln Court of 1863. Most accounts of the Civil War highlight Chief Justice Roger B. Taney's antiadministration opinion in *ex parte Merryman* during the spring of 1861 and then feature the Court's proadministration pragmatism in the *Prize Cases* during the winter of 1863, with little indication of what the Court did or how it was constituted during those critical months in between, when emancipation became official Union policy.

But the mere fact that Lincoln did not speak openly of the Supreme Court while he wrestled with emancipation does not mean it played no role in his deliberations. Indeed, his silence on such matters is logical, and consistent with his caution and reticence on all matters related to the Court in 1861 and 1862. We know that Lincoln was examining the possible impact of his proclamation from all sides: political, economic, military, social, and cultural. It would have been strange had this lifelong attorney failed to assess the legal ramifications of his actions and the perspective of the nation's highest legal institution. Moreover, by placing Lincoln's apparently baffling speculations on compensation and the supposed limitations of the Emancipation Proclamation in the light of the Supreme Court's latent hostility to emancipation and the Lincoln administration in general, we may be able to achieve a better understanding of his actions.

LINCOLN WAS SWORN INTO OFFICE on March 4, 1861, by Chief Justice Roger B. Taney, then in his eighty-fourth year. Observers wondered what Taney was thinking as he administered the oath to a new president whose political party and antislavery ideology he despised. Taney was the first person to shake Lincoln's hand after the swearing-in ceremony, and one reporter noted that he "listened with utmost attention to every word" of the inaugural address. Another bystander observed that "the Chief Justice seemed very agitated, and his hands shook perceptively with emotion" as he administered the oath.[13]

When Lincoln became president, Taney's notorious court opinion, *Dred Scott v. Sandford,* was only four years old, and it was still the law of the land. It has rightly been called the most racist Supreme Court decision in American history, a moment during which the nation's highest tribunal saw fit to declare that African Americans (not just slaves, but all Americans of African descent) "were not intended to be included, under the word 'citizen' in the Constitution, and can therefore claim none of the rights and privileges which that instrument provides for and secures to the citizens of the United States."[14] Lincoln himself repeatedly denounced the racist content of the decision during the late 1850s, referring at one point to "Dred Scottism" as a "burlesque on judicial decisions" and a "slander and profanation upon the honored names, and sacred history of republican America."[15] Many Americans felt the same way.

There was, however, another feature of "Dred Scottism" that aroused less attention than its overt bigotry. The case offered powerful federal protection of individual property rights, not just for slaveowners but as an abstract right possessed by all Americans. The chief justice's majority opinion gave a very expansive reading of the Fifth Amendment, with its guarantee that the federal government could take no private property without "due process" or "just compensation." This constitutional restraint on federal authority was, to Taney's mind, substantive and unassailable. The powers to take private property "are not only not granted to Congress, but are in express terms denied, and they are forbidden to exercise them. . . . [I]t is a total absence of power everywhere within the dominion of the United States, and . . . guards [American citizens] as firmly and plainly against any inroads which the General Government might attempt, under the plea of implied or incidental powers."[16]

Taney's purpose here was to demolish the argument that territorial governments, under the aegis of Washington, D.C., could interfere with a slaveowner's right to take a slave like Dred Scott into a Western territory. But the language was more sweeping and general than this relatively narrow constitutional point. *Dred Scott* would make it extraordinarily difficult for a future federal official to take any private property from an American citizen without paying careful attention to "due process" and rendering "just compensation." The tenor of Taney's opinion indicated that the Court would interpret the due process and just compensation clauses with an eye toward protecting the individual property holder from government interference. This was all the more true for any federal attempts to take slave "property" from their rightful owners, because much of Taney's *Dred Scott* opinion was aimed at erasing the distinction between a slave and an inanimate piece of property.

Dred Scott was a tremendous blow to the abolitionist cause and the Republican Party in 1857 and was condemned by Lincoln and other party leaders. Lincoln even went so far as to suggest the wisdom of rethinking the Court's traditional role as arbiter of a law's constitutionality. Nothing really came of this, however, and four years later *Dred Scott* remained on the books, without reversal. As Lincoln took the oath of office, he faced the hard fact that the old man standing across from him with trembling hand and cold stare was the architect of a serious legal barrier to Republican antislavery aspirations, and neither the old man or his barrier had yet to be removed.

Lincoln received a rude reminder of just how potent an adversary Taney could be a month later, when the chief justice issued his ruling in *ex parte Merryman,* a federal circuit court case involving the president's right to suspend the writ of habeas corpus and impose martial law on unruly Confederate sympathizers in Maryland. Responding to the military arrest of a Marylander named John Merryman, Taney angrily denounced Lincoln as a military despot who had violated the basic citizenship rights of John Merryman when he ordered Union soldiers to effect his arrest. "I can only say," Taney acidly observed, that "the people of the United States are no longer living under a government of laws, but every citizen holds life, liberty and property at the will and pleasure of the army officer in whose military district he may happen to be found."

But Taney aimed higher than the army officers making the arrests. He made clear in *ex parte Merryman* that, as far as he was concerned, the ultimate culprit was executive power run amok. *Merryman* was an exercise in strict interpretation of the Constitution's grant of authority to the president. "It is the second article of the constitution that provides for the organization of the executive department, enumerates the powers conferred on it, and prescribes its duties," Taney pointed out, and "if the high power over the liberty of the citizen now claimed, was intended to be conferred on the president, it would undoubtedly be found in plain words in this article; but there is not a word in it that can furnish the slightest ground to justify the exercise of the power." For the chief justice, the need to limit Lincoln's authority extended beyond the specific matter of the writ of habeas corpus. A fair portion of *ex parte Merryman* was devoted to a detailed reading of Article II in its entirety and to Taney's broad claim that the Framers, by narrowly proscribing the president's prerogatives "show[ed] the jealousy and apprehension of future danger which [they] felt in relation to that department of the government, and how carefully they withheld from it many of the powers belonging to the executive branch of the English government which were considered as dangerous to the liberty of the subject; and conferred (and that in clear and specific terms) those powers only which were deemed essential to secure the successful operation of the government."

This particularly included his military powers, which, far from being a grant of expansive authority, must be all the more carefully limited. "Nor can any argument be drawn from the nature of sovereignty, or the necessity of government, for self-defence in times of tumult and danger," he wrote. "The government of the United

States is one of delegated and limited powers; it derives its existence and authority altogether from the constitution, and neither of its branches, executive, legislative or judicial, can exercise any of the powers of government beyond those specified and granted."[17]

Ex parte Merryman was a relatively rare judicial ruling on the extent of the president's wartime authority; indeed, it was one of the first cases to offer a Supreme Court justice's observations on the nature of the presidency as a whole.[18] Lincoln responded by ignoring the *Merryman* decision. Various circumstances made this strategy feasible: Congress ratified the president's actions after the fact when it convened later in the summer, the president's swift response to the Maryland situation kept that state in the Union (and the capital in Washington, D.C., which would have been abandoned if pro-Confederates like Merryman had been allowed to spread mayhem unchecked), and *ex parte Merryman* was, after all, only a federal circuit court opinion, rendered by one Supreme Court justice acting in his capacity as a circuit judge (the Court's justices performed this double duty back then). It did not bear the imprimatur of the entire Supreme Court. This fact lessened its legal and political impact, particularly in light of an earlier Marshall Court decision—*Martin v. Mott*—that granted the president broad discretionary authority as commander in chief. Whether *Merryman's* new narrow reading of Article II from a lower federal circuit court could trump *Martin v. Mott's* older, broader reading from the nation's highest tribunal was an open question.[19]

Nevertheless, the president had to tread carefully. In an early draft of his July 1861 address to Congress, Lincoln wanted to point out, "I have been reminded from a high quarter that one who is sworn to 'take care that the laws be faithfully executed' should not himself be one to violate them." In the final draft he omitted even this oblique reference to Taney, stating instead that "the legality and propriety of what has been done [in Maryland] are questioned," and went on to argue that the Constitution supported his actions and to ask "are all the laws, *but one,* to go unexecuted, and the government itself go to pieces, lest that one be violated?" In offering this defense of his administration, Lincoln never directly mentioned Taney or the Court.[20]

So, as the nation careened toward civil war, Lincoln had two large reminders—*Dred Scott* and *Merryman*—that he faced a hostile Supreme Court. This was true politically speaking, because (as his reticence in the July 4 speech makes clear) he felt he could not afford to criticize the Court too directly, lest he arouse the ire of moderate and conservative Americans who still put great stock in the Court's opinion. It was also true, however, in terms of the law and the Constitution, for in those two opinions the Taney court had placed the weight of the judicial branch in the way of his administration's war-making capabilities, and (with *Dred Scott*) in the way of any moves he might make toward emancipation.

Meantime, other events both helped and harmed Lincoln's position regarding the Court. Justice Peter V. Daniel died nine months before Lincoln took office, and President Buchanan failed to nominate a replacement. Then, in rapid succession, two more justices left the Court: seventy-six-year-old John McLean died, and Southerner John Campbell defected to the Confederacy. This left Lincoln three vacancies to fill on the Court, a situation that might normally have been a golden opportunity for a president to put his stamp on the nation's highest tribunal. The administration, however, lost a potential friend in McLean; Lincoln had cited with approval his dissent in *Dred Scott,* and he generally respected the elderly judge's legal acumen.[21] Campbell backed Taney in *Dred Scott,* and now he was gone, but there remained on the Court what might be called a *Dred Scott* bloc, consisting of five of the seven men who voted in the majority on that case: Roger Taney, John Catron, James Wayne, Samuel Nelson, and Robert Grier. Nathan Clifford, appointed in 1858 to succeed Benjamin Curtis (the only other dissenting voice in *Dred Scott*), was a Democrat who greatly admired Roger Taney—"He is truly my friend," Clifford wrote his wife—and could be expected to side with the chief justice on most matters.[22] Opposing these six men were three empty seats.

This was not a pro-Lincoln Court. Of course, the five *Dred Scott* judges would not necessarily be adamant opponents of the president. There had been many fissures and disagreements within the *Dred Scott* majority, even as the justices came together to decide Scott's fate, and the judges who signed off on the *Dred Scott* decision were not necessarily pro-Southern or pro-Confederate.[23] Tennessean John Catron, for example, was such a staunch Unionist that he tried gamely to hold federal court sessions in his home state, at the risk of arrest by Confederate authorities. Even Taney remained nominally loyal to the North, though he thought a peaceful separation of the sections would be best for all concerned. There were also persistent rumors of his imminent resignation because of poor health, and Catron was experiencing physical problems, as well.[24] Perhaps, in view of the quirks of old age and sickness, Lincoln might be able to soon appoint two more justices and effect a decisive swing on the Court in his direction.

Maybe—but then again, maybe not. Acts of nature aside, there was no reason to think the Court's makeup would change so drastically anytime soon. The irascible old chief justice would likely cling to his seat as long as possible, if for no other reason than to stand as a self-appointed bulwark against the president's alleged tyranny. Lincoln had good reason to believe that the four men who voted with Taney in *Dred Scott,* and Clifford—the man who felt the chief justice was "truly my friend" and a great jurist—might be easily persuaded to side with Taney on whatever controversial wartime issues came before them. When Lincoln looked at the Court, he must have seen the potential of a formidable six-judge majority arrayed against him.

With this in mind, the president gave two of the vacant seats to men he could trust. He allowed the rest of 1861 to expire without acting; the Court did not convene from March onward, and Lincoln had many more pressing matters to attend. Finally, in January 1862, he submitted the name of Ohio lawyer Noah H. Swayne to the Senate, which quickly confirmed him. Six months later, Lincoln nominated Iowan Samuel F. Miller, who also received swift approval. Both men had solid antislavery and Republican pedigrees and could be expected generally to support the administration.[25] By July 1862—just as he was unveiling the Emancipation Proclamation to his cabinet—Lincoln faced a Supreme Court with the *Dred Scott* block of five justices, Taney ally Clifford, two men he could reasonably count on to be friendly toward his policies, and one remaining vacancy.

That last seat went to Illinois judge David Davis, Lincoln's campaign manager and longtime friend from the Illinois circuit. The president could count on Davis as an ally, though the process of selecting him was difficult. Both Davis and Orville Browning—an Illinois lawyer and another old friend—badly wanted the job and brought significant political resources to bear on the president.

Davis had the better personal claim, but Browning boasted strong credentials: he was a native Kentuckian who was well connected politically with conservative ex-Whig types in the party, a constituency Lincoln felt he could not alienate, particularly in the border states.[26]

For a while, it looked as though this would be the deciding factor. "There has never been a day when if I had to act I should not have appointed Browning," Lincoln said, and when this quote got back to Davis and his supporters they assumed their cause was lost. But after renewing their pressure on Lincoln, the president suddenly and without explanation switched course and decided upon Davis as his man. The decision was made in August 1862, and, unlike the previous year, Lincoln was unwilling to wait for the Court to resume its winter term before making the appointment. In fact, Lincoln took the highly unusual step of appointing Davis when the Senate was recessed; this was so unusual that he asked his attorney general to furnish a written opinion affirming its propriety. The Attorney General did so, and on October 17, 1862, Lincoln formally offered his old friend the last Supreme Court vacancy.[27]

The timing and nature of this decision is interesting. Davis was a safer bet to support emancipation than the mercurial Browning, who later broke with the administration over that issue and blamed Lincoln's proclamation for the Republicans' poor showing in the 1862 elections. Lincoln chose Davis just as he was decisively committing his administration to black freedom. He then rushed Davis's nomination in an unprecedented fashion, and for no discernible reason, except that perhaps Lincoln wanted Davis already on the bench when the Emancipation Proclamation took effect on January 1, 1863. The president no doubt picked Davis and hurried his nomination for a variety of reasons, but it is reasonable to speculate that he hoped Davis could protect emancipation if it came before the Court.[28]

Lincoln must also have reflected that, though having Davis join the two other administration appointees on the bench helped, it would not be enough. As emancipation loomed just over the horizon in the fall of 1862, Lincoln still faced a majority of six Supreme Court justices who were likely hostile to the measure. Moreover, he had now played all the cards in his hand. Barring a sudden resignation or death, the Court's lineup was complete.

The career lawyer in the White House could easily imagine a plausible test case involving a loyal border state slaveowner from, for instance, Kentucky, who after losing his slaves under the new presidential order brought a lawsuit to recover his human "property," a lawsuit that would surely land on the Supreme Court's docket. Lincoln also would have had no difficulty piecing together in his mind the elements of a majority opinion, written by the chief justice and at least his four *Dred Scott* allies, which would destroy emancipation before it even began.

The centerpiece of such an opinion would have been a reaffirmation of *Dred Scott* itself, which now enjoyed the status conferred upon it by *stare decisis*. That case gave Taney the tools he needed to strike down Lincoln's emancipation decree, and he could do so at a relatively low political cost, without resurrecting the controversy over black citizenship. The chief justice need only reaffirm *Dred Scott's* substantive reading of the Fifth Amendment's takings clause, ruling that presidential emancipation without compensation was unconstitutional. Taney did not have to address the social status of blacks directly; instead, he could appeal to abstract principles of property rights, principles supported by a majority of Americans, whatever their feelings on slavery.

If the damage wrought to black Americans' aspirations were not enough, Taney could in the same opinion strike a telling blow against his other Lincoln administration bugaboo: the growth of wartime executive authority. As we have seen, this was the essence of his opinion in *ex parte Merryman*. By later 1862, *Merryman* was essentially a dead letter, but now an executive order freeing the slaves, written as a war measure, could be used by Taney to dredge up the entire matter of presidential "tyranny" again. This section of Taney's antiemancipation opinion could read the president's powers to emancipate as narrowly as *Merryman* read his power to suspend the writ of habeas corpus. Granted, the power to emancipate and the power to enforce wartime internal security were on the surface unrelated. The sweeping indictment of *all* manifestations of presidential power in *Merryman*, however, would give the chief justice the legal hook he needed to hang a new denunciation of Lincoln's tyrannical emancipation of the slaves and subsequent erasure of white property rights.

To make matters worse, Lincoln risked the embarrassment of possibly seeing one or both of his new appointees side with the Taney-led majority on the executive powers issue. Both Swayne and Miller were supporters of antislavery principles, but both were also wary of Lincoln's authority as commander in chief. Later in the war, Swayne expressed concern over what he saw as overly zealous pursuit of suspected Confederate sympathizers by the army, and Miller contacted Lincoln seeking relief for what he believed was the arbitrary arrest of an elderly Kentucky man.[29] Both men were generally supportive of the president, but if Taney was shrewd enough to couch his opposition to emancipation in a manner calculated to arouse his colleagues' fears of presidential excess, he stood a decent chance of killing black freedom with a near-unanimous Court on his side.

Even if Taney ended up commanding only a bare five-four majority, an antiemancipation ruling would have done incalculable legal and political damage to the Lincoln administration and the Union's cause. It would make emancipation that much more difficult, add more legal chains to the black man's plight, and, by further narrowing Lincoln's war necessity arguments, make the war harder to prosecute. Finally, it would have reinforced the two most potent antiemancipation, antiadministration opinions issued by the Court: *Dred Scott* and *ex parte Merryman*. Those two cases, now connected to a third one striking down emancipation, would have formed an anti-Lincoln iron triangle, forged by an implacably hostile chief justice and his allies, with each ruling reinforcing the other.

We do not know whether all of this ran through Lincoln's mind during the last half of 1862, but there is the circumstantial evidence of his hurried attempt to get Davis appointed to his new job, which suggests that the Court was at least in the back of the president's mind as he formulated administration policies on emancipation. More generally there is Lincoln's status as a lawyer who had spent twenty-five years of his life litigating cases in courtrooms where the judge's demeanor made all the difference. Above all, there was the fact that Lincoln could not see into the future. He could not know in the fall of 1862 that Taney's health would soon make him a nonfactor on the bench. Nor could he foresee the *Prize Cases* ruling of March 1863, a tremendous legal victory for his administration that signaled a sea change in the

Court's attitude toward the war and the administration and gave Lincoln flexibility in defining the nature of the war and Confederates' legal rights. In the fall of 1862, all Lincoln knew was that, first, the Emancipation Proclamation was fundamentally a legal document, second, that the nation's highest legal tribunal stood a good chance of knocking it down, and third, that such a ruling would be a severe setback for his presidency, his party, and the hopes of millions of African Americans.

What, though, could the president have done about it? Lincoln's best bet for heading off an antiemancipation Supreme Court were the two features his abolitionist critics found so disagreeable: compensated emancipation and the exclusion of border state and occupied Americans in the Emancipation Proclamation.

A viable compensation program would have solved a variety of problems for Lincoln, but one of its chief uses was legal. Compensating slaveholders for their losses would have defused Taney's potential Fifth Amendment argument. Had Congress and the border states responded to Lincoln's request for compensated emancipation, Taney would have found it much more difficult to construct a case for emancipation constituting an unlawful seizure of property without the "just compensation" required by the Framers.

Nevertheless, compensation also had serious limitations. Enactment of a compensation plan was not up to Lincoln. He could not appropriate the money from the federal treasury without congressional action; in the end, he could only beg Congress to do so, while Congress in turn begged the states to cooperate. The president underscored this point in his March 1862 message to Congress. "The proposition now made," he pointed out, was "an offer only," and he sounded almost plaintive by adding that, "while it is true that the adoption of the proposed resolution [to appropriate money for voluntary compensation] would be merely initiatory, and not within itself a practical measure, it is recommended in the hope that it would soon lead to important results."

Lincoln also felt that Congress could not force the states to act upon his request. Compensated emancipation "sets up no claim of a right, by federal authority, to interfere with slavery within state limits," he claimed; rather "it is proposed as a matter of perfectly free choice with them."[30] He felt this was necessary to placate the border states, and it was also consistent with the long-stated

Republican position that it had no desire to meddle with slavery where it already existed. It did, however, seriously weaken the plan's legal impact. If only one border state chose not to take advantage of Congress's offer, and Lincoln subsequently issued an emancipation decree freeing all American slaves, that recalcitrant state would be full of potential litigants, at least one of whom would be willing to test the whole program in court.

But the worst weakness of all was the fact that, by the fall of 1862, compensation was dead in the water. Congress was willing enough, but border state leaders were not. An exasperated Lincoln gave it one last try in December 1862. He proposed to Congress a series of constitutional amendments that together would have created an ambitious national compensation program. The states that chose to pursue emancipation before 1900 would be given federal government bonds and congressional aid in "colonizing free colored persons, with their own consent, at any place or places without the United States." Lincoln couched his proposal in terms of the states' (and the nation's) pecuniary self-interest. "Without slavery the rebellion could never have existed; without slavery it could not continue," he declared, and then provided detailed financial data showing that compensation would cost far less than the monetary burden imposed by fighting the war. As Congress read the president's proposal, the Emancipation Proclamation was almost upon them, its January deadline only four weeks away.[31]

This last-ditch effort at compensated emancipation has provided more grist for the mills of Lincoln's critics, who see it as further evidence of his weak moral conviction to end slavery cleanly. "Lincoln distanced himself further from the Proclamation by campaigning . . . for a gradual emancipation program that contradicted and imperiled the Emancipation Proclamation he had signed," according to Bennett.[32]

Lincoln's moral convictions aside, compensated emancipation could have played an invaluable legal role by heading off potential Fifth Amendment litigation.[33] Otherwise, why did he pitch his ideas as constitutional amendments? Why did he choose the most difficult political and constitutional format available, one that would have required a lengthy and extensive ratification process? Why did he not instead field the same ideas as proposed congressional legislation? This would have achieved the same basic policy results with a higher probability of success.

As with so much else, we cannot be certain what Lincoln's thinking was in this regard. It seems reasonable, though, to suggest that he chose this course of action because constitutional amendments were the only way to place *some* sort of emancipation plan beyond the reach of the Supreme Court. Compensated emancipation was better than no emancipation at all—still a distinct possibility in December 1862, with Taney alive and the *Dred Scott* bloc intact. Lincoln was not "distancing himself," as Bennett alleges. Rather, he was trying to establish what any good lawyer knew was sound strategy in the event of a defeat: a fallback position.

The best position of all, however, would be to keep an antiemancipation lawsuit from ever reaching the Court's docket in the first place. Lincoln knew that border state slaveholders were the most likely source of any such litigation. Like pro-Confederate Southerners, they still possessed all of the rights guaranteed United States citizens. Unlike the Confederates, however, border state slaveowners still enjoyed unfettered access to the federal court system.

Hence Lincoln's other option: eliminate border state slaveowners as potential litigants by allowing them to keep their slaves. Again, modern Lincoln critics such as Bennett—as well as more radical antislavery contemporaries like Horace Greeley and Salmon Chase—objected strongly to the Emancipation Proclamation's exemptions for border state and loyal slaveowners.[34] Even more moderate types such as Secretary of State William Seward wondered whether this was such a good idea. According to Secretary of the Navy Welles, "Chase advised that fractional parts of States ought not to be exempted." Welles added, "I think he is right," citing possible conflicts between state and local authorities. Chase objected to excluding any of the slaves in the United States, believing it would "impair the moral effect of the Proclamation."[35]

Lincoln, however, insisted that the exemptions must remain in place, despite the objections of radicals on moral grounds and moderates on political and legal grounds. He couched his stance in terms of border state and Reconstruction politics, telling his cabinet that he could not afford to alienate conservatives and moderates in the border states and the occupied South. There was a lot more going on underneath the surface, however. Even as Lincoln allowed border state slaveowners to keep their human "property," he began working quietly behind the scenes to persuade legislators in Kentucky, Missouri, Maryland, and Delaware to enact their emancipation plans, and he pressed for passage of a constitutional amendment that would make slavery a thing of the past nationwide. The president also well knew that events on the battlefront were quickly eradicating slavery everywhere, as runaway slaves flooded into Union lines and Yankee soldiers proved increasingly willing to help them escape from bondage. "Although Lincoln may not have been 'touching' slavery in the South," historian Philip Paludan observes, "his generals were roughing it up rather dramatically."[36]

Thus, Lincoln had good reason to be confident that, come what may, slavery would die everywhere in America, including the border states. The army was killing it with its bullets and bayonets, Congress was killing it via property confiscation and what would eventually become the Thirteenth Amendment, and he was doing his best to kill it with the Emancipation Proclamation and various quiet political efforts in the border states. Only one national institution might possibly try to intervene and stop slavery's nosedive to extinction—the Taney Court—but Taney had to have a test case to do so, and the proclamation's exemptions removed the only realistic plaintiffs. Surely the opprobrium directed at Lincoln by radical critics (and some modern observers) was a small price to pay for keeping the author of *Dred Scott* and his allies out of the emancipation process entirely.

The course of events would, in the end, work to Lincoln's benefit. Taney's health would begin its final decline in early 1863, and by the middle of that year he would cease to be a serious threat to the president or the war effort. He did file a vigorous dissent—with Justices Nelson, Catron, and Clifford—in the *Prize Cases,* and he groused at Secretary of Treasury Chase about the creation of an income tax to fund the war effort. Lincoln worried enough about the influence of Taney and his Court allies that he pressed for, and received, a modest "court-packing" scheme that added a tenth justice to the bench. Meantime, Taney remained a thorn in the president's side until the chief justice's death on October 13, 1864.[37]

But he never had a chance to rule on the constitutionality of emancipation. In light of his views on race, the war, and Lincoln, there is little doubt what such a ruling would have looked like. Critics of Lincoln's policies on black freedom might do well to remember that the future of African Americans—indeed, the future of American liberty—might have been very different had the author of *Dred Scott* been given the final word on the matter.

MICHAEL VORENBERG

SLAVERY REPARATIONS
IN THEORY AND PRACTICE
Lincoln's Approach

Almost a century and a half ago, at Gettysburg, Pennsylvania,
Abraham Lincoln helped to bury not only thousands of soldiers but also the Constitution "as it is"—or, rather, as it was.
By invoking the framers of the Declaration of Independence
rather than the framers of the Constitution at his Gettysburg
Address, and by declaring a "new birth of freedom," Lincoln,
in a move so well described by Garry Wills, told the nation
that a Constitution sanctioning slavery could no longer guide
a nation fighting for freedom.[1] Or, as he put it eloquently in
his December 1862 message to Congress, "the dogmas of the
quiet past are inadequate to the stormy present."[2]

Yet the Gettysburg Address, for all of its poetry, was in-
complete. Its terms were vague. Not one of the three words
usually used by Lincoln in his public statements—Union,
Constitution, slavery—appeared in the address. Nor was
there any direct call for a specific measure to give legal or
constitutional force to the "new birth of freedom" that he
proclaimed. Such a call was missing also from the Emancipation Proclamation, signed on January 1, 1863, which
Lincoln himself conceded might be outlawed by the
Supreme Court or Congress, rescinded by his successor if
he were defeated for reelection, or simply have no standing

once the war was over. Lincoln's omission in the Gettysburg Address of a specific measure to guarantee freedom is understandable: adding specific proposals to the speech would have detracted from its poetic majesty and might have been seen as a callous move, using a memorial to past soldiers to promote a present agenda. Yet, one naturally wonders whether Lincoln at Gettysburg had in mind the idea of amending the Constitution to abolish slavery, a proposal that was gaining popularity at the moment that he delivered the speech. If such a measure had been on Lincoln's mind, he kept silent about it, and for a long time. Not until June 1864, seven months after the amendment had been introduced in Congress, eight months after the Gettysburg Address, and eighteen months after the Emancipation Proclamation, did Lincoln finally endorse the antislavery amendment in public. Indeed, there is no evidence that he supported the measure even in private during this time. Only later, after he had been renominated and reelected, did Lincoln publicly support the amendment. Ultimately, he helped secure congressional passage of the resolution sending the amendment to the states for ratification. But why had he maintained such silence early on?[3]

Compared to the subject of what Lincoln did or did not do for emancipation in the months and years leading up to the Emancipation Proclamation, the subject of what Lincoln did to secure black freedom *after* the proclamation is relatively untouched by historians. Most scholars assume that the Thirteenth Amendment was simply an obvious afterthought to the proclamation and thus that they should focus most of their attention on the proclamation. One of the few exceptions to this scholarly trend was a 1976 article in *Ebony* magazine on the final debate in Congress on the resolution for the Thirteenth Amendment. The author of the article was Lerone Bennett.

Thus, it is rather surprising and disappointing that Bennett's grand work, *Forced into Glory*, published almost twenty-five years after the *Ebony* article, paid little attention to Lincoln's approach to emancipation in the last years of the Civil War. To the question of what Lincoln learned between the time that he began to support emancipation to the time that he helped to make emancipation a part of the Constitution, Bennett's book seems to answer, "Not much."

Although Lincoln's overall attitudes on race may offer a poor model of how we might think about race today, his thinking about race did evolve, especially over the course of the Civil War. It is precisely the human capacity for intellectual self-development demonstrated by Lincoln that can offer optimism for today, even as we acknowledge with pessimism—as Bennett does—the racism that plagued Lincoln all his life.

To highlight Lincoln's evolution as a thinker about race, this chapter focuses on three issues that follow roughly a chronological path in his developing racial attitudes: his approach to African American colonization; his attitudes toward education for African Americans; and his belief in restitution due to African Americans because of their former enslavement, what today goes by the general term of "reparations." After examining these matters, one inevitably wishes, as Bennett does, that Lincoln had been more progressive in his racial views, but one also might be struck by Lincoln as still a role model, albeit in a limited way, in racial thinking.

FIRST, LET US LOOK AT Lincoln's efforts to colonize African Americans abroad. For many years, historians battled over the question of exactly when—or even if—the president relinquished his idea of settling black people outside of the country. Bennett assumes that Lincoln never gave up this particular "white dream" (Bennett's term), even though scholars in the past twenty years have tended to take the opposite position. The last documented time Lincoln supposedly talked of colonization is to General Benjamin Butler in the spring of 1865. Because of meticulous detective work done by Mark E. Neely, Jr., we now know that Butler's account of this meeting was a fabrication. Neely helps to get Lincoln off the hook, to show that he had given up on colonization by at least the end of the Civil War.[4] Even without Neely's research, there is the record of John Hay, who, in his diary at July 1, 1864, wrote that Lincoln had finally "sloughed off" that idea of colonization. Many have read that passage as evidence that Lincoln held onto colonization until at least July 1, 1864, but Hay's entry allows for the possibility that Lincoln gave up the idea well before that date. Indeed, it is most likely that Hay mentioned Lincoln's "sloughing off" of colonization on this particular date simply because a bill rescinding funds for colonization had just crossed his desk. Despite the continued assumption of Bennett and others that Lincoln never gave up on colonization, all evidence suggests otherwise. For a scholar of a positivist persuasion, one who relies mainly on evidence rather than speculation, it is easy to follow Neely's lead and take Lincoln off the hook of colonization.[5]

Yet, perhaps focusing only on the recorded evidence is limiting. Yes, Butler did not have the conversation with Lincoln that he purported to have. Yes, Lincoln probably did not say to John Hay on July 1, 1864, "Today, and only today, I have given up on colonization." With detective work and a positivist methodology that assumes that hard digging can reveal all the answers that really matter, historians thus make advances. But this same approach can also close off avenues of inquiry. After all, might it be possible that Butler and Lincoln did have a conversation some time in late 1864 or early 1865, that Butler remembered the date wrong, that Butler told Lincoln his various schemes for using African soldiers abroad, and Lincoln nodded approvingly, perhaps because he liked the idea, or more likely because he wanted to end the conversation with a general whom he did not much like?

A less positivist, more speculative approach has merit, and it may indeed lead to the conclusion that Lincoln never stopped dreaming of a future in which all African Americans left the country. At the very least, he never stopped thinking that African Americans were better served by gradual rather than immediate emancipation. He conceded that the circumstances of war, more than other factors, forced him toward immediate abolition. Over and over during the period after he signed the proclamation, Lincoln expressed his concern that the former slaves would become "a laboring, landless, and homeless class" if they were immediately emancipated.[6] According to Alexander Stephens, the vice president of the Confederacy, at Hampton Roads, Lincoln told Stephens that, if he were in the Georgian's place, he would persuade the governor of his state to assemble the legislature and instruct the newly elected body to recall the state's troops, elect members to Congress, and ratify the antislavery amendment "prospectively, so as to take effect—say in five years."[7] Stephens's story is suspicious at best. Surely Lincoln would have doubted the constitutionality of prospective ratification. Also, he knew that no program of gradual emancipation could exist in the face of a constitutional amendment declaring that "neither slavery nor involuntary servitude . . . shall exist." Yet, it is quite possible that Lincoln did retain his private concerns about the fate of the slaves if they were freed immediately. Just a few days before his death, he supposedly told an Alabama man that, were it up to him, he might allow "gradual emancipation, say running through twenty years," to take place, but the matter was out of his hands because of the constitutional amendment "now before the people."⁸ Perhaps at Hampton Roads, Lincoln made a similar statement to Stephens, who twisted it to make Lincoln sound as if he believed gradual emancipation and the abolition amendment were compatible—something Lincoln surely could not have believed.

As he continued to voice his preference for gradual over immediate abolition, Lincoln may well have still harbored a desire for a future in which blacks and whites lived separately, even though as president he knew that he must work toward a different, biracial future. When he met with his cabinet in February 1865, he again made his plea for funds to pay compensation to loyal slaveowners for the loss of their freed slaves, a plea that was summarily rejected.⁹ But, tellingly, he did not make a plea for colonization, even though, in the past, he had always joined colonization and compensation in his policies. It is clear that he knew, at least by early 1865, though probably well before, that colonization was a hopeless, unworkable, and unpopular cause.

But does that mean that Lincoln stopped dreaming of black colonization? If the United States had unlimited funds to colonize African Americans abroad, if it had recently laid claim to a newly discovered large continent in the central Atlantic filled with rich land, ports, and navigable rivers, and, most important, if African Americans themselves were unified in a desire to leave the country and settle abroad, would Lincoln not have tried to make his white dream a reality? Are historians really supposed to believe that Lincoln instead would have given up his dream and argued that Americans would be better off if the races learned to live together, whether in the United States or in the newly discovered continent?

Of course, like other exercises in counterfactual history, this speculative approach fails to explain why history played out the way it did. It does, however, expose in a quick flash the textures of Lincoln's complex views on race. Yes, Lincoln would have said yes to colonization if he had faced this unlikely scenario. So, at least in one respect—by taking a highly speculative approach—a historian can agree with Bennett that Lincoln never gave up the white dream.

Although a speculative approach is not inherently ahistorical, it does seem so when it is used to understand Lincoln, who was far more pragmatic than speculative. Although historians might muse about the imagined scenario above, Lincoln would never have done so. He had dreams, to be sure, but he kept those dreams *as* dreams, never working to implement them as policy to the detriment of some higher cause such as Union. And that point must preface and overshadow any discussion of Lincoln's dream, white or otherwise. He dreamed, yes—he even spoke of his dreams in rare moments— but when he acted as president, he left the dreams behind.

So, WHAT THEN, WAS LINCOLN'S waking dream? That is, what realistic vision of the future for African Americans did he have in mind in the months after the Emancipation Proclamation? Was he the white supremacist or the racial egalitarian? For a moment, let us put all labels that strictly involve race aside and simply call Lincoln, instead, a Whig. The notion of Lincoln as a Whig in the White House is not a new one: more than forty years ago, David Herbert Donald used the Whig model to characterize Lincoln's style of presidential leadership.[10] Putting aside the long-debated question of whether Lincoln saw himself more as a Whig or a Republican, one cannot deny that he had been a Whig for almost thirty years before joining the Republican Party and that he undoubtedly still identified with Whig ideology, even if he no longer identified with the defunct party. Lincoln scholars must therefore take stock of scholarship on Whig ideology, especially the work of Daniel Walker Howe, who argues, among other things, for a distinctive Whig approach to race.[11] It is a natural step to assume that the Whig mentality, aside from governing Lincoln's administrative behavior, also influenced his social sensibilities as president, including his attitudes toward race.

As a Whig, Lincoln held an optimistic vision of a positive, though limited, role of the federal government in promoting social reform. He came to the White House with the belief that federal authorities should encourage but seldom compel the state and local authorities to help the nation achieve its glorious mission.

Second, as a Whig, Lincoln believed that all people were inherently equal—that is, that they had equal capacities even if they did not share the same attributes. Slaves and the descendants of slaves, however, were different. Lincoln and most other Whigs believed that, through years of racial oppression, the moral and intellectual development of African Americans was stunted, posing an almost insurmountable obstacle to their achieving equality with whites. Here Lincoln's thinking was much in line with the thinking of most Democrats, including Thomas Jefferson, but Lincoln diverged from the Jeffersonian tradition in his belief that blacks, like whites, were capable of improving themselves, though such improvement might take some time. This guarded optimism distinguished Lincoln from his contemporaries among the Democrats, almost all of whom believed that the slaves, once freed, would suffer and die. One Democrat, Samuel Barlow, General George McClellan's advisor and political manager, penned a statement that captured perfectly his party's thinking on black freedom: "Freedom of the blacks must lead to a speedy annihilation of the race," he wrote. "Perhaps this is necessary," he speculated, "perhaps it is wise that they shall be freed from the restraints as well as the duties which are now enforced by their masters and be allowed to follow in the footsteps of the red man, be allowed to reap the inevitable consequences of inferiority of race, surrounded by a civilization the advantages of which they cannot share and under the vices of which they must succumb."[12] Barlow's sentiment was shared also by many former Democrats who had joined the Republican Party, including the crusty Jacksonian Francis P. Blair, Sr., who wrote to William Lloyd Garrison in 1864 that there was no "better hope of the amalgamation of the Africans with our race" than there was of the amalgamation of Native Americans with the white race.[13]

Certainly, Lincoln retained his own doubts about the African American potential for success right up until the end of the war. At the Hampton Roads conference in February 1865, when the Confederate commissioner Robert M. T. Hunter argued that the emancipation of the slaves would lead to the ruin of the South and the decimation of the African American race, the president tried to lighten the mood by giving his own version of what would happen to the freed people. As usual, he used a story to demonstrate his point, in this case the hoary tale of farmer Case of Illinois. Case had found an economical way of feeding his hogs by planting potatoes and letting the animals root them out themselves. In this way, the hogs were fed, and the potatoes harvested. But what would happen, asked a neighbor, when the ground froze a foot deep during the winter. "Well," stammered

Lincoln's farmer, "it may come pretty hard on their *snouts,* but I don't see but that it will be 'root, hog or die!'"[14] "Root, hog or die" later became the catch phrase of Reconstruction-era conservatives who demanded that the federal government not concern itself with the fate of African Americans. For Lincoln in 1865, the phrase reflected a similar fatalistic attitude toward the future of the freed people, but it also revealed that Lincoln, unlike many of his political opponents, had become convinced that some of the blacks would, to use his metaphor, root successfully. This was the narrow scope of Lincoln's progressive vision: he did not foresee all blacks locked into the same dismal future but instead believed that some of them would flourish.

The key to the African American future, believed Lincoln (and here was the final way in which Whig ideology infused his racial vision), was education. Lincoln embraced the Jeffersonian notion that a successful democracy depended on a well-educated electorate, but he went beyond Jefferson in suggesting that African Americans—at least some of them—were as capable as whites of becoming educated citizens. If Lincoln at first resisted black suffrage, he did so less because of raw, racist feelings of white superiority than because of specific fears, emanating from his Whig background, that an uneducated electorate of any color could be easily manipulated by dangerous enemies, domestic or foreign.

For Lincoln, it was education, much more than race, that defined a person, and a nation. As a young boy, he scribbled in one of his school books, "Good boys who to their books apply / Will all be great men by and by."[15] In his first political campaign, running for the Illinois state legislature in 1832, he called education "the most important subject which we as a people can be engaged in," and he spoke of a future when learning could be extended to all. "I desire to see a time," he said, "when education, and by its means, morality, sobriety, enterprise and industry, shall become much more general than at present."[16] Lincoln came to define himself by his education. In the two autobiographical sketches he prepared during the year preceding the 1860 election, he paid particular attention to his schooling. His father, he gratuitously pointed out, was uneducated, but young Abraham was determined to improve himself intellectually. His autobiographies reflect humility and even humiliation at having to contend with political opponents like Stephen Douglas and William Henry Seward, who had attended private academies or colleges. Lincoln wrote of himself, "He regrets his want of education, and does what he can to supply the want."[17] Yet, in his self-deprecation, he helped ingrain education into the Lincoln myth. Whereas Andrew Jackson, the quintessential Democrat, would become known as the self-*made* man; Lincoln, the quintessential Whig, would become known as the self-*taught* man.

Education, then, became the focus of Lincoln's vision of a successful African American future. Before the war, especially in his debates with Douglas, Lincoln had frequently shared with Douglas doubts about what Lincoln called the "moral and intellectual endowment" of blacks.[18] His concern that Southern blacks had intellects that were, in his words, "clouded by Slavery," led him to believe, as he told a delegation of black leaders in 1862, that the race had little future in America.[19] In that speech, Lincoln recommended colonization abroad to the black delegation as a solution to their intellectual shortcomings. Once the wartime experiments in free black labor began to prove successful, Lincoln emphasized education, not colonization, as the key to African American self-sufficiency. "Education for young blacks," Lincoln wrote to General Nathaniel Banks in the summer of 1863, should be included in Louisiana's reconstruction plan. In his Reconstruction Proclamation in December of 1863, he encouraged all Southern states to provide for the education of the freed people. By 1865 the president was handing out compliments to those military officials in the South who helped foster what he called the "moral and physical elevation" of the newly freed African Americans.[20]

Yet Lincoln knew that more was needed than white philanthropic efforts at educating blacks in order to ensure a successful future for both races. He knew that for real success blacks would need the self-motivation to educate themselves. Prior to becoming president, Lincoln probably was skeptical of African Americans' desire for education. Life as president in Washington, D.C., during the Civil War changed that. Here, Lincoln had the first opportunity of his life to see just how self-motivated African Americans could be in acquiring education. Lincoln's model for self-education was, of course, Frederick Douglass. Self-directed and self-taught, Douglass, by his very existence, must have challenged the president's preconception of the former slave as morally and intellectually destitute. Lincoln trusted Douglass's political savvy as well as his moral code, and he read the abolitionist's speeches and sought his advice three times during the war. The president and the abolitionist conferred in 1863 about equal pay for black soldiers, in 1864 about the emancipation issue in the presidential election, and in 1865 about Lincoln's second inaugural. In a way, Douglass even delivered his own Gettysburg Address, although his talk came about one hundred miles to the east, in Philadelphia, and about two weeks after Lincoln's more famous speech. In his address, Douglass used words much like Lincoln's at Gettysburg. "What business . . . have we to fight for the old Union?" asked Douglass. "We are not fighting for it," he answered, "We are fighting for something incomparably better than the old Union. We are fighting for unity; unity of idea; unity of sentiment, unity of object, unity of institutions, in which there shall be no North, no South, no East, no West, no black, no white, but a solidarity of the nation, making every slave free, and every free man a voter."[21] Aside from Douglass's explicit mention of the issue of black suffrage, the words could just as well have been Lincoln's. And if we are willing to concede that Lincoln's racial views changed through his relationship with Douglass and that the president's attitudes grew closer to Douglass's as the war's end approached, we might also accept the possibility that Lincoln, had he lived, would have made black suffrage not just a suggestion but a mandate.

Douglass was not the only educated African American that Lincoln met during the war. In his daily life at home he had constant dealings with educated black servants such as Elizabeth Keckley, his wife's dressmaker, and his valet, William Slade, who accompanied him to Gettysburg. In his official capacity as president, Lincoln had the opportunity to meet powerful black abolitionists such as Sojourner Truth and Martin Delany, people who had simply been names on a page during his years in Illinois. The president's position exposed him to black ministers, black educators, and even black officials from the newly recognized republics of Haiti and Liberia.

It was Lincoln's meeting with two highly educated leaders of the black community in New Orleans that probably did more than anything else to convince him that at least some Southern blacks should be granted the ballot. These men, Jean Baptiste Roudanez and Arnold Bertonneau, presented Lincoln on March

12, 1864, with a petition demanding black suffrage signed by more than a thousand literate African Americans, some of whom had fought under Andrew Jackson at the Battle of New Orleans in 1815.[22] Impressed by Roudanez, Bertonneau, and the people they represented, he sat down the next day to write his now-famous though then-private letter to Governor Michael Hahn suggesting that intelligent blacks and black veterans be allowed to vote. It was the president's face-to-face contact with black educated elites, as well as his favorable impression of the African American soldiers, that allowed him, for the first time in his life, to consider blacks as potential actors on America's political stage.

Lincoln's newfound appreciation of black self-determination during the war helped convince him of what is obvious to us today: most African Americans were as eager for education, if not more so, as Lincoln had been. He expressed his guarded optimism about the potential for black self-improvement to African Americans directly only once, in a speech that he made to a group of Washington African Americans who came to serenade him after Maryland voted to free its slaves in the fall of 1864. In response to the serenade, Lincoln congratulated the blacks on Maryland's edict of freedom, and he added a final word of advice: "I hope that you, colored people, who have been emancipated, will use this great boon which has been given to you to improve yourselves both intellectually and morally."[23] Clearly, the president still held to a vestige of his belief that freedom was something given to rather than sought by the slaves, and he still carried with him an assumption that most African Americans were largely ignorant. But at least he was ready to acknowledge an "ambition for education," to use the words he once used to describe himself, on the part of the African Americans.[24] Lincoln's speech on this occasion stands in sharp contrast to his speech of two years before—the only other speech in which he addressed African Americans directly—when he implored blacks to leave the country. Now the president was willing to entertain a biracial vision of the country, a vision that depended on blacks maintaining an appetite for education.

Speculation and disagreement about what would have happened had Lincoln survived the assassin's bullet will never end, but, on the basis of Lincoln's policies and attitudes while alive, it is reasonable to assume that at the very least he would have supported government funding of African American education. Most likely, he would have preferred that the state governments play the major role and the federal government the minor one in funding education for blacks, much as happens today in all education programs. In his effort to make the federal army an instrument of bringing education to African Americans, however, he made clear his desire to use the federal government as a resource for African Americans to use as they sought to improve themselves.

That approach on Lincoln's part is ironic, really, when one considers the effort among some African American activists and lawyers today to secure reparations for slavery. If one can get past the mischaracterization of the reparations movement as purely an effort by African Americans for cash handouts, one is left with a fairly modest proposal by most advocates of reparations. Some seek specific damages in civil suits against private corporations, but for the most part, all that most seek is funding from the government for black education, usually in the form of federally funded programs and scholarships exclusively for African Americans. If there is a consensus among those who believe that there should be reparations for slavery, it is that some money should be paid by the government for black education as compensation to a people who were denied education for so long because of the institution of slavery.

Would not have Lincoln agreed with this position? He might not have seen the matter in terms of compensation for slavery, but he certainly would have believed that something was owed to those of African descent for the horrors wreaked upon them. He said as much in his second inaugural, of March 1865:

> If we shall suppose that American Slavery is one of those offences which, in the providence of God, must needs come, but which, having continued through His appointed time, He now wills to remove, and that He gives to both North and South, this terrible war, as the woe due to those by whom the offence came, shall we discern therein any departure from those divine attributes which the believers in a Living God always ascribe to Him? Fondly do we hope—fervently do we pray—that this mighty scourge of war may speedily pass away. Yet, if God wills that it continue, until all the wealth piled by the bondman's two hundred and fifty years of unrequited toil shall be sunk, and until every drop of blood drawn with the lash, shall be paid by another drawn with the sword, as was said three thousand years ago, so still it must be said "the judgments of the Lord, are true and righteous altogether."[25]

Here was as powerful a statement in favor of reparations as was ever made. Reparations here meant war and mass death as payment for slavery. Surely Lincoln would have preferred the less bloody and less expensive alternative of government funding of black education as payment for slavery. In this very limited way, might Lincoln not have smiled upon efforts by African Americans today to educate themselves in any possible way, including an effort to use the law, one of Lincoln's favorite instruments, to get the money to educate themselves?

YET, PARADOXICALLY, LINCOLN'S emphasis on education for the freed people may have helped sow the seeds of failure during the Reconstruction era, and funding for African American education today may again do only half the work that is needed. While emphasizing education for blacks, the president said almost nothing during the war about the need to educate *whites* for a biracial society. There is something unsettling about Lincoln standing on the porch of the White House and telling newly freed African Americans that they were not ready for freedom, that they must educate themselves for freedom. The enslaved blacks were ready for freedom, and they had been ready for freedom since the guns had fired in Charleston Harbor four years before. It was the whites who had yet to be educated for black freedom, and it was Lincoln's failure to see this basic truth that represents a genuine failing. His dream of an educated society was a black dream, a dream in which only blacks needed education. He might have considered, and today's advocates for reparations might also consider, how public monies might be used to fund education for whites as well—specifically, for programs where whites and Americans of all races might be educated about what it means to live in a pluralistic society.

We should not expect Lincoln to have been so progressive as to see the need for multicultural education—even the most radical of his peers rarely took such a position—but perhaps he could have had a better understanding that the proper waking dream was not a purely white dream or a black dream but a dream of *all* of society's members adopting his own model of self-education and educating themselves in a quest to learn to live in harmony with one another.

DENNIS K. BOMAN

ALL POLITICS ARE LOCAL

Emancipation in Missouri

Numerous scholars have noted that President Abraham Lincoln's policy toward slavery was complicated by many different considerations. Lincoln's conservatism and constitutional beliefs made him suspicious of rapid and radical reform and unwilling to encroach upon the rights guaranteed to others—even the right of property in slaves. One of the thorniest and most important problems he confronted was preserving the border states in the Union. The population of these slave states was divided among enthusiastic supporters of secession, unionists, and those who wished to remain neutral in the conflict. Of these, perhaps Missouri presented the most challenging set of circumstances and policy issues, representing a microcosm of the same intransigent problems Lincoln faced throughout the country. As a statesman he did not have the luxury to stand upon purely moral or ideological grounds and ignore the consequences that might proceed from the implementation of an abolitionist policy. Lincoln's Missouri policies demonstrate the complicated and delicate nature of presidential decision making.[1]

When Lincoln assumed office in March 1861, several states in the Deep South had already seceded and others of the Upper South were holding conventions to consider secession. Secession in Missouri also seemed probable with the election of Claiborne F. Jackson as governor, his sympathies being strongly pro-Southern and proslavery; however, because a large majority of unionist delegates were elected to Missouri's convention, no secession resolution was ever submitted to the people. Instead the unionists, led by Hamilton R. Gamble, former chief justice of Missouri's Supreme Court, proclaimed that no reason existed to justify secession in Missouri. This same convention met again in July following the flight of Governor Jackson and the legislature from the state after coming into conflict with Nathaniel Lyon, the commander of federal troops stationed at the St. Louis Arsenal. The convention then took the bold action of ousting Governor Jackson, other state officials, and the legislature, and electing Gamble as provisional governor.[2]

Throughout the controversy between unionists and secessionists, Lincoln had sought to calm the turbulent waters of Missouri politics without success. With the secessionists having formed an army under the leadership of former Governor Sterling Price, Lincoln's first challenge was to protect the provisional government and to reestablish peace. At this time very few unionists supported emancipation and Governor Gamble reassured Missourians that his administration would protect slavery. This policy was uncontroversial except among some segments of the German population and other small groups of abolitionists centered primarily in St. Louis. During the course of the war, however, military and political developments strengthened the abolitionists, dividing unionists into two camps. These factions increasingly became alienated from one another, confronting Lincoln with a number of perplexing issues to solve.[3]

Another matter with the potential of undermining the provisional government and its military security was the misbehavior of regiments from other states. Many of these regiments' officers and men hated slavery and sought to undermine it in Missouri. Some regiments quickly became notorious for aiding the escape of slaves and taking extraordinary measures against civilians, especially those they believed were proslavery. In his first message to Missouri, delivered on August 3, 1861, Governor Gamble promised to stop the practices on the part of the military which have occasioned so much irritation throughout the State—such as arresting citizens who have neither taken up arms against the Government, nor aided those who are in open hostility to it, and searching private houses without any reasonable ground to suspect the occupants of any improper conduct and unnecessarily seizing of and injuring private property.[4]

In his statement, Gamble had in mind not only troops from other states but the Home Guard militia units, composed mainly of immigrant German troops who had been hastily organized into companies and regiments to meet the secession emergency. Gamble later complained to Lincoln that the actions of these out-of-state troops and the Home Guard militia had made enemies of many former unionists and had "continually embarrassed" him in his efforts to restore peace.[5]

To understand the complexities in forming a Missouri policy, Lincoln first turned to those in Washington familiar with the circumstances there, including congressmen and two of his cabinet members from Missouri, Postmaster General Montgomery Blair and Attorney General Edward Bates. Blair and his brother Frank, a congressman from St. Louis, provided insight into the inner workings of Missouri's Republican Party. Bates, a Whig until the eve of the 1860 presidential election, was well acquainted with that party's leadership. Most of Missouri's Whigs, while against secession, were proslavery in sentiment and unenthusiastic about Lincoln's election to the presidency. Bates helped to reassure the Whig leadership that Lincoln had no intention of interfering with slavery in Missouri or elsewhere. Bates also happened to be the brother-in-law of Governor Gamble and was well situated to help both Lincoln and Gamble understand the policies, motivations, and the character of the other. Moreover, Lincoln received reports from acquaintances in St. Louis with whom he had previously formed connections through his legal work and political activities. Two of these acquaintances, Samuel T. Glover and James O. Broadhead, were Republicans and as members of the St. Louis Committee of Public Safety had planned and coordinated unionist efforts during the first months of 1861. Through them Lincoln became acquainted with others representing the broad spectrum of support for the Union throughout the state.[6]

Complicating matters further, Lincoln's appointment of John C. Fremont as military commander over Missouri was unfortunate. Fremont's strong support for emancipation conflicted with the majority whose values were represented in Governor Gamble's policy to preserve slavery. German immigrants in St. Louis, along with some native Missourians, supported Fremont who increasingly was influenced by their animosity and distrust of Governor Gamble and proslavery unionists. During this difficult and dangerous time Fremont's mistrust of Gamble led to misunderstandings between them.[7]

Consistent with his understanding of the causes of the conflict and his mistrust of Missouri's provisional government, Fremont issued a proclamation on August 30. In it he declared martial law, promised to shoot all persons in arms against the United States, and stated his intention to confiscate the property of those in arms and those who had aided the enemy. Moreover, their slaves were to be "declared freemen."[8]

While approving of Fremont's decision to declare martial law, Lincoln objected to the proclamation's provisions regarding the shooting of prisoners of war, confiscation, and emancipation. He believed the first of the provisions unwise—not to mention inhumane—for it would provoke similar treatment of Union prisoners of war. Lincoln required his approval before any sentences of death could be executed. Furthermore, the provisions concerning the confiscation of property and emancipation were in violation of Congress's confiscation act of August 6, 1861, and, therefore, must be repealed.[9]

Fremont replied that he preferred that Lincoln write a public letter ordering him to rescind the objectionable provisions of the proclamation. Fremont stated that his own revocation of them would be an admission that he had not considered the matter fully and had made a mistake. More probably, Fremont feared alienating his German supporters by moderating his severe-war stance. Concerning the provision of the proclamation promising to shoot the enemy Fremont stated, "I do not think the enemy can either misconstrue or urge anything against it, or undertake to make unusual retaliation. . . . The article does not at all refer to prisoners of war." The reaction of two Confederate commanders, however, demonstrated that, regardless of Fremont's intentions, they believed he intended to execute Confederate prisoners.[10]

Fremont's proclamation became a huge political headache for Lincoln as well, for it undermined his policy of leaving slavery alone and focusing the war effort upon reuniting the South to the United States. Those who wished to make the conflict a war for abolition now had someone around whom to rally. Moreover, this effort posed a significant threat to the war effort, for a large number of unionists in Missouri and other border states conditioned their support of the Lincoln administration on the promise that slavery would be left alone. The proclamation also helped Confederate recruiters for Price's army and probably inspired many to provide aid and comfort to his invading army. John B. Henderson, who lived in northeast Missouri and would soon become one of Missouri's United States senators, explained the negative impact of Fremont's proclamation to James O. Broadhead, one of Lincoln's friends in St. Louis. The letter, which was forwarded to Lincoln, demonstrated the frustration of many with Fremont:

> You know the sensitiveness of our people on the question of *nigger* and especially *free nigger* and there is no use of losing Union strength by threatening anything but *death* to these men. . . . Again I find that the idea is busily being created in Illinois adjoining to us that this proclamation shows the true object of the war to be the emancipation of slaves. This foolish and accursed notion came near ruining our county, the soundest in the State, but I sincerely hope I have it now checked for a time.[11]

At the time of this controversy, the military situation in Missouri had quickly deteriorated. Despite the frequent urgings of many to reinforce Lyon, who was in command of a Union force near Springfield, Fremont, without taking any action, had allowed a superior enemy force under Price to defeat Lyon's army on August 10. Following this disaster Fremont proved to be incapable of energetic leadership. His incompetence became increasingly evident as Price operated in Missouri with impunity, defeating another Union army on September 20 at Lexington. Even after this Lincoln decided to give Fremont one more chance to redeem himself, while at the same time placing more pressure on him to act quickly to protect the state. Moreover, Lincoln hoped that the influence upon Fremont of General David Hunter, whom Lincoln had sent to serve as Fremont's chief of staff, would lead to a reversal of the dismal situation. Undoubtedly he also desired to avoid the political fallout and subsequent harm to the war effort in the border states that might result from Fremont's dismissal.[12] To ascertain what was really happening, Lincoln sent others to investigate Fremont's command. Undoubtedly, Lincoln wanted to learn whether the reports he had received were accurate, both out of fairness to Fremont and to document his incompetence if it became necessary to remove him. This was especially important, in light of Fremont's powerful friends, who were certain to protest his removal and characterize his detractors as disloyal and proslavery. One of the complaints of Fremont's critics was that he had secluded himself from everyone, even refusing to see those with important information about military affairs. Fremont's indifference to the military situation and impractical measures taken to that point reinforced the opinion of most that he lacked a plan of action, common sense, and the requisite administrative and military skills necessary to command the military district competently. Most damning of all was his inaction in the face of military defeats and the mounting disasters suffered by unionists throughout Missouri. Eventually Lincoln concluded that Fremont must be replaced, although he still believed him to be a good man who had intended to support his country. Consistent with this conclusion, Lincoln sent General Samuel R. Curtis orders to relieve Fremont if he was not then in the field conducting a campaign against the enemy. These orders reached Fremont on November 2, and Hunter was given temporary command.[13]

Not long after this Lincoln appointed General Henry W. Halleck, a Mexican War veteran and expert on military law and tactics, to command both the state militia and federal forces in Missouri. Upon assuming command, Halleck sized up the situation and reported to General McClellan that northern Missouri was "in a state of insurrection. The rebels have organized in many counties, taken Union men prisoners, and are robbing them of horses, wagons, provisions, clothing." To restore law and order, Halleck believed that only martial law, which provided the military with wide-ranging authority, would be effective. In response to this report, Lincoln authorized Halleck "to exercise martial law as you find it necessary."[14]

Halleck immediately made full use of these powers. He first ordered that persons providing aid and comfort to the enemy were liable to execution, as were spies and saboteurs. He also warned that the property of those captured in arms against the government was liable to confiscation. To pay the expenses of the war and provide resources to unionist refugees, Halleck proposed quartering them in the homes of wealthy secessionists in St. Louis. Moreover, he took prompt military action against guerrilla forces operating throughout the state. In all these endeavors, Governor Gamble supported and encouraged Halleck and recommended that he arrest federal commanders who were then using their military positions for personal revenge and to strike at slavery in Missouri. In particular, Gamble had in mind commanders of regiments from Kansas who sought to settle old scores in western Missouri.[15]

The problems along the Kansas-Missouri border had begun in 1854 when armed bands of Missourians had entered Kansas to attack abolitionists and others opposed to slavery. Missourians, led by United States Senator David R. Atchison, sought to guarantee that Kansas would be a slave state by organizing large groups to vote illegally in its territorial elections to choose delegates for a state constitutional convention. This and other fraudulent actions were successful in ensuring a proslavery document was drafted at Lecompton, Kansas, where the convention met. Animosity between the border residents of both states increased after each murdered and committed atrocities against the other. From Illinois, Lincoln had monitored these events closely and had even traveled to Kansas in 1859 to meet the people and observe what was happening.[16]

From the beginning of the war, despite the decision of Kansas and Missouri to oppose secession, the residents of both states anticipated renewed trouble along their shared border. These concerns prompted Charles Robinson, the territorial governor of Kansas, to write Fremont, warning him about potential trouble if James Lane, a radical abolitionist leader in Kansas, was not relieved of his command. These fears were realized when troops under Lane's and Charles R. Jennison's command entered Missouri and began to steal property and free slaves. For this reason, Governor Gamble wrote to Lincoln that he did not want Lane made the commander of the proposed military department in Kansas.[17]

Halleck, although a stern disciplinarian, discovered that it was very difficult to prevent volunteer, free-state troops from committing depredations, especially against Missouri slaveholders. Most of these troops had never before observed slavery and blamed the institution for the war. For this reason, many volunteers disobeyed orders and helped slaves escape. The concerns of Missourians only intensified after reports circulated about the recruitment of many blacks along the border where they were easily brought into Kansas, causing many to fear that runaway slaves might return to exact revenge or to lead a slave insurrection. Efforts to quell violence against the property and lives of civilians in Missouri were never completely successful. Particularly difficult was the protection of slaves as property, sometimes leading to mistrust between the leadership of federal troops and state militia forces.[18]

Early in the war radical leaders, wishing to transform the war into a crusade against slavery, protested when Halleck and other commanders enforced federal and state laws protecting the institution. Moreover, these commanders, who were following orders, were denounced in newspapers throughout the country. These protests complicated Lincoln's task of maintaining his policy of fighting the war exclusively to reunite the country. These efforts soon forced Lincoln to reconsider the policy and seek a compromise.[19]

In formulating his emancipation policy, Lincoln did not abandon his concerns about the preservation of slaveholders' constitutional rights. Unlike his radical critics, he was unwilling to embrace immediate emancipation, believing such a course to be both unwise and unjust, although he was also convinced that either immediate or gradual emancipation could be employed as a military necessity. In devising his emancipation scheme, Lincoln sought to weaken the enemy without alienating the military leadership and rank-and-file soldier upon whom the fate of the nation rested. Having concluded that the border states were secure, Lincoln proposed in March 1862 that Congress pass legislation to encourage them voluntarily to end slavery gradually.[20]

In his message to Congress, Lincoln argued that the abolition of slavery in the border states was "one of the most efficient means" of preserving the Union available to him, for it deprived the Confederate leadership of the hope that the loyal slave states might yet secede from the Union. His proposal, he took pains to make clear, was voluntary, for the federal government did not have the authority to interfere with slavery in the loyal states. He believed it was best for each to work out the details, but he expected each state to submit the matter to its voters before adopting a plan of gradual and compensated emancipation. Moreover, Lincoln asserted that, by promoting a quicker end to the war, compensated emancipation was economical when one compared this to the great daily cost of fighting the war. In a private letter to Henry J. Raymond, editor of the *New York Times,* Lincoln demonstrated that the cost of freeing all the slaves in the border states at $400 each would cost no more than the expense of fighting the war for only eighty-seven days.[21]

Before making his proposal to Congress, Lincoln had quietly cultivated the support of some abolitionists. Once his plan had been adopted, Lincoln devised schemes for the colonization of former slaves, recognizing that the vast majority of unionist sentiment was strongly against granting equal social and political rights to free blacks. Remarkably, Lincoln's proposal gained the commendation of a majority of Northern public opinion and of Congress.[22]

Unfortunately, the border state congressmen, including members from Missouri, were overwhelmingly opposed to the plan. Their attitudes reflected the values of their constituents, most of whom were not yet ready to yield their right to slavery. One member argued that agitation of the slavery question had caused the war and he could not see how its reintroduction into the public debate could be useful. A second member objected to Lincoln's proposal. noting the number of Missourians who had flocked to the army of Confederate General Sterling Price after the promulgation of Fremont's proclamation. Yet another member denied that slavery was the cause of the rebellion, but rather its real cause was "the belief that [slavery] will be destroyed." This was his way of blaming the North for the South's decision to secede. Moreover, it was observed that different members of Congress had already proposed measures to provide help for the new freedmen and freedwomen with little success. This legislation had not passed after the impracticability of the plans became evident. Missouri's congressmen also noted the unwillingness of Northerners to invite former slaves to their states and communities, most of which had stringent discriminatory laws that either reduced free blacks to a status with few civil and political rights or prohibited them from residing there completely. Despite their own reservations, however, some of Missouri's congressmen indicated that they were willing to submit Lincoln's proposal to their constituents, while one of their number, Frank Blair Jr., the brother of Postmaster General Montgomery Blair, unreservedly supported Lincoln's proposal and offered an amendment to colonize the former slaves.[23]

After passing a resolution promising compensation to the loyal slave states accepting gradual emancipation, the particulars of the matter, as Lincoln had envisioned, were to be settled by the border states. In Missouri this led to a policy debate concerning the wisdom and practicality of emancipation. Most conservatives believed emancipation to be a mistake for a variety of reasons. One of the first objections to Lincoln's proposal concerned provisions in the state constitution that prohibited the legislature from emancipating slaves "without the consent of their owners, or without paying them" in full before the emancipation of slaves. Slaveowners were also responsible for ensuring their former slaves did "not become a public charge." Moreover, the constitution prohibited any restrictions against emigrants bringing slaves to Missouri. Many agreed with their representatives in Washington, who feared that the policy would create a larger and more determined foe. Some demagogic opponents warned that emancipation would mean black equality, that former slaves would be armed and led by Kansas Jayhawkers, and that whites would lose the benefit of black labor. More responsible opponents to emancipation believed sincerely that the institution was too completely interwoven into the fabric of society for anyone to make Missouri a free state. These critics also argued that slavery benefited blacks as much as whites and rejected the radical assertion that anyone against emancipation was disloyal.[24]

The supporters of the president's policy in Missouri were found mostly among German immigrants in St. Louis. These immigrants brought to Missouri a foreign culture and an animosity for slavery and conservative politicians. It would be a mistake, however, to presume that no disagreement existed among them. While the vast majority of Germans voted for Lincoln in 1860, and general agreement remained in their desire to end slavery, disagreement was evident concerning how best to achieve this goal. Two German newspapers in St. Louis, the *Anzeiger des Westons* and the *Westliche Post,* reflected these different views. The *Post,* the more conservative of the two, supported amending the state constitution and thereby removing that obstacle. The *Anzeiger,* however, basing its position on natural rights theory, argued that the proslavery sections of the constitution were already void.[25]

Before passing a resolution promising compensation for any state adopting gradual emancipation, Congress, reflecting the nation's hardened attitude toward anyone supporting the rebellion, passed a bill prohibiting the military from returning slaves to their masters. In July 1862, Congress next prohibited the return of slaves of disloyal masters after coming into the lines of the Union army.[26]

In June 1862 the state convention, responding to Governor Gamble's call, convened to decide a number of pressing matters. On June 6 it deliberated upon Lincoln's proposition when Samuel M. Breckinridge, a conservative from St. Louis, offered "an ordinance to provide for submitting to a vote of the people of Missouri certain amendments to the constitution, and a scheme for the gradual emancipation of slaves." Arguing that the war would soon extinguish slavery as a viable institution in Missouri, Breckinridge wanted to make the transition to free labor as smooth as possible. Moreover, he was impressed with the fairness of Lincoln's proposition to which, he argued, the convention owed a respectful answer. He also believed that with emancipation would come the end of the South's attempt to bring Missouri into the new confederacy. Breckinridge, however, made clear that newly emancipated slaves must leave Missouri, for he considered free blacks "a pest upon her bosom—a class necessarily inferior and depraved."[27]

United States Senator John B. Henderson—who also happened to be a member of the state convention—supported Breckinridge's ordinance. Having voted in favor of Lincoln's proposal in the Senate, he argued that the war's continuance, even for a brief duration, made emancipation inevitable. A majority of soldiers were now convinced that slavery was the cause of the war. Moreover, Lincoln as commander in chief, with whom Henderson had consulted on this subject, believed he had the power to emancipate the slaves as a war measure. Henderson agreed with Lincoln that without slavery Missouri would never become a member of the Confederacy.[28]

Opposition to Breckinridge's ordinance was led by former Missouri Supreme Court Justice James H. Birch. Born in Virginia, Birch strongly supported slavery and threatened to side with the South if the convention accepted Lincoln's proposal. He also claimed that emancipation would cost too much and asserted that as a constitutional right slavery could not be abolished. Another member stated that emancipation would convert the Southern states into a wasteland controlled "by brutal negroes alone." Apparently, the majority of the convention agreed, or more probably believed that emancipation was still then unnecessary, for Breckinridge's recommendation was quickly put aside by a vote of fifty-two to nineteen.[29]

Having monitored the convention's deliberations, Governor Gamble intervened to encourage the delegates at least to make a respectful reply to Lincoln's proposal. Such courtesy seemed proper and expedient, Gamble believed, for Lincoln had provided funds, arms, and federal troops to defend Missouri. Other members, however, disagreed, revealing a strong animus for Lincoln and emancipation. After debating the issue for some time, however, the delegates voted thirty-seven to twenty-three for the resolution, expressing "its profound appreciation" to Lincoln for "the liberality" of his proposition.[30]

Perhaps disappointed that Gamble had not addressed the issue of emancipation in his message to the state convention, abolitionists decided to hold their own assembly. Meeting shortly after the adjournment of the state convention, the main goal of the abolitionists was to urge the passage of legislation presenting to the people the issue of emancipation in 1864. By this measure Missouri could benefit from federal aid offered by Lincoln and supported by the resolution of Congress. The abolitionists wanted to free all slaves born after the adoption of the law. To enable them to take care of themselves, slaves would not be freed until they were twenty-five years of age. Such *post-nati* laws—legislation affecting only those slaves born after the bill's passage—had been adopted by many of the Northern states during and after the American Revolution.[31]

By the end of the congressional session, nothing had come of Lincoln's proposal to provide compensation to the border states for the emancipation of their slaves. Perhaps frustrated by the failure of Missouri and the other border states to act, in July 1862 Lincoln asked the border state congressmen to meet with him on July 12 at the White House. In the meeting, he urged them upon their return home to press the leaders and people of their states to adopt his plan. The reply of the majority was disappointing. They complained that too little time was available for them to consult their constituents, that the funding of compensation was unconstitutional and would create a huge debt, and that agitation of the slavery question would undermine support for the Union in their states. Furthermore, while the minority of border state congressmen agreed with Lincoln that the South would be weakened by striking at slavery, it was doubtful the congressmen's support could persuade the majority in their states to agree even to gradual emancipation.[32]

In part, because of the rejection of his compensated emancipation plan, Lincoln edged toward using his powers as commander in chief to end slavery in the rebellious states as a war measure. This conclusion led to Lincoln's decision in September 1862, after a great deal of agonizing and deliberation, to issue the preliminary emancipation proclamation announcing that on January 1, 1863, all slaves held in rebellious states would be free. He believed this measure would shore up his support in the North, where many had lost their enthusiasm for a war that would not end slavery. Moreover, Lincoln hoped to deny to the South the labor of slaves who were employed to do much of its menial work.[33]

As many critics of Lincoln's emancipation policy have noted, the measure freed no slaves immediately. Another deficiency, according to critics, was that it did not free slaves in the loyal border states, leading to the oft-repeated criticism that the Emancipation Proclamation declared slaves free where it had no authority while accomplishing nothing for those in the loyal states. Lincoln disagreed with his critics, although, desperately wanting the border states to accept his offer of compensation, he still believed that his constitutional authority to end slavery extended only to those states which had seceded. For this reason, the issue of slavery was far from decided in Missouri and became a very important matter during the fall 1862 election.[34]

During its June 1862 session, the delegates of the Missouri State Convention had debated the propriety of holding wartime elections. The consensus among the delegates—a majority of whom were conservatives—was that it would be unwise to hold elections for the state executive offices, for Governor Gamble and Lieutenant-Governor Willard P. Hall had proven themselves to be very effective leaders and had developed good relationships with Lincoln and his cabinet. Nevertheless, the absence of a state legislature to deliberate upon fiscal and internal matters had proven to be a handicap, and it was decided that elections for legislators should be conducted in the fall. Besides, if Missouri was to have representatives in Congress, an election must be held. However, to ensure that the members of the legislature supported the Union, the state convention required all candidates and voters to take a loyalty oath and delayed the election until November to enable out-of-state Missouri regiments to vote.[35]

The fall campaign marked the organization of an official opposition to the Gamble administration. These radicals, as they sometimes referred to themselves, made gradual emancipation a major plank of their party and criticized many of the provisional government's policies. In particular, they faulted Gamble for not having urged the state convention to pass an emancipation bill in his opening message to its June 1862 proceedings. In August 1862 a committee of radicals traveled to Washington, D.C., to convince Lincoln that Gamble should be replaced by a military governor and place Samuel R. Curtis in command of the District of Missouri, which had been created after General Henry W. Halleck's departure from St. Louis. This effort proved fruitless, in part because of the Lincoln administration's fear that the radicalization of the state government would cause the loss of conservative support for the Union. Unfortunately, the attempt to replace Gamble with Curtis also led to mistrust between both. This mistrust festered over the next few months and made it very difficult for Lincoln to gain cooperation from both men.[36]

Having failed in their attempt to remove Governor Gamble and install a more radical military commander over Missouri, the opposition soon concentrated on electing members to Congress and to Missouri's General Assembly who would support emancipation and the use of more severe measures in the prosecution of the war. The opposition came to be known as the Charcoals, the radical wing of the Republican Party. In turn, the radicals referred to moderate members of their own party as Claybanks. Remarkably, the election, although marred by some minor irregularities, was conducted successfully. This success was largely due to the efforts of the state militia forces to prevent violence and interference in the campaign and the voting.[37]

The majority of candidates elected to Congress and the legislature favored Lincoln's plan for emancipation. This result demonstrated the wisdom of the state convention's measures to prevent the disloyal from voting and from holding office. As a result, five Republicans, one Democrat in favor of emancipation, two unconditional unionists, and two proslavery Democrats were elected to Congress. Moreover, the majorities elected to both houses of Missouri's General Assembly could be expected to elect members to the United States Senate with similar views.[38]

When Missouri's General Assembly convened in early 1863, Governor Gamble presented to the legislature a message in which he urged its members to pass emancipation legislation. Gamble proposed providing for the emancipation of slave children born after the plan's passage. The owners of these slaves' mothers would raise them until they reached maturity and could take care of themselves. This plan, though not freeing slaves then living before the bill's passage, had the advantage of reducing significantly the cost of compensating slaveowners and circumventing the need to gain their consent, both requirements of the state constitution. Gamble believed that gradual, compensated emancipation would encourage free immigration into Missouri and secure the state for the Union.[39]

Nevertheless, despite a majority of the Twenty-second General Assembly's members favoring emancipation, the inexperience of these legislators proved to be a major obstacle preventing the passage of legislation. Moreover, a significant minority of ideologues on both sides of the slavery issue were unwilling to compromise.[40] From the start of the legislative session, the Charcoals took charge of the legislature's operations through the election of radical officers to the House and Senate, most of whom turned out to be inexperienced parliamentarians. The radicals also refused to compromise on the emancipation issue, insisting that only immediate emancipation was acceptable and that radical leader B. Gratz Brown should become Missouri's next United States senator. By holding these positions, radical legislators represented well the position of their constituents, especially those in St. Louis. These policies, however, increasingly alienated moderate Republican members. For this reason the business of the General Assembly bogged down, and debate often degenerated into personal vituperations. Additionally, time was consumed by investigations into election irregularities and challenges to some members' right to serve in the legislature. Well into the legislative session, the radicals, recognizing that they could not force an immediate emancipation bill through the legislature, instead sought to establish a new state convention. By this means, the radicals hoped to supersede the old convention and elect enough radicals to the new convention to ensure the passage of an emancipation bill to their specifications.[41]

By the end of the legislative session of the Twenty-second General Assembly, in mid-March 1863, a permanent break occurred between the two wings of the Republican Party. Despite their attempts to reunite in April for the city commission election in St. Louis, the radicals and moderates discovered little common ground upon which a compromise and cooperation might be forged.[42]

While the Missouri legislature debated emancipation in Jefferson City, Lincoln supported Representative John W. Noell's and Senator John B. Henderson's sponsorship of congressional bills providing for compensated emancipation in Missouri. Both Missourians had supported Lincoln's plan for gradual, compensated emancipation the previous summer. Noell's bill allocated $10,000,000 for immediate emancipation, and Henderson's legislation provided $25,000,000 for gradual emancipation. In circumstances similar to those in the Missouri legislature, opposition to the bills in Congress emerged from both sides of the slavery issue. Some Northern congressmen objected to compensated emancipation because they thought it unjust to require their constituents to pay to free slaves in Missouri or elsewhere. And besides, as a senator from Indiana injudiciously and indelicately stated, he doubted the genuine nature of "the loyalty of Missouri," which he compared to "the purchased love of the prostitute." Other congressmen, representing a more moderate view, thought Congress lacked authority from the United States

Constitution to appropriate funds for such a purpose. Still others argued that it would be inexpedient to free the slaves, for no place had been provided where they could live as freedmen. Moreover, they asserted that this circumstance would end in the freedmen's destruction, or at least greatly to their detriment. Missouri congressmen, except for the sponsors, opposed the compensation bills for different reasons. Thomas L. Price, whose district was strongly proslavery, blamed the war on "Northern radicalism" and Northerners' refusal "to agree to just and liberal terms of compromise." This measure to compensate slaveholders in Missouri, Price complained, was just another component of the conspiracy "of the Abolition radicals." James S. Rollins, another representative from Missouri, opposed the measure because, according to him, even $20,000,000 was inadequate compensation to provide for the loss of slave property in Missouri.[43]

After the failure of Missouri's legislature and Congress to pass an emancipation law of some kind, Governor Gamble, convinced that slavery in Missouri was doomed, sent out a proclamation to reconvene the state convention to consider "some scheme of Emancipation" to be adopted. By the spring of 1863, political and military pressures made this decision necessary. As already noted, both radicals and moderates insisted upon the destruction of slavery. Believing that whites and blacks had the natural right to freedom and equality, many, but not all, radicals sought immediate emancipation regardless of its impact upon the war effort. Most radicals, however, also argued that the destruction of slavery would precipitate the war's end. On the other hand, moderates, in agreement with Lincoln, considered emancipation a war measure to deprive the South of an important labor source supporting their military efforts. These two views might be summarized thus: conservatives and moderates regarded emancipation as a means only; radicals considered it an all-important end. Therefore, if unity was ever to return to the Union effort in Missouri, the issue of slavery must somehow be settled and removed from the public forum.[44]

Prior to the commencement of the final session of the state convention, radical elements in St. Louis continued their attacks upon Gamble, which had been almost unrelenting in the German newspapers since the fall of 1862. The radicals believed that Gamble had only called the convention together to preempt their attempt to establish a new convention whose members, they hoped, would support immediate emancipation. The radicals, especially the German element, distrusted Gamble for they still considered him to be proslavery in sentiment. Their frustration and feelings of powerlessness had been exacerbated recently when Lincoln had categorically and firmly rejected resolutions passed at a radical meeting in St. Louis, calling for the removal of his two Missouri cabinet members, Blair and Bates, and the sacking of Halleck. Moreover, most devastating was Lincoln's statement that he preferred gradual to immediate emancipation.[45]

On June 15, 1863, the state convention convened in Jefferson City. In a message to the delegates Governor Gamble explained why he had called them together. State constitutional constraints had prevented the legislature from passing an emancipation ordinance; therefore, only through amendment or the action of an extraconstitutional body, such as the state convention, could the issue of slavery be resolved conclusively. Noting the controversial nature of the issue, he urged the delegates to work together to find a reasonable compromise. In devising a workable plan, however, Gamble urged the delegates to take care not to deprive citizens of their rights "farther than is necessary to make the public benefit certain and sure."[46]

In response to his message, the convention established a committee on emancipation and appointed Gamble as chair. A majority being composed of conservatives, it was not surprising that the committee soon presented to the convention a plan for gradual emancipation. The plan repealed those sections of the constitution requiring the consent and compensation of owners in a state emancipation bill. Slavery would end on July 4, 1876, a century after the traditional date of the Continental Congress signing the Declaration of Independence. The committee also stipulated that all slaves brought into the state owned by nonresidents would be free. One member of the committee objected to the plan, wanting instead an earlier date for emancipation and a prohibition upon slave sales. Another member argued that blacks benefited from slavery and that emancipation would harm many white families.[47]

Early in the debate, some of the delegates, whether as a real concern or as an argument to forestall action, expressed concern that Lincoln would not respect the convention's decision. This matter came to Lincoln's attention when General John M. Schofield, who was then commander of forces in Missouri, sent a telegram requesting Lincoln to direct him on the matter. Lincoln, who to this point had not interfered in the convention's deliberations, responded that he would support the convention's action so long as military necessity did not dictate otherwise; however, he stated his preference for gradual emancipation, believing that such a policy was beneficial "for both black and white." For this reason, he perceived little possibility that the military would interfere with slavery in Missouri, especially if the temporary transitional period to emancipation was brief.[48]

As the delegates debated the committee's emancipation plan, amendments were presented and voted upon. These amendments addressed a number of concerns and objections to the committee's plan and represented the wide range of opinion among the delegates. Representing the radicals' position and filling one of the convention's vacant seats was Charles D. Drake, who soon led the opposition to the Gamble and Lincoln administrations in Missouri. Early in the deliberations, Drake had presented a plan to emancipate the slaves on January 1, 1864, and to establish an apprenticeship system to provide slaves and masters with a transition from slavery to freedom. This moderate plan was shelved until the committee on emancipation had presented its work to the convention. As the debate unfolded, Drake accused Gamble of having called the convention together to pass an emancipation ordinance "so feeble and inert as to prolong Slavery in this State, with a continuance of the wretchedness it has brought upon us, until some distant day." Later Drake offered an amendment to establish January 1, 1866, for emancipation and challenged Gamble to vote for it. Perhaps to demonstrate that he was not conspiring to save slavery, Gamble voted for Drake's amendment. Soon, however, Drake changed course again, advocating absolute and immediate emancipation. United States Senator Henderson, who was also a delegate to the state convention, noted the inconsistency of Drake's positions on slavery, inferring that Drake and his radical supporters were more interested in preserving slavery as a political issue than they were in solving it conclusively. It is interesting to note that radical delegates joined with proslavery delegates in supporting a move to require a vote on any emancipation measure passed by the convention. Some of the moderate delegates noted this agreement of members on opposite poles of the slavery issue, suggesting that the measure was meant to kill emancipation.[49]

After debate had continued for some time and the delegates had been unable to come to any agreement, Gamble moved to table the issue until a new convention could be elected to revisit the matter. This suggestion may have been calculated to spur the delegates to action. If so, the maneuver worked, for the majority passed a final compromise meeting the criteria of both Gamble and Lincoln in their messages to the convention. First, the measure repealed the state's constitutional prohibitions to emancipation. According to the plan, slavery was to cease on July 4, 1870; however, the plan established an intermediate condition for slaves as "servants" to their former masters, allowing a transition for both slave and master and preventing an interruption in the supply of laborers in Missouri. Those slaves more than forty years of age on July 4, 1870, would remain servants for life. Those younger than twelve would remain servants until they reached the age of twenty-three, while the remainder would be released from their temporary servitude on July 4, 1876. The convention also prohibited the sale of slaves and their removal from the state after July 4, 1870. This measure anticipated the possibility that the South might win its independence and have a ready market for slaves after the war.[50]

Much to Lincoln's chagrin, passage of the emancipation ordinance did not end the controversy between unionists in Missouri. Instead, the radicals intensified their attacks upon Gamble and many of the officers of state militia forces whom he had appointed. By the spring of 1863, if not sooner, Lincoln considered himself caught in the middle of the Missouri dispute and perceived no resolution that could satisfy either faction. Having heard many misrepresentations, or at least very one-sided accounts, from both conservatives and radicals, Lincoln had sought, often without success, to ascertain the facts about various matters. In addition to the slavery controversy, the disputes concerned martial law, the proper extent of free speech during wartime, the appointment of state militia officers, and assessments against the disloyal. Each difference of opinion tended to exacerbate the struggle between the radicals and Gamble and his supporters. These matters came to a head in late September 1863, when a radical delegation from Missouri traveled to Washington seeking the ouster of Schofield.[51]

Heading the delegation was Charles D. Drake, one of the harshest critics of both Lincoln and Gamble since the convention. As related in his diary, Lincoln's private secretary, John Hay, recorded a conversation he had with Lincoln before the meeting. According to his account, Hay had warned Lincoln that without the radicals' help he could not carry Missouri in the upcoming presidential election. Lincoln did not disagree with Hay's analysis or his assertion that on the whole the radicals' principles were more in agreement with them than were the conservatives in Missouri. Lincoln, however, was under no illusion about the radicals' attitude toward him. Acknowledging the political danger of his position, Lincoln, nevertheless, reaffirmed his determination not to "do anything contrary to my convictions to please these men, earnest and powerful as they may be."[52]

On September 30, 1863, the delegation of seventy men met with Lincoln for two hours in the White House. Drake read his prepared address, in which he presented a rather lengthy account of the issues and circumstances in Missouri. He first asserted the premise upon which all radical policy rested: slavery was the cause of the war; therefore, the only effective way to win the war was through the complete and immediate eradication of the institution. The conservatives, Drake claimed, were for the most part disloyal men, former rebels, sympathizers with the rebellion, and those opposed to the Emancipation Proclamation and the abolition of slavery. This characterization was ingenious and misleading, for it did not distinguish conservatives who favored secession from those who did not. The vast majority of conservative delegates at the state convention, although against immediate emancipation, had supported Lincoln from the beginning of the war at considerable personal risk when it seemed probable that Missouri would secede. Many of the radicals, including Drake himself, had not shared in these dangers nor had many of them served in the military.[53]

Next, Drake claimed that Governor Gamble had called together the state convention to prevent the election of a new convention and the passage of a real plan for emancipation. In reference to the gradual emancipation plan adopted by Gamble and the conservatives, Drake asserted that it was "adverse to true loyalty, and to the vital interests of our State. . . . The policy of our State Executive represses and chills the loyal heart of Missouri, as a pro-Slavery policy represses and chills loyal hearts everywhere." Moreover, Drake accused Gamble of coddling rebels and "interpos[ing] his official influence to screen disloyal men from military measures deemed necessary to subdue the spirit of treason." All of these measures, according to Drake, had the darker purpose of secretly helping the rebellion in Missouri.[54]

As Lincoln had anticipated, Drake sought to persuade him to remove Schofield and replace him with General Benjamin Butler as commander of the Department of Missouri. According to Drake, Schofield was in league with Gamble and the conservatives, was seeking to suppress freedom of speech and the press, had illegally suspended the writ of habeas corpus in ordering the conscription of Missourians into the militia, had supported Gamble's desire to remove federal troops from Missouri, and had ordered the arrest of an officer commissioned to recruit blacks into the military. In conclusion, Drake asserted that, during Schofield's tenure as commander, conditions in Missouri had worsened progressively. He also demanded that the civil and military government sustain the election laws.[55]

Lincoln's response to the delegation demonstrated his determination to pursue his own policies. Hay, who was present, strongly disliked Drake, whom he described as having read his speech "pompously as if it were full of matter instead of wind." In contrast, Hay described the president's performance in dealing with Drake and the rest of the radical delegation as demonstrating Lincoln's superior logic and strength of character. At the end of their personal conference, Lincoln promised the delegation to make a written reply after considering their demands.[56]

On October 5, Lincoln drafted his reply to the radical delegation, although he waited until the fourteenth to release it. In it, he provided the radicals with his own analysis of the circumstances in Missouri and the motives of the actors involved. The radicals, Lincoln noted, had demanded that Schofield be replaced by Butler; that the state militia should be replaced by national forces; and that those "who are not entitled to vote" not be allowed to do so. Lincoln observed that Drake and the committee had cited many instances of unionists' suffering as proof that Schofield and the state government were responsible for the prolonged warfare in Missouri. He came to a different conclusion, however, stating that "the whole can be explained on a more charitable and, as I think, a more rational hypothesis. We are in civil war."[57]

To emphasize this point Lincoln next enumerated the different beliefs of unionists in Missouri to demonstrate how these led to unnecessary disagreements and disunity. Of these unionists there were

> those who are for the Union with, but not without, slavery; those for it without, but not with; those for it with or without, but prefer it with; and those for it with or without, but prefer it without. Among these, again, is a subdivision of those who are for gradual, but not for immediate, and those who are for immediate, but not for gradual, extinction of slavery. It is easy to conceive that all these shades of opinion, and even more, may be sincerely entertained by honest and truthful men, yet all being for the Union, by reason of these differences each will prefer a different way of sustaining the Union. At once sincerity is questioned and motives are assailed. Actual war coming, blood grows hot and blood is spilled; thought is forced from old channels into confusion; deception breeds and thrives, confidence dies, and universal suspicion reigns.[58]

This condition of affairs having continued from the beginning of the war until then, Lincoln disagreed with the radicals' assertion that Schofield was culpable and declined to replace him. In answer to the demand for federal troops to replace militia forces in Missouri, Lincoln asked from where the radicals proposed he remove federal forces. Moreover, he emphasized the important role regiments formerly in Missouri had played during the summer when Grant's command had been threatened by Confederate General Joseph Johnston's move to reinforce the garrison at Vicksburg. Finally, Lincoln agreed to meet only one of the radicals' demands in ordering Schofield to ensure that Missouri's election laws be enforced.[59]

Although never completely quieted, Lincoln's strong reply to the radical delegation and his refusal to take sides in the unionists' internecine struggle in Missouri served as a warning to those who sought to enlist the president in their partisan conflicts. Soon after this controversy, the radicals won significant victories in the fall elections, sending majorities to both the state legislature and to Congress. In the 1864 session, Missouri's legislature passed an ordinance to hold elections in the fall to choose delegates to a new convention to be held in early 1865. In the election, Missouri gave Lincoln a majority, and a radical governor, Thomas C. Fletcher, was elected, thus ending the authority of the provisional government that had guided Missouri's ship of state through the troubled waters of civil war.[60]

The fall 1864 election also produced a new convention largely composed of radicals, most of whom were political novices. The legislative act mandated that the convention amend the state constitution to ensure immediate emancipation, restrict voting to the loyal, and promote the public welfare. Because of his dominance of the convention, the document which emerged was named the Drake Constitution, after Charles D. Drake. The convention quickly passed an ordinance for immediate emancipation replacing the old convention's act. At about the same time, in February 1865, the General Assembly ratified the Thirteenth Amendment to the United States Constitution, thereby conclusively ending slavery in Missouri and the nation.[61]

IN WRITING HISTORY, the complexities of issues can be lost when one anticipates the conclusion of events and therefore neglects the many and sundry steps leading to the seeming eventuality. Of course, Lincoln and his contemporaries could not know certainly who would win the war and what its consequences would be. Writing many years after the American Civil War, historians and others sometimes forget the uncertainties that plagued Lincoln and his contemporaries. Considering the historiography of another period, Ronald Syme in his great work *The Roman Revolution* wrote of this problem and the failure of historians to suspend their knowledge of how things would turn out during the crisis of the Roman Republic in the first century BC:

The tale has often been told, with an inevitability of events and cul-
mination, either melancholy or exultant. The conviction that it all
had to happen is indeed difficult to discard. Yet that conviction ruins
the living interest of history and precludes a fair judgement upon the
agents. They did not know the future.[62]

In much the same way, some fail to suspend their knowledge
of the concluding events in the American Civil War and impose
their own ethical standards upon its participants. This presentism
has blinded many to the significance of much of what Lincoln
did. Moreover, others have sought to mold their accounts of Lincoln's presidency to conform to their political agendas. These
agenda-driven accounts often present Lincoln as a Machiavellian
character, manipulative and in control of events to an extraordinary degree.[63] Such characterizations are simplistic at best and
tend to portray Lincoln as darkly as possible. When one considers
the extent to which events were out of Lincoln's control, especially in light of the testimony of his contemporaries and of Lincoln himself, it is remarkable, indeed, that such conspiratorial accounts have gained credibility with some. Certainly,
Attorney-General Bates and Governor Gamble believed that Lincoln lacked the firm resolve of a successful statesman. Gamble
went so far as to write to Lincoln thus:

> If you will carry out your own sense of right and justice, breaking
> down every person who stands in the way, be he General, Senator,
> Governor, or Citizen, not of a party merely but of the American peo-
> ple, and your name will stand fair and bright, upon the page of his-
> tory. It requires boldness and courage.[64]

Moreover, Lincoln himself never claimed to have governed circumstances, even after many of his policies had proven successful: "I claim not to have controlled events, but confess plainly
that events have controlled me."[65]

NOTES

Abbreviations

CW	*The Collected Works of Abraham Lincoln*
Drake Autobiography	Charles D. Drake, "Autobiography," Western Historical Manuscripts Collection, State Historical Society of Missouri, Columbia, Missouri
Gamble papers	Hamilton R. Gamble papers, Missouri Historical Society, St. Louis, Missouri
Journal, June 1863	*Journal of the Missouri State Convention, Held in Jefferson City, June 1863*
Lincoln papers	Abraham Lincoln papers, Library of Congress Archives, Washington, D.C.
Official Records	*The War of the Rebellion: A Compilation of the Official Records of the Union and Confederate Armies*
Proceedings, June 1863	*Proceedings of the Missouri State Convention Held in Jefferson City, June 1863*

Introduction

1. Lincoln, remarks to Ohio Regiment, August 22, 1864, Roy P. Basler, ed., *The Collected Works of Abraham Lincoln* (New Brunswick, N.J.: Rutgers University Press, 1953; hereinafter cited as *CW*), vol. 7: 512.

2. James M. McPherson, *Abraham Lincoln and the Second American Revolution* (New York: Oxford University Press, 1991), 22.

3. Frank J. Williams, *Judging Lincoln* (Carbondale: Southern Illinois University Press, 2002), 30; Stephen B. Oates, *Abraham Lincoln: The Man behind the Myths* (New York: Harper Perennial, 1984), 57; see also, generally, Harry V. Jaffa, *A New Birth of Freedom: Abraham Lincoln and the Coming of the Civil War* (New York: Rowman and Littlefield, 2000), esp. 227–28; LaWanda Cox, *Abraham Lincoln and Black Freedom: A Study in Presidential Leadership,* 2nd ed. (Columbia: University of South Carolina Press, 1994); William K. Klingaman, *Abraham Lincoln and the Road to Emancipation* (New York: Viking Press, 2000), esp. chap. 9; and the essays by Gabor Boritt and Allen Guelzo in Gabor Boritt, ed., *The Lincoln Enigma: The Changing Face of an American Icon* (New York: Oxford University Press, 2001).

156 *Notes to Pages 6–12*

4. George M. Frederickson, "A Man, but Not a Brother: Abraham Lincoln and Racial Equality," *Journal of Southern History,* 41 (February 1975): 55, 57.

5. Lerone S. Bennett, *Forced into Glory: Abraham Lincoln and the White Dream* (Chicago: Johnson Publishing, 2000), 2, 337.

6. Thomas J. DiLorenzo, *The Real Lincoln: A New Look at Abraham Lincoln, His Agenda, and an Unnecessary War* (Roseville, Calif.: Prima Publishing, 2002), ix, 36, 53.

1—"Paradox Though It May Seem"

1. *CW,* vol. 1: 74–75, vol. 4: 65; Paul Simon, *Lincoln's Preparation for Greatness: The Illinois Legislative Years* (Urbana: University of Illinois Press, 1965), 132–34.

2. *CW,* vol. 2: 239, 270, 461; vol. 5: 537.

3. *CW,* vol. 1: 348; vol. 2: 270, 320.

4. William Lee Miller, *Lincoln's Virtues: An Ethical Biography* (New York: Alfred A. Knopf, 2002), 14.

5. *CW,* vol. 2: 255, 256, 266. George M. Fredrickson, "A Man but Not a Brother: Abraham Lincoln and Racial Equality," *Journal of Southern History,* 41 (February 1975): 39–58; and Don E. Fehrenbacher, "Only His Stepchildren: Lincoln and the Negro," *Civil War History,* 20 (December 1974): 293–310, offer judicious overviews of Lincoln's racial attitudes. Arthur Zilversmit, "Lincoln and the Problem of Race: A Decade of Interpretations," *Papers of the Abraham Lincoln Association,* 2 (summer 1980): 22–45, provides a historiographic review of the subject.

6. *Aggregate Amount of Persons Within the United States in the Year 1810* [third census] (Washington, D.C.: Government Printing Office, 1811), 72–74; Simon, *Lincoln's Preparation for Greatness,* 128.

7. *Abstract of the Returns of the Fifth Census* (Washington, D.C.: Government Printing Office, 1832), 35; *CW,* vol. 3: 511; vol. 4: 62; vol. 7: 281; Douglas L. Wilson and Rodney O. Davis, eds., *Herndon's Informants: Letters, Interviews, and Statements about Abraham Lincoln* (Urbana: University of Illinois Press, 1998), 457; Leon F. Litwack, *North of Slavery: The Negro in the Free States, 1790–1860* (Chicago: University of Chicago Press, 1961), 70–71; Emma Lou Thornbrough, *The Negro in Indiana: A Study of a Minority* (Indianapolis: Indiana Historical Bureau, 1957), 121–28; Andrew R. L. Cayton, *Frontier Indiana* (Bloomington: Indiana University Press, 1996), 296–97; Benjamin Quarles, *Lincoln and the Negro* (New York: Oxford University Press, 1962), 16–19.

8. Paul Finkelman, "Slavery and the Northwest Ordinance: A Study in Ambiguity," *Journal of the Early Republic,* 6 (winter 1986): 343–70; Peter Onuf, "From Constitution to Higher Law: The Reinterpretation of the Northwest Ordinance," *Ohio History,* 94 (winter–spring 1985): 5–33; James E. Davis, *Frontier Illinois* (Bloomington: Indiana University Press, 1998), 101, 116–17; David Brion Davis, "The Significance of Excluding Slavery from the Old Northwest in 1787," *Indiana Magazine of History,* 84 (March 1988): 75–89; Eugene Berwanger, *The Frontier against Slavery: Western Anti-Negro Prejudice and the Slavery Extension Controversy* (Urbana: University of Illinois

Press, 1967), 7–29; Paul Finkelman, "Slavery, the 'More Perfect Union,' and the Prairie State," *Illinois Historical Journal*, 80 (winter 1987): 248–69; Robert P. Howard, *Illinois: A History of the Prairie State* (Grand Rapids, Mich.: William B. Eerdmans, 1972), 130–31.

9. Theodore Calvin Pease, *The Frontier State, 1818-1848*, vol. 2 of Clarence Walworth Alvord, ed., *The Centennial History of Illinois* (Chicago: A. C. McClurg, 1922), 47, 49; Howard, *Illinois*, 131; Davis, *Frontier Illinois*, 166–67; Finkelman, "Slavery and the Northwest Ordinance," 369.

10. *Abstract of the Returns of the Fifth Census*, 38; manuscript U.S. Census, Sangamon County, Illinois, 1830; Sangamon County Commissioners Record, Illinois State Archives, Springfield, Illinois, March 7, 1827, March 4, 1834; Sangamon County Indentures of Apprenticeship, Illinois State Historical Library, Springfield, Illinois; Richard E. Hart, "Honest Abe and the African Americans: A Groundbreaking Study of How Blacks in Early Springfield Influenced Lincoln's Views on Race and Society," *Illinois Times*, 23 (February 12, 1998): 6–11; Richard E. Hart, "Springfield's African Americans as a Part of the Lincoln Community," *Journal of the Abraham Lincoln Association*, 20 (winter 1999): 35–54; Elmer Gertz, "The Black Laws of Illinois," *Journal of the Illinois State Historical Society*, 56 (autumn 1963): 454–73.

11. Springfield *Sangamo Journal*, December 17, 1836; manuscript U.S. Census, Springfield, Illinois, 1840; Sangamon County Indentures of Apprenticeship, Illinois State Historical Library, Springfield, Illinois. Ninian Edwards, Benjamin Edwards, John Calhoun, and Edward Baker all kept African American servants, as did William Butler while Lincoln boarded with him.

12. To his credit, Enos never answered the letter, which prompted a renewed request a month later for information about the "colour boy" who was rumored to be for sale. Thomas William Taylor to Pascal P. Enos, April 26, May 15, 1830, Pascal P. Enos Papers, Illinois State Historical Library, Springfield, Illinois; Sangamon County Commissioners Record, Illinois State Archives, Springfield, Illinois, December 6, 1831; Springfield *Sangamo Journal*, March 2, 1833.

13. Springfield *Sangamo Journal*, April 28, 1838, and February 18, 1842; Springfield *Illinois State Register*, August 15, 1845.

14. Essential analyses of the colonization movement during this period appear in P. J. Staudenraus, *The African Colonization Movement, 1816–1865* (New York: Columbia University Press, 1961), 27–29; Floyd J. Miller, *The Search for a Black Nationality: Black Emigration and Colonization, 1787–1963* (Urbana: University of Illinois Press, 1975), 54–90; Leonard P. Curry, *The Free Black in Urban America, 1800–1850: The Shadow of the Dream* (Chicago: University of Chicago Press, 1981), 232–37; Louis Filler, *The Crusade against Slavery, 1830–1860* (New York: Harper, 1960), 20; George M. Fredrickson, *The Black Image in the White Mind: The Debate on Afro-American Character and Destiny, 1817–1914* (New York: Harper & Row, 1971), 6–32; Litwack, *North of Slavery*, 20–24.

15. Springfield *Sangamo Journal*, November 17, 1832, August 31, 1833, and August 23, October 4 and 18, and November 2, 1839; Springfield *Illinois State Register*, October 5, 1839, and July 10, 1840; Sangamon County Indentures of Apprenticeship; Davis, *Frontier Illinois*, 258.

16. Springfie d *Sangamo Journal*, August 23, October 4 and 18, and November 2, 1839, and January 23, 1845; Springfield *Illinois State Register*, October 5, 1839, July 10, 1840, and January 17, 1845; Springfield *Illinois Journal*, June 1, 1852; Manuscript Poll Books, Sangamon County, Illinois, Illinois State Historical Library, Springfield, Illinois, 1848.

17. Springfield *Sangamo Journal*, June 25, 1836, October 28, 1837; Springfield *Illinois State Register*, June 7, 1844; Filler, *Crusade against Slavery*, 78–81; Michael Feldberg, *The Turbulent Era: Riot and Disorder in Jacksonian America* (New York: Oxford University Press, 1980), 43–53.

18. *CW*, vol. 1: 48; vol. 2: 498; Simon, *Lincoln's Preparation for Greatness*, 121–37, provides the most succinct summary of Lincoln's attitudes toward slavery and racial equality during his legislative career.

19. *CW*, vol. 1: 260, 320, and 323; Joshua F. Speed, *Reminiscences of Abraham Lincoln and Notes of a Visit to California* (Louisville: John P. Morton, 1884), 39–40; Robert L. Kincaid, "Joshua Fry Speed, 1814–1882: Abraham Lincoln's Most Intimate Friend," *Filson Club History Quarterly*, 17 (April 1943): 63–123, esp. 67, 69.

20. John J. Duff, *Abraham Lincoln, Prairie Lawyer* (New York: Bramwell House, 1960), 86–87.

21. Duff, *Abraham Lincoln, Prairie Lawyer*, 130–49; David Herbert Donald, *Lincoln* (New York: Simon and Schuster, 1995), 103–104; Filler, *Crusade against Slavery*, 200.

22. Donald W. Riddle, *Congressman Abraham Lincoln* (Urbana: University of Illinois Press, 1957), 164, 166, 171–72, and 178–79.

23. Springfield *Sangamo Journal*, November 7, 1835, and March 16, April 20, 1848; *Illinois Constitution* (1848), art. 13, sec. 16; Arthur Charles Cole, ed., *The Constitutional Debates of 1847* (Springfield: Illinois State Historical Library, 1919), xxvi–xxvii, 201–202; Arvarh E. Strickland, "The Illinois Background of Lincoln's Attitude toward Slavery and the Negro," *Journal of the Illinois State Historical Society*, 56 (autumn 1963): 474–94; Litwack, *North of Slavery*, 70–71; Berwanger, *Frontier against Slavery*, 44–45; Finkelman, "Slavery and the Northwest Ordinance," 358.

24. Analysis of support for the restrictive clause in Springfield is based on the two-hundred fifty-two voters who participated in the constitutional referendum in March 1848 and remained in the city long enough to appear in the 1850 census; Manuscript Poll Books, Springfield, Illinois, Illinois State Historical Library, Springfield, Illinois, 1848, linked with Manuscript U.S. Census, Springfield, Illinois, 1850.

25. Manuscript Poll Books, Springfield, Illinois, 1848, linked with Manuscript U.S. Census, Springfield, Illinois, 1850; Cole, *Constitutional Debates of 1847*, 861; Springfield *Illinois Journal*, April 1, 1854; Gertz, "Black Laws of Illinois," 466; James P. Jones, "The Illinois Negro Law of 1853: Racism in a Free State," *Illinois Quarterly*, 40 (winter 1977): 5–22.

26. Wilson and Davis, *Herndon's Informants*, 597; Lloyd Ostendorf and Walter Oleksy, *Lincoln's Unknown Private Life: An Oral History of His Black Housekeeper, Mariah Vance, 1850–1860* (Mamaroneck, N.Y.: Hastings House, 1995), 23, 34, 36; Hart, "Springfield's African Americans," 46; Quarles, *Lin-*

coln and the Negro, 194–95; Roy P. Basler, "Lincoln, Blacks, and Women," in Cullom Davis, Charles B. Strozier, Rebecca Monroe Veach, and Geoffrey C. Ward, eds., *The Public and the Private Lincoln: Contemporary Perspectives* (Carbondale: Southern Illinois University Press, 1979), 38–53. Ruth Burns is also known by her married name, Ruth Stanton; Allen C. Guelzo, "Did the Lincoln Family Employ a Slave in 1849–1850?" *For the People: A Newsletter of the Abraham Lincoln Association,* 3 (autumn 2001): 1, 6–7.

27. Manuscript U.S. Census, Springfield, Illinois, 1850 and 1860; Lloyd Ostendorf, "The Story of William Florville, Mr. Lincoln's Barber," *Lincoln Herald,* 79 (spring 1977): 29–32.

28. Springfield *Sangamo Journal,* September 6, 1834; Springfield *Illinois Journal,* January 23, 1850; Manuscript U.S. Census, Springfield, Illinois, 1850; Hart, "Honest Abe and the African Americans," 9; Larry Gara, "The Underground Railroad in Illinois," *Journal of the Illinois State Historical Society,* 56 (autumn 1963): 508–28; Hart, "Springfield's African Americans," 47; Stanley W. Campbell, *The Slave Catchers: Enforcement of the Fugitive Slave Law, 1850–1860* (Chapel Hill: University of North Carolina Press, 1968). Jenkins also appears in historical records as Jimison Jenkins.

29. Springfield *Illinois Journal,* January 17, 22, 23, and 25, 1850.

30. *CW,* vol. 2: 130–32; Staudenraus, *African Colonization Movement,* 242–43. Mark E. Neely, Jr., "American Nationalism in the Image of Henry Clay: Abraham Lincoln's Eulogy on Henry Clay in Context," *Register of the Kentucky Historical Society,* 73 (January 1975): 31–60, provides an essential analysis of Lincoln's eulogy. For an analysis of Lincoln's devotion to colonization, see Michael Vorenberg, "Abraham Lincoln and the Politics of Black Colonization," *Journal of the Abraham Lincoln Association,* 14 (summer 1993): 23–45; Gabor S. Boritt, "The Voyage to the Colony of Lincolnia," *The Historian,* 37 (August 1975): 619–33; Mark E. Neely, Jr., "Abraham Lincoln and Black Colonization: Benjamin Butler's Spurious Testimony," *Civil War History,* 25 (March 1979): 77–83; Gary R. Planck, "Abraham Lincoln and Black Colonization: Theory and Practice," *Lincoln Herald,* 72 (summer 1970): 61–77; and Jason H. Silverman, "'In Isles Beyond the Main': Abraham Lincoln's Philosophy on Black Colonization," *Lincoln Herald,* 80 (fall 1978): 155–22.

31. *CW,* vol. 2: 130–32.

32. *CW,* vol. 2: 298–99.

33. *CW,* vol. 2: 228, 232, 404; Springfield *Illinois Journal,* January 15, 1854; Larry Gara, "Slavery and the Slave Power: A Crucial Distinction," *Civil War History,* 15 (March 1969): 5–18; William E. Gienapp, "The Republican Party and the Slave Power," in Robert H. Abzug and Stephen E. Maizlish, eds., *New Perspectives on Race and Slavery in America: Essays in Honor of Kenneth M. Stampp* (Lexington: University Press of Kentucky, 1986), 51–78.

34. *CW,* vol. 2: 255, 256, 266; vol. 4: 67.

35. Don E. Fehrenbacher, *The Dred Scott Case: Its Significance in American Law and Politics* (New York: Oxford University Press, 1978).

36. *CW,* vol. 2: 405–406.

37. *CW,* vol. 2: 405; Eric Foner, *Free Soil, Free Labor, Free Men: The Ideology of the Republican Party before the Civil War* (New York: Oxford University Press, 1970).

38. Don E. Fehrenbacher, *Slavery, Law, and Politics: The Dred Scott Case in Historical Perspective* (New York: Oxford University Press, 1981), 244–72, and *Prelude to Greatness: Lincoln in the 1850s* (Stanford, Calif.: Stanford University Press, 1962), 106–12; Allan Nevins, *The Emergence of Lincoln* (New York: Charles Scribner's Sons, 1950), 1: 250–79. Essential analyses of the Lincoln-Douglas Debates include Harry V. Jaffa, *Crisis of the House Divided: An Interpretation of the Issues in the Lincoln-Douglas Debates* (Chicago: University of Chicago Press, 1959); and David Zarefsky, *Lincoln, Douglas and Slavery: In the Crucible of Public Debate* (Chicago: University of Chicago Press, 1990).

39. *CW*, vol. 2: 461–69.

40. Wilson and Davis, *Herndon's Informants*, 163, 267, 438, 442.

41. *CW*, vol. 2: 465–66, 513, 514, 519–20; vol. 3: 1–12.

42. *CW*, vol. 3: 16, 249.

43. *CW*, vol. 2: 255, 281; vol. 3: 14, 96, 113.

44. *CW*, vol. 1: 374: vol. 2: 461; vol. 3: 16.

2—*Greeley, Colonization, and a "Deputation of Negroes"*

1. D. David Bourland, "TO BE OR NOT TO BE: E-Prime as a Tool for Critical Thinking," p. 3, at www.generalsemantics.org/ARTICLES/TOBECRIT.HTM (February 2003).

2. Georges Santayana, *Skepticism and Animal Faith* (New York: Scribner, 1929), 123.

3. David Hackett Fisher, *Historian's Fallacies* (New York: Harper & Row, 1970).

4. A search through Earl Schenck Meiers, ed., *Lincoln Day by Day: A Chronology* (Dayton, Ohio: Morningside, 1991), finds only two identifiable minstrel-like shows that Lincoln attended: July 6, 1848, and February 24, 1863. He was far more interested in Shakespeare, attending twelve performances.

5. The incident is described in William Miller, *Lincoln's Virtues* (New York: Alfred A. Knopf, 2002), 356–57, n. On the basis of a comment by John Nicolay in 1899 that this recollection was untrustworthy, Don E. and Virginia Fehrenbacher, *Recollected Works of Abraham Lincoln* (Stanford, Calif.: Stanford University Press, 1996), grade the story as "a quotation about whose authenticity there is above average doubt," 389–90. I am inclined to accept the story because of the lateness of Nicolay's testimony, thirty-five years after the incident took place, and because it squares with Lincoln's generally warm attitude toward African Americans in his presence. See also Randall Kennedy, *Nigger: The Strange Career of a Troublesome Word* (New York: Pantheon, 2002).

6. See homepage of the Alabama Knights of the Ku Klux Klan (www.kukluxklan.net/menu.html), which quotes Lincoln's words about separating the races (February 2003). Lincoln haters come out when a book like Thomas DeLorenzo's *The Real Abraham Lincoln: A New Look at Abraham Lincoln, His Agenda, and an Unnecessary War* (New York: Prima Lifestyles, 2002) is published. This dishonest and ignorant attack on Lincoln has evoked almost a hundred reader's reviews on Amazon.com—most of them favorable.

7. James M. McPherson, "Who Freed the Slaves?" in *Drawn with the Sword: Reflections on the American Civil War* (New York: Oxford University

Press, 1998), 192–207; Ira Berlin, "Who Freed the Slaves? Emancipation and Its Meaning," in Michael Perman, ed., *Major Problems in the Civil War and Reconstruction*, 2nd ed. (Boston: Houghton Mifflin, 1998), 288–97; Richard Hofstadter, *The American Political Tradition and the Men Who Made It* (New York: Alfred A. Knopf, 1948), chap. 5; Lerone Bennett, *Forced into Glory: Abraham Lincoln's White Dream* (Chicago: Johnson Publishing, 2000).

8. *CW*, vol. 4: 388–89.

9. Gideon Welles, "History of Emancipation," *Galaxy*, December 1872, 842–43; Phillip Shaw Paludan, *The Presidency of Abraham Lincoln* (Lawrence: University Press of Kansas, 1994), 146–48.

10. For Southern fears of the erosion of slavery see William Freehling, *The Road to Disunion*, vol. 1, *Secessionists at Bay, 1776–1854* (New York: Oxford University Press, 1990); and *The South vs. the South: How Anti-Confederate Southerners Shaped the Course of the Civil War* (New York: Oxford University Press, 2001), chap. 2.

11. Bennett, *Forced into Glory;* and Susan-Mary Grant and Brian Holden Reid, eds., *The American Civil War* (Harlow, Eng.: Longman, 2002), 71.

12. *CW*, vol. 1: 368–70.

13. *CW*, vol. 4: 428–29.

14. Sunday *Times Book Review Section*, February 10, 2002; Bennett, *Forced into Glory*. Bennett uses "ethnic cleansing" on pp. 465, 507, and 516 and as the title of chap. 10. On 516, he specifically discusses Bosnia and Kosovo. He avoids putting the term in his index. High school teachers who attended Foner's summer seminar on Civil War issues report that Foner used "ethnic cleansing" as describing colonization. This information came to me in a personal conversation at Galesburg, Illinois, September 28, 2002, during a conference on Lincoln's writings.

15. *CW*, vol. 3: 541.

16. *CW*, vol. 2: 131–32. Robert Remini, *Henry Clay: Statesman for the Union* (New York: Norton, 1991), 179, 491–92, 696–97, does not show Clay's forced colonization idea, but the claim is made in Marvin Cain, "Lincoln's views on Slavery and the Negro," *Historian*, 26 (1964): 508. Cain also notes that Jefferson favored voluntary colonization. Michael Vorenberg, "Abraham Lincoln and the Politics of Black Colonization," *Journal of the Abraham Lincoln Association*, 14 (1993): 26, n. 6.

17. *CW*, vol. 5: 48.

18. Gideon Welles, *Diary of Gideon Welles*, 3 vols. (New York: Houghton-Mifflin, 1911), 1: 152; *CW*, vol. 5: 535; Don and Virginia Fehrenbacher, eds., *Recollected Works of Abraham Lincoln* (Stanford, Calif.: Stanford University Press, 1996), 474–75. The American Colonization Society also advocated voluntary colonization. See *African Repository*, 18, no. 2 (February 1862): 47, 49: The object of the society was "the removal of the free people of color *with their own consent*" to Africa. "The idea of compulsion must not be associated with the scheme."

19. See Benjamin Quarrels, *Lincoln and the Negro* (New York: Oxford University Press, 1962); Mark E. Neeley, Jr., *The Abraham Lincoln Encyclopedia* (New York: Da Capo Press, 1982), 62–63.

20. See Philip S. Paludan, *The Presidency of Abraham Lincoln* (Lawrence: University Press of Kansas, 1994), 150–54.

21. *United States Statutes at Large* (Boston: Little, Brown, 1863–1869), 4 volumes, vol. 2: 1268–69. Dudley Cornish, *The Sable Arm: Negro Troops in the Union Army, 1861–1865* (New York: W. W. Norton, 1966), 69–71.

22. *African Repository*, vol. 40, no. 9 (September 1864): 282–83; Michael Burlingame and John Turner Ettlinger, eds., *Inside Lincoln's White House: The Complete Civil War Diary of John Hay* (Carbondale: Southern Illinois University Press, 1997), 217.

23. *CW*, vol. 5: 219, 223–24.

24. *CW*, vol. 5: 317–19.

25. See Vorenberg, "Politics of Black Colonization," 33.

26. *CW*, vol. 5: 370–71, fn.

27. See Philip Foner, *Life and Writings of Frederick Douglass* (New York: International Publishers, 1952), 281–84; *African Repository and Colonial Journal*, 40, no. 9 (June 1864): 282–83; 18, no. 12 (December 1862): 359–62.

28. Frederick Douglass, *The Life and Times of Frederick Douglass* (London: Collier, 1962), 347, 359; Don E. Fehrenbacher, "Only His Stepchildren: Lincoln and the Negro," *Civil War History*, 20 (1974): 293–310.

29. The literature on nineteenth-century racism is large, ranging from Jacque Voegeli, *Free but Not Equal: The Midwest and the Negro during the Civil War* (Chicago: University of Chicago Press, 1969), and George Frederickson, *The Black Image in the White Mind: The Debate on Afro-American Character and Destiny, 1817–1914* (New York: Harper and Row, 1972), to David Roedigger, *The Wages of Whiteness: Race and the Making of the American Working Class* (London: Verso, 1991), and Eric Lott, *Love and Theft: Blackface Minstrelsy and the American Working Class* (New York: Oxford University Press, 1993).

30. See Thomas Jefferson, "Query XVIII" in *Notes on the State of Virginia* as printed in *Thomas Jefferson, Writings* (New York: Library of America, 1984). Don E. Fehrenbacher, *The Slaveholding Republic: An Account of the United State Government's Relations to Slavery*, completed and edited by Ward M. McAfee (New York: Oxford University Press, 2001), is only the most recent survey to emphasize the impact of slavery on white experience in the coming of the war.

31. *CW*, vol. 5: 370–75, contains Lincoln's meeting with the "Deputation of Negroes." All subsequent descriptions of that meeting rely on these pages.

32. Philip S. Foner, ed., *The Life and Writings of Frederick Douglass*, 4 vols. (New York: International Publishers, 1950), 3: 267–70.

33. Gabor Boritt, *Lincoln and the Economics of the American Dream*, 2nd ed. (Urbana: University of Illinois Press, 1994), 258–66, in a fine discussion, recognizes the free labor dream implicit in Lincoln's plans, even while considering the process impractical. See Eric Foner, *Free Soil, Free Labor, Free Men: The Ideology of the Republican Party before the Civil War*, 2nd ed. (New York: Oxford University Press, 1995), for this free labor vision.

3—*Abraham Lincoln, Jeffersonian*

1. The most noted recent student of Lincoln to portray him thus is Harry V. Jaffa. Compare his *Crisis of the House Divided* (Chicago: University

of Chicago Press, 1959), *A New Birth of Freedom* (Lanham, Md.: Rowman & Littlefield, 2000), and *Original Intent and the Framers of the Constitution: A Disputed Question* (Chicago: Regnery Publishing, 1993), along with numerous topical essays in journals, scholarly and popular.

2. Allen C. Guelzo, *Abraham Lincoln: Redeemer President* (Grand Rapids, Mich.: William B. Eerdmans, 1999), 5–9, 18.

3. Ibid., 195.

4. Ibid., 195, 455–56. For Lincoln's negative general appraisal of Jefferson, compare ibid., 458, 460.

5. William Lee Miller, *Lincoln's Virtues: An Ethical Biography* (New York: Alfred A. Knopf, 2002), 353.

6. For Lincoln, see ibid., 359, and George M. Fredrickson, "A Man but Not a Brother: Abraham Lincoln and Racial Equality," *Journal of Southern History*, 61 (1975): 39–58; for Jefferson, see Peter S. Onuf, *Jefferson's Empire: The Language of American Nationhood* (Charlottesville: University Press of Virginia, 2000).

7. Harry V. Jaffa, *Crisis of the House Divided: An Interpretation of the Issues in the Lincoln-Douglas Debates*, 2nd ed. (Chicago: University of Chicago Press, 1982), 385–86.

8. James M. McPherson, *Battle Cry of Freedom: The Civil War Era* (New York: Oxford University Press, 1988), 509. There were occasional colonization efforts spearheaded by blacks in the antebellum period, it should be noted, but little came of them. Floyd J. Miller, *The Search for a Black Nationality: Black Emigration and Colonization, 1787–1863* (Urbana: University of Illinois Press, 1975).

9. Fredrickson, "A Man but Not a Brother," 39–40.

10. Joseph J. Ellis, *American Sphinx: The Character of Thomas Jefferson* (New York: Alfred A. Knopf, 1997).

11. Holly Brewer, "Entailing Aristocracy in Colonial Virginia: 'Ancient Feudal Restraints' and Revolutionary Reform," *William and Mary Quarterly*, 3d series, vol. 54 (1997): 307–46.

12. Richard Bland, "An Inquiry Into the Rights of the British Colonies, Intended as an Answer to the Regulations Lately Made Concerning the Colonies . . . ," in Robert L. Scribner, ed., *Revolutionary Virginia: The Road to Independence* (Charlottesville: University Press of Virginia, 1973), vol. 1: 28–44.

13. K[evin]. R. Constantine Gutzman, "Jefferson's Draft Declaration of Independence, Richard Bland, and the Revolutionary Legacy: Giving Credit Where Credit Is Due," *Journal of the Historical Society*, 1 (2001): 137–54, describes Jefferson's debt to Bland.

14. For an extended consideration of the myth of Jefferson as abolitionist and antislavery leader, see Paul Finkelman, *Slavery and the Founders: Race and Liberty in the Age of Jefferson*, 2nd ed. (Armonk, N.Y.: M. E. Sharpe, 2001), 105–96. For historiographic disputes over Jefferson and race, see Scot A. French and Edward L. Ayers, "The Strange Career of Thomas Jefferson: Race and Slavery in American Memory, 1943–1993," in Peter S. Onuf, ed., *Jeffersonian Legacies* (Charlottesville: University Press of Virginia, 1993). Also see Lucia C. Stanton, "'Those Who Labor for My Happiness': Thomas Jefferson

and His Slaves," in Onuf, ed., *Jeffersonian Legacies*, 147–80; Annette Gordon-Reed, *Thomas Jefferson and Sally Hemings: An American Controversy* (Charlottesville: University Press of Virginia, 1997); and Onuf, *Jefferson's Empire*. An anti-Jefferson philippic on the race issue may be found at Conor Cruise O'Brien, *The Long Affair: Thomas Jefferson and the French Revolution, 1785–1800* (Chicago: University of Chicago Press, 1996), 254–325.

15. Jefferson to Edward Coles, August 25, 1814, Thomas Jefferson, *Writings*, ed. Merrill D. Peterson (New York: Library of America, 1984), 1343–46.

16. Those who discuss Jefferson's and others' scientific racism tend to describe it as "pseudo-scientific," evidently because ideas this distasteful could not be grounded in science. In fact, however, science is a morally neutral method, and it can be employed for good or for ill; in Jefferson's case, his predisposition to see blacks as inferior led him down the latter path. Ironically, those who describe Jefferson's racism in this way betray their own Jeffersonian faith in science. Compare Daniel Gasman, *Haeckel's Monism and the Birth of Fascist Ideology*, Studies in Modern European History, vol. 33 (New York: Peter Lang Publishing, 1998).

17. The standard edition is Thomas Jefferson, *Notes on the State of Virginia*, ed. William Peden (Chapel Hill: University of North Carolina Press, 1954).

18. Ibid., xv, xi.

19. Ibid., 162–63.

20. For a brilliant treatment of Jefferson's notion of American nationality, see Onuf, *Jefferson's Empire*. Blacks' place in Jefferson's conception is the subject of chap. 5, "To Declare Them a Free and Independant People," 147–88, which has had an enormous influence on my understanding of related questions.

21. For Jefferson's linking George III and slavery in Virginia, see Pauline Maier, *American Scripture: Making the Declaration of Independence* (New York: Alfred A. Knopf, 1997).

22. "Query XIV. Laws," Thomas Jefferson, *Notes on the State of Virginia*, 130–49, revision at 136–49, slaves at 137–43.

23. "A Bill Declaring Who Shall Be Deemed Citizens of this Commonwealth," Thomas Jefferson, *Writings*, 374–75, at 374. Interestingly, when Congressman Jefferson proposed legislation for the governance of the Western territories in 1784, the presence of non-Southerners in Congress required him to refer to "free" population without implicitly excluding non-whites. Thomas Jefferson, "Report on Government for Western Territory," March 1, 1784, Jefferson, *Writings*, 376–78, at 376.

24. Finkelman, *Slavery and the Founders*, 145.

25. The Haitian Revolution is chronicled in Cyril Lionel Robert James, *The Black Jacobins: Toussaint L'Ouverture and the San Domingo Revolution* (New York: Random House, 1963); it is also the topic of Madison Smartt Bell, *All Souls' Rising* (New York: Penguin Books, 1996), a historical novel based on shockingly gruesome firsthand accounts.

26. Edmund Burke and James T. Boulton, eds., *A Philosophical Enquiry into the Origin of Our Ideas of the Sublime and Beautiful* (1757) (South Bend: University of Notre Dame Press, 1968).

27. Ironically, by the time of the republication of *Notes on the State of Virginia* in North America, Jefferson may himself have embarked upon a career of fathering several children by one of his own slaves. Annette Gordon-Reed makes a compelling argument that Jefferson did so; however, the woman in question may have been legally white under Virginia's racial classification scheme. Gordon-Reed notes that as the daughter of a white man and a half-white mother, she was legally a quadroon "according to the legal classifications of the day." She omits that a subsequent revision of the law made the woman "white." Annette Gordon-Reed, *Thomas Jefferson and Sally Hemings*, passim. and 160.

28. A recent Nott biography is Reginald Horsman, *Josiah Nott of Mobile: Southerner, Physician and Racial Theorist* (Baton Rouge: Louisiana State University Press, 1987). Nott was a leading scientific racist of the nineteenth century. Thomas Dixon, *The Clansman : An Historical Romance of the Ku Klux Klan*, 2nd ed. (Armonk, N.Y.: M. E. Sharpe, 2000), is a 1905 "vindication" of the Reconstruction-era Ku Klux Klan; full of viciously racist images and language, it was the source of the classic D. W. Griffith film "The Birth of a Nation." Dixon's appraisal of blacks, whites, and mulattos was eerily similar to Jefferson's, with the addition of the motif of black men as animalistic would-be rapists. Chester M. Morgan, *Redneck Liberal: Theodore G. Bilbo and the New Deal* (Baton Rouge: Louisiana State University Press, 1985). Bilbo, a Mississippi governor and United States senator, advocated colonization of blacks in the most lurid terms in the 1930s and 1940s.

29. O'Brien, *The Long Affair*, includes a plaintive plea to pull down the Jefferson statuary on the basis of this passage and others like it.

30. Thomas Jefferson to Benjamin Banneker, August 30, 1791, Jefferson, *Writings*, 982–83.

31. Thomas Jefferson to Henri Grégoire, February 25, 1809, ibid., 1202.

32. For the whole sordid story in its proper context, see Don Fehrenbacher, *The Slaveholding Republic: An Account of the United States Government's Relations to Slavery*, completed and edited by Ward M. McAfee (New York: Oxford University Press, 2001).

33. For a full account, see Douglas R. Egerton, *Gabriel's Rebellion: The Virginia Slave Conspiracies of 1800 & 1802* (Chapel Hill: University of North Carolina Press, 1993).

34. Ibid., 111.

35. Ibid., 112.

36. Ibid., 153.

37. Ibid., 154.

38. The letter discussed in this and the following paragraphs is Thomas Jefferson to the Governor of Virginia (James Monroe), November 24, 1801, Jefferson, *Writings*, 1096–99.

39. Egerton, *Gabriel's Rebellion*, 155.

40. Ibid., 156.

41. Thomas Jefferson to John Holmes, April 22, 1820, Jefferson, *Writings*, 1433–35; Thomas Jefferson to Albert Gallatin, December 26, 1820, ibid., 1447–50, at 1448–50.

42. Thomas Jefferson to Jared Sparks, February 4, 1824, ibid., 1484–87.

43. Thomas Roderick Dew, "Abolition of Negro Slavery," in Drew Gilpin Faust, ed., *The Ideology of Slavery* (Baton Rouge: Louisiana State University Press, 1981), 23–77.

44. Perhaps the wave of Irish immigration resulting from the Great Famine of the late 1840s changed some American calculations in this regard. I am grateful to George Forgie for this observation.

45. This account will focus on Lincoln's public pronouncements. For the private discussions and personal recollections, see Lerone Bennett, Jr., *Forced into Glory: Abraham Lincoln's White Dream* (Chicago: Johnson Publishing, 2000).

46. *CW*, vol. 5: 518–37, at 530.

47. Robert V. Remini, *Henry Clay: Statesman for the Union* (New York: W. W. Norton, 1991), 483.

48. *CW*, vol. 5: 518–37, at 520–21.

49. *CW*, vol. 5: 433–36, at 434.

50. David Donald, *Lincoln* (New York: Simon & Schuster, 1995), 343.

51. *CW*, vol. 3: 1–37, at 29.

52. *CW*, vol. 3: 121–32, e.g., at 127.

53. *CW*, vol. 3: 128–29.

54. Remini, *Henry Clay*, 507, 696–97.

55. See p. 55.

56. Some historians have made the contrary argument concerning tactical necessity. In support of my assertion that Lincoln went further than political necessity dictated, consider the following quotation from Lincoln's September 18, 1858, debate with Douglas. Are the last two sentences of this quotation strictly necessary, or had he already said enough to ingratiate himself with his audience? Other examples of Lincoln's saying more in a racist vein than political necessity might be thought to have mandated are not difficult to identify. Jaffa, whose praise of Lincoln has included favorable comparisons to Aristotle, differs from some Lincoln apologists in noting the Lincolnian colonization talk's "manifest seriousness" at the same time as he notes that this talk paved the way for public acceptance of Lincoln's goal of putting slavery on a path to ultimate extinction. Jaffa, *Crisis of the House Divided*, 61.

57. Bennett, *Forced into Glory*, 90–95.

58. *CW*, vol. 3: 145–201, at 145–46. Lincoln apologists have made Herculean efforts to wipe this passage from the record of Lincoln's life. Lawanda Cox, for example, plays on a misdefinition of the word "inasmuch," taking it to mean "if" when it actually means "in like degree; in like manner; seeing that; considering that; since." Lawanda Cox, *Lincoln and Black Freedom: A Study in Presidential Leadership* (Columbia: University of South Carolina Press, 1981), 21; dictionary.com, "inasmuch" (citing *Webster's Unabridged Dictionary*, 1996, 1998). The same source lists synonyms of "inasmuch" as "because," "since," "for," and "as," none of which is conditional, *pace* Cox.

59. See p. 55.

60. *CW*, vol. 2: 398–410.

61. For an example of the exculpatory explanation, one from which Lincoln's attribution of responsibility for the Civil War to blacks'

mere presence in America is omitted, see Donald, *Lincoln,* 367; see *CW,* vol. 5: 370–75. In his Pulitzer Prize–winning history of the period, the leading historian of the time, Princeton's James M. McPherson, wrote, contrary to voluminous evidence that Lincoln had advocated colonization for decades, that this idea came to Lincoln in the context of the 1862 election campaign and was proposed only for tactical purposes; although the electorate was racist, in McPherson's account, Lincoln was merely Machiavellian. McPherson, *Battle Cry of Freedom: The Civil War Era* (New York: Oxford University Press, 1988), 508.

62. Recall Jaffa's notion that this seeming insult actually was a tribute to the controverted political capacity of blacks. See p. 48.

63. As in Donald, *Lincoln,* 368. The colonization speculation is at Phillip Shaw Paludan, *The Presidency of Abraham Lincoln* (Lawrence: University Press of Kansas, 1994), 132. It seems that Lincoln's statement to the black delegation with whom he met at the White House on August 14, 1862, that, "Now if you gave a start to white people, you might open the door for many to be made free," upon which Paludan relies here, meant not that the preliminary success of the colonizing enterprise would persuade white Americans of free blacks' worthiness to join them in American citizenship, as Paludan implies, but that its success would persuade whites of the likelihood that freed blacks would leave the country. In this passage, as at 151, Paludan's understanding of Lincoln's and his associates' state of mind regarding colonization in the late 1850s seemingly mirrors Gabor Boritt's. Yet, only two pages earlier, he notes that Lincoln long had been an advocate of colonization; his conclusion that Lincoln must not really have believed colonization to be a workable option seems to have led Paludan to his conclusion that Lincoln's advocacy of it was a ruse. Again, however, recent events may have made colonization seem practical: the Irish Great Famine ended only a decade before Lincoln's election to the presidency, and more than one million Irishmen emigrated as a result of that disaster.

64. Bennett, *Forced into Glory,* is an example of a book whose author has followed the straightforward, though apparently inadequate, hermeneutical approach of reading Lincoln's words and drawing from them the conclusion that, as he made clear many times, Lincoln accepted the necessity of abolition only as a war measure and a last resort. Gabor Boritt, "Did He Dream of a Lily-White America? The Voyage to Linconia," in *The Lincoln Enigma: The Changing Faces of an American Icon* (New York: Oxford University Press, 2001), 305, asserts that Bennett "distorts history," though Boritt gives not a single example of such distortion. A contrary example is Fredrickson, "A Man but Not a Brother."

65. Boritt, "Did He Dream of a Lily-White America?" 51. Desire to use the Lincoln image for contemporary purposes has driven many other historians to endeavor to square his nineteenth-century actions with contemporary sensibilities, too. For example, see Miller, *Lincoln's Virtues,* 354, et seq.

66. Boritt, "Did He Dream of a Lily-White America?" 17, 12.

67. Thomas Jefferson to James Heaton, May 20, 1826, Jefferson, *Writings,* 1516.

68. Joseph T. Glatthaar, "Black Glory: The African-American Role in Union Victory," in Gabor S. Boritt, ed., *Why the Confederacy Lost* (New York: Oxford University Press, 1992), 133–62.

69. Abraham Lincoln to Charles D. Robinson, August 17, 1864, *Collected Works of Abraham Lincoln*, 7:499–502, at 499–500.

70. Paludan, *The Presidency of Abraham Lincoln*, 189.

71. Kenneth J. Winkle, *The Young Eagle: The Rise of Abraham Lincoln* (Dallas: Taylor Trade Publishing, 2001), 265.

72. *CW*, vol. 8: 399–405, at 403.

73. Fredrickson, "A Man but Not a Brother," 51. For dubious evidence to that effect, see ibid., 57.

74. Fredrickson wrote that Lincoln remained a Clay colonizationist to his dying day. "A Man but Not a Brother," 43–44.

75. William S. McFeely, *Grant: A Biography* (New York: W.W. Norton, 1982); Edmund David Cronon, *Black Moses: The Story of Marcus Garvey and the Universal Negro Improvement Association*, 2nd ed. (Madison: University of Wisconsin Press, 1969).

4—*The Difficulties of Understanding Abe*

1. Lerone Bennett, Jr., *Forced into Glory: Abraham Lincoln's White Dream* (Chicago: Johnson Publishing, 2000); Richard N. Current, *The Lincoln Nobody Knows*, 2nd ed. (New York: Greenwood Press, 1980), quote from Vardaman on pp. 230–36; Donald E. Fehrenbacher, "Only His Stepchildren," in *Lincoln in Text and Context: Collected Essays* (Stanford, Calif.: Stanford University Press, 1987): 95–112; and Oates, *Abraham Lincoln: The Man behind the Myth*, 26.

2. Fehrenbacher, "The Changing Image of Lincoln in American Historiography," in *Lincoln in Text and Context*, 181–96.

3. David Lowenthal, *The Past Is Another Country* (New York: Cambridge University Press, 1985).

4. Bennett, *Forced into Glory*, 327. Fehrenbacher has criticized the broad and indiscriminate use of the word "racist" in "Only His Stepchildren," 102, whereas George Fredrickson has emphasized the differences in degree and emphasis between white racists' ideas in "A Man but Not a Brother: Abraham Lincoln and Racial Inequality," *Journal of Southern History*, 41, no. 1 (February 1975): 44–47.

5. David Donald, *Lincoln* (New York: Simon & Schuster, 1995), n. 633.

6. George M. Fredrickson, *The Black Image in the White Mind: The Debate on Afro-American Character and Destiny, 1817–1914* (New York: Harper Row, 1971), 46–64.

7. Cited in Donald, *Lincoln*, 220–23. See also LaWanda Cox, *Lincoln and Black Freedom*, 2nd ed. (Charleston: University of South Carolina Press, 1994), 19–36.

8. "Address on Colonization to a Deputation of Negroes," August 14, 1862, *CW*, vol. 5: 370–75.

9. Quoted in Fredrickson, "A Man but Not a Brother," 39.

10. Myrdal, *An American Dilemma: The Negro Problem and Modern Democ-*

racy, vol. 1 (New Brunswick and London: Transaction Publishers, 2002 [1944]).
11. David A. Nichols, *Lincoln and the Indians: Civil War Policy and Politics* (Urbana: University of Illinois Press, 1978), 2–4.
12. "Speech to Indians," March 27, 1863, *CW,* vol. 6: 151–53.
13. Phillip Shaw Paludan, *The Presidency of Abraham Lincoln* (Lawrence: University Press of Kansas, 1994), 116–17; and "Speech to Germans at Cincinnati, Ohio," February 12, 1861, *CW,* vol. 4: 201–203.
14. Nichols, *Lincoln and the Indians,* 175–92.
15. "Speech to Indians."
16. "Speech in U.S. House of Representatives: The War with Mexico," January 12, 1848, *CW,* vol. 1: 431–42; Donald, *Lincoln,* 122–26; Mark E. Neely, Jr., "Lincoln and the Mexican War: An Argument by Analogy," *Civil War History,* 26, no. 1 (March 1978): 5–24, and "War and Partisanship: What Lincoln Learned from James K. Polk," *Journal of the Illinois State Historical Society,* 74, no. 3 (fall 1981): 199–216.
17. "Fifth Debate with Stephen A. Douglas at Galesburg, Illinois," October 7, 1858, *CW,* vol. 3: 235.
18. "Second Lecture on Discoveries and Inventions," February 11, 1859, *CW,* vol. 3: 356–63.
19. Ibid.
20. Hegel, *The Philosophy of History,* trans., J. Sibree (Buffalo, New York: Prometheus Books, 1991); and John Patrick Diggins, *On Hallowed Ground: Abraham Lincoln and the Foundations of American History* (New Haven, Conn.: Yale University Press, 2000), 152–58.
21. Sandburg, *Abraham Lincoln, the Prairie Years* (New York: Blue Ribbon Books, 1926), 91.
22. P. M. Zall, ed., *Abe Lincoln Laughing: Humorous Anecdotes from Original Sources by and about Abraham Lincoln* (Berkeley: University of California Press, 1982), 154.
23. Theodore W. Allen, *The Invention of the White Race: The Origin of Racial Oppression in America* (London: Verso, 1997); Noel Ignatiev, *How the Irish Became White* (New York: Routledge, 1996); Alexander Saxton, *The Rise and Fall of the White Republic: Class Politics and Mass Culture in Nineteenth Century American* (London: Verso, 2003).
24. Matthew Frye Jacobson, *Whiteness of a Different Color: European Immigrants and the Alchemy of Race* (Cambridge, Mass.: Harvard University Press, 1998), 22–52; and Fredrickson, *The Black Image in the White Mind,* 90–91, 97–108. See also Reginald Horsman, *Race and Manifest Destiny: The Origins of American Racial Anglo-Saxonism* (Cambridge, Mass.: Harvard University Press, 1981).
25. David R. Roediger, *The Wages of Whiteness: Race and the Making of the American Working Class* (London: Verso Press, 1991), 142–43.
26. "Speech at Chicago, Illinois," July 10, 1858, *CW,* vol. 2: 484–502. See also "Speech at Springfield, Illinois," June 26, 1857, *CW,* vol. 2: 398–410.
27. "Speech at Carlinville, Illinois," August 31, 1858, *CW,* vol. 3: 77–81.
28. "Third Debate with Stephen A. Douglas at Jonesboro, Illinois," September 15, 1858, *CW,* vol. 3: 102–44; and "Fifth Debate with Douglas at Galesburg, Illinois," October 7, 1858, *CW,* vol. 3: 207–44.

29. Diggins, *On Hallowed Ground*, 3–5.
30. "Fragment on Slavery," April 1, 1854, *CW*, vol. 2: 222–23.
31. Quoted in George Sinkler, *The Racial Attitudes of American Presidents, from Abraham Lincoln to Theodore Roosevelt* (Garden City, N.Y.: Doubleday, 1971), 32–37.
32. Donald, *Lincoln*, 201–202.
33. Diggins, *On Hallowed Ground*, 28–31, 41–48.
34. Bennett, *Forced into Glory*, 303–14.
35. "Address before the Young Man's Lyceum of Springfield, Illinois," January 27, 1838, *CW*, vol. 1: 109–15.
36. Brian R. Dirck, *Lincoln and Davis: Imagining America, 1809–1865* (Lawrence: University Press of Kansas, 2001), 129–30.
37. Quoted in David M. Potter, *The Impending Crisis, 1848–1861* (New York: Harper and Row, 1976), 342–44.
38. John Locke, *Second Treatise of Government*, ed. C. B. Macpherson (Indianapolis: Hackett Publishing, 1980 [1690]), 8–10; Jean-Jacques Rousseau, "Discourse on the Origin of Inequality," in *The Basic Political Writings* (Indianapolis: Hackett Publishing, 1987), 37–38, 81; and James Woelfel and Sarah Trulove, *Patterns in Western Civilization*, 2nd ed. (New York: Simon and Schuster, 1998), 308–309.
39. Diggins, *On Hallowed Ground*, 48–49, 177–81.
40. Robert F. Berkhofer, Jr., *The White Man's Indian: Images of the American Indian from Columbus to the Present* (New York: Alfred A. Knopf, 1978), 48–49.
41. Horsman, *Race and Manifest Destiny*, 250–51.
42. James D. Bilotta, *Race and the Rise of the Republican Party, 1848–1865* (New York: Peter Lang, 1992), 75–82; and Fredrickson, "A Man but Not a Brother," 40–43.
43. "Eulogy on Henry Clay," July 6, 1852, *CW*, vol. 2: 121–32.
44. "Seventh and Last Debate with Stephen A. Douglas at Alton, Illinois," October 15, 1858, *CW*, vol. 3: 283–325.
45. Bilotta, *Race and the Rise of the Republican Party*, 365–97; and "Speeches at Clinton, Illinois," September 2, 1858, *CW*, vol. 3: 81–84.
46. Fredrickson, *White Supremacy*, 160–61; Boritt, *Lincoln and the Economics of the American Dream*, 155–74; and Foner, *Free Soil, Free Labor, Free Men*, 295–300.
47. "Speech at Peoria, Illinois," October 16, 1854, *CW*, vol. 2: 275. See also "Speech at Chicago, Illinois," July 10, 1858, *CW*, vol. 2: 500–501.
48. "Speech at Springfield, Illinois," June 26, 1857, *CW*, vol. 2: 398–410. See also Potter, *The Impending Crisis*, 344–47.
49. Dirck, *Lincoln and Davis*, 132–35; Potter, *The Impending Crisis*, 338–53; "Speech at Peoria," *CW*, vol. 3: 263–66; and "Fifth Debate with Douglas," *CW*, vol. 3: 225–26
50. Donald, *Lincoln*, 165–66. See also Paludan, *The Presidency of Abraham Lincoln*, 130–33.
51. Fredrickson, *The Black Image in the White Mind*, 135–52; Fredrickson, "A Man but Not a Brother," 49–51; "Address on Colonization to a Dep-

utation of Negroes," August 14, 1862, *CW*, vol. 5: 370–75; and Neely, "Lincoln and the Mexican War."
    52. Nichols, *Lincoln and the Indians,* 76–118.
    53. Cox, "Lincoln and Black Freedom," in Gabor Boritt, ed., *The Historian's Lincoln: Pseudohistory, Psychohistory, and History* (Urbana: University of Illinos Press), 175–96. See also Oates, *Abraham Lincoln,* 99–112.
    54. Cited in Cox, *Lincoln and Black Freedom,* 25.
    55. Fredrickson, "A Man but Not a Brother," 52–58; Oates, *Abraham Lincoln,* 112–19; Paludan, *The Presidency of Abraham Lincoln,* 221–23, 263–64; commentary by Oates on LaWanda Cox, in Boritt, ed., *Historian's Lincoln,* 197–203.
    56. Bennett, *Forced into Glory,* 79–80; Vincent Harding, *There Is a River: The Black Struggle for Freedom in America* (New York: Harcourt, Brace and Jovanovich, 1981), 235–36, 277–78; Paludan, *The Presidency of Abraham Lincoln,* 18–20; and Oates, *Abraham Lincoln,* 26–30.
    57. Dirck, *Lincoln and Davis,* 121–23.

5—Abraham Lincoln, Emancipation, and the Supreme Court

    1. David Homer Bates, *Lincoln in the Telegraph Office* (Lincoln: University of Nebraska Press, 1995 [1907]), 138–41.
    2. Mark E. Neely, Jr., *The Last Best Hope of Earth: Abraham Lincoln and the Promise of America* (Cambridge, Mass.: Harvard University Press, 1993), 109.
    3. Francis B. Carpenter, *The Inner Life of Abraham Lincoln: Six Months at the White House* (Lincoln: University of Nebraska Press, 1995 [1866]), 20–21; he may have discussed a draft of the proclamation with Hannibal Hamlin on June 18, but the evidence is sketchy on that point; see David Donald's observations in *Lincoln* (New York: Simon and Schuster, 1995), 363, 654.
    4. See generally Neely, *Last Best Hope of Earth,* 108–109.
    5. *CW,* vol. 5: 144–46; see also ibid., 5: 152–53, 160, and 169.
    6. Richard Hofstadter, *The American Political Tradition and the Men Who Made It,* 2nd ed. (New York: Alfred A. Knopf, 1989), 130–31.
    7. *CW,* vol. 6: 28–29.
    8. Lerone S. Bennett, *Forced into Glory: Abraham Lincoln's White Dream* (Chicago: Johnson Publishing, 2000), 532.
    9. Garrison quotes in Henry Mayer, *All On Fire: William Lloyd Garrison and the Abolition of Slavery* (New York: St. Martin's, 1998), 542–44.
    10. Bennett, *Forced into Glory,* 415 (emphases in original); Vincent Harding, *There Is a River: The Black Struggle for Freedom in America* (New York: Harcourt, Brace and Jovanovich, 1981), 236; George M. Fredrickson, "A Man but Not a Brother: Abraham Lincoln and Racial Equality," *Journal of Southern History,* 51 (February 1975): 56; David Brion Davis, "The Emancipation Moment," in Gabor S. Boritt, ed., *Lincoln the War President: The Gettysburg Lectures* (New York: Oxford University Press, 1992), 87; Oates, *Abraham Lincoln: The Man behind the Myths* (New York: Harper Perennial, 1984), 21–30, offers a useful overview of the literature that is critical of Lincoln's race policies.

11. David Donald, *Lincoln* (New York: Simon and Schuster, 1995), 342–45; William Lee Miller, *Lincoln's Virtues: An Ethical Biography* (New York: Alfred A. Knopf, 2002), 355; also see his remarks in his essay, "A. Lincoln, Politician," in his *Lincoln Reconsidered*, 2nd ed. (New York: Vintage Press, 1984), esp. 67–69; Mark Neely also emphasizes the role of the border state problem in Lincoln's thinking; see *Last Best Hope of Earth*, 105–107; as does Oates in *With Malice toward None: A Life of Abraham Lincoln*, 2nd ed. (New York: Harper Perennial, 1994), 297, and *Abraham Lincoln*, 106–107; and so does James M. McPherson, *Abraham Lincoln and the Second American Revolution* (New York: Oxford University Press, 1991), 32–33; see also Jan Morris, *Lincoln: A Foreigner's Quest* (New York: Da Capo Press, 2000), 120–21; William E. Gienapp, *Abraham Lincoln and Civil War America* (New York: Oxford University Press, 2002), 117–18, emphasizes the role of Northern politics and Democratic Party opposition.

12. One exception is Allen C. Guelzo, *Abraham Lincoln, Redeemer President* (Grand Rapids, Mich.: William B. Eerdmans, 1999), 344.

13. *New York Times*, March 5, 1861.

14. *Dred Scott v. Sanford* 60 U.S. 393 (1856).

15. Lincoln, fragment of a speech, circa December 28, 1857, *CW*, vol. 2: 454.

16. *Dred Scott v. Sandford* 60 U.S. 393 (1857); see also Don E. Fehrenbacher, *The Dred Scott Case: Its Significance in American Law and Politics* (New York: Oxford University Press, 1978), 380–82.

17. *Ex parte Merryman* Fed. Case 9487 (1861).

18. The only other major rulings on presidential war-making powers were *Martin v. Mott* 12 U.S. 19 (1827), which gave the president wide discretionary authority in calling upon the state militias in times of emergency (see below); and *Bas v. Tingy* 4 U.S. 37 (1800), which allowed the president to define and execute limited war actions without congressional approval; neither offered the sweepingly narrow reading of Article II preferred by Taney in *Merryman*.

19. *Martin v. Mott* 12 U.S. 19 (1827).

20. *CW*, vol. 4: 429–30.

21. *CW*, vol. 2: 400, 417.

22. David M. Silver, *Lincoln's Supreme Court* (Urbana: University of Illinois Press, 1998), 22–23.

23. For the definitive analysis of similarities and differences between the justices in the *Dred Scott* majority, see Fehrenbacher, *The Dred Scott Case*, esp. chap. 17.

24. Silver, *Lincoln's Supreme Court*, 3–4, 15, 58.

25. Ibid., 57–66.

26. On Lincoln's relationship with Browning, see Donald, *Lincoln*, 245–46, 293–94.

27. See Leonard Swett's reminiscences quoted in William Herndon, *Herndon's Life of Lincoln* (New York: Da Capo Press, 1983), 406–408; also *CW*, vol. 5: 465–66; a good general overview of this process can be found in Silver, *Lincoln's Supreme Court*, 77–81.

28. On Browning opposition to Lincoln and emancipation, see Philip S. Paludan, *The Presidency of Abraham Lincoln* (Lawrence: University Press of Kansas, 1994), 157; and Oates, *With Malice toward None*, 320, 330.

29. Silver, *Lincoln's Supreme Court*, 62–63, 68.

30. *CW*, vol. 5: 145.

31. *CW*, vol. 5: 531–33.

32. Bennett, *Forced into Glory*, 26.

33. LaWanda Cox makes a somewhat similiar point, suggesting that the December 1862 proposal would have given Lincoln "legal security"; see Cox, *Lincoln and Black Freedom: A Study in Presidential Leadership* (Columbia: University of South Carolina Press, 1994), 10.

34. Bennett, *Forced into Glory*, 526–27.

35. Exerpt from Welles diary in James D. Richardson, ed., *A Compilation of Messages and Papers of the Confederate States of America, Including the Diplomatic Correspondence*, 2 vols. (Nashville: Publishing, 1905), 1: 209; John Niven, *Salmon P. Chase: A Biography* (New York: Oxford University Press, 1995), 304–306.

36. Paludan, *The Presidency of Abraham Lincoln*, 148; see also Cox, *Lincoln and Black Freedom*, 4; James M. McPherson, "Lincoln and Liberty," in *Abraham Lincoln and the Second American Revolution* (New York: Oxford University Press, 1990), 32–34 and passim; Michael Vorenberg, *Final Freedom: The Civil War, the Abolition of Slavery, and the Thirteenth Amendment* (Cambridge, Mass.: Harvard University Press, 2001).

37. See generally Silver, *Lincoln's Supreme Court*, 83–92, 128–30, who takes a more sympathetic approach to Taney's position; and Stuart L. Bernath, *Squall across the Atlantic: American Civil War Prize Cases and Diplomacy* (Berkeley: University of California Press, 1970), 31–32.

6—*Slavery Reparations in Theory and Practice*

1. Garry Wills, *Lincoln at Gettysburg: The Words that Remade America* (New York: Simon & Schuster, 1992),121–47.

2. *CW*, vol. 5: 537.

3. See Michael Vorenberg, *Final Freedom: The Civil War, the Abolition of Slavery, and the Thirteenth Amendment* (New York: Cambridge University Press, 2001), esp. 176–85.

4. Mark E. Neely, "Abraham Lincoln and Black Colonization: Benjamin Butler's Spurious Testimony," *Civil War History*, 25 (March 1979): 77–83.

5. For details on Lincoln's dabbling with colonization, as well as my own argument that Lincoln did indeed give up on colonization well before the end of the Civil War, see Michael Vorenberg, "Abraham Lincoln and the Politics of Black Colonization," in Thomas F. Schwartz, ed., *"For a Vast Future Also": Essays from the Journal of the Abraham Lincoln Association* (New York: Fordham University Press, 1999), 35–56.

6. *CW*, vol. 7: 55.

7. Alexander H. Stephens, *A Constitutional View of the Late War Between the States* (Philadelphia: National Publishing, 1870), 611–14.

8. W. C. Bibb, "Visit of an Alabamian to Washington City in the Spring of 1865," transcription from the *Gulf Messenger*, 6 (1893): 16, Carl Sandburg papers, Illinois Historical Survey, University of Illinois at Urbana-Champaign; see Carl Sandburg, *Abraham Lincoln: The War Years* (New York: Harcourt, Brace, 1939), 4:238–40.

9. Francis Fessenden, ed., *Life and Public Services of William Pitt Fessenden* (Boston: Houghton, Mifflin, 1907), 2:8; *CW*, vol. 8: 261–61; see also Ludwell H. Johnson, "Lincoln's Solution to the Problem of Peace Terms," *Journal of Southern History*, 34 (November 1968): 582–86.

10. David Donald, *Lincoln Reconsidered: Essays on the Civil War Era*, 2nd ed. (New York: Vintage, 1961), 187–208.

11. Daniel Walker Howe, *The Political Culture of the American Whigs* (Chicago: University of Chicago Press, 1979).

12. Samuel L. M. Barlow to Henry Stebbins, February 1, 1864, Samuel L. M. Barlow letter books, Henry E. Huntington Library, San Marino, Calif.

13. Francis P. Blair, Sr., to William Lloyd Garrison, June 21, 1864, Blair Family manuscripts., Manuscript Division, Library of Congress. Laura Giddings Julian, wife of U.S. Representative George Julian, had a conversation with the elder Blair in early 1864 in which he said that if all the blacks were not sent to Texas they would perish like the Native Americans. "Poor old man," wrote Mrs. Julian to her sister, "[he] can never work off that colonization scheme. . . ." Laura A. Julian to Mollie Giddings, February 27, 1864, George W. Julian MSS., Indiana State Library, Indianapolis.

14. See Carl Sandburg, *Abraham Lincoln: The War Years*, 4 vols. (New York: Harcourt, Brace), vol. 4: 43–44. John A. Campbell, another of the commissioners at Hampton Roads, was probably the first to record Lincoln telling the story; his account is reprinted in John A. Campbell, *Reminiscences and Documents Relating to the Civil War during the Year 1865* (Baltimore: John Murphy, 1887), 14. Henry J. Raymond, *The Life and Public Services of Abraham Lincoln* (New York: Derby and Miller, 1865), 745–46, has Lincoln telling Raymond that he did indeed tell the "root, hog or die" story at Hampton Roads.

15. William Henry Herndon and Jesse William Weik, *Abraham Lincoln: The True Story of a Great Life*, 3 vols. (New York: Belford, Clarke, 1889), vol. 1: 38.

16. *CW*, vol. 1: 8.

17. *CW*, vol. 4: 62; for the full text of his autobiographic sketches, see *CW*, vol. 3: 511–12, vol. 4: 60–67.

18. See, for example, Lincoln's speech at Springfield, Ill., *CW*, vol. 2: 405–406; and his speech at Ottawa, Ill., August 21, 1858, *CW*, vol. 3: 16.

19. *CW*, vol. 5: 372.

20. *CW*, vol. 6: 365, vol. 7: 55, vol. 8: 325.

21. Proceedings of the American Anti-Slavery Society at its Third Decade, Held in the City of Philadelphia, December 3 and 4, 1863, cited in Foner, *Life and Writings of Frederick Douglass*, vol. 3: 386.

22. See James M. McPherson, *The Negro's Civil War* (Urbana: University of Illinois Press, 1982), 277–80.

23. P. J. Staudenraus, *Mr. Lincoln's Washington: Selections from the Writings of Noah Brooks, Civil War Correspondent* (New York: Thomas Yoseloff, 1967), 382–83.

24. For the phrase "ambition for education," see autobiography for Jesse W. Fell, December 20, 1859, *CW,* vol. 3: 511.

25. *CW,* vol. 8: 333.

7—*All Politics Are Local*

1. Only a few examples of the varied scholarly perspectives on Lincoln's emancipation policy can be provided here. James G. Randall, *Constitutional Problems under Lincoln* (Urbana: University of Illinois Press, 1951); Richard N. Current, ed., *The Political Thought of Abraham Lincoln* (New York: Macmillan and Collier Macmillan, 1967); James M. McPherson, *Abraham Lincoln and the Second American Revolution* (New York: Oxford University Press, 1990); David Brion Davis, "The Emancipation Moment," in Gabor S. Borritt, ed., *Lincoln the War President* (New York: Oxford University Press, 1992); Philip Shaw Paludan, "Hercules Unbound: Lincoln, Slavery, and the Intentions of the Framers," in Donald G. Nieman, ed., *The Constitution, Law, and American Life: Critical Aspects of the Nineteenth-Century Experience* (Athens: University of Georgia Press, 1992); Ira Berlin, "Who Freed the Slaves? Emancipation and Its Meaning," in David W. Blight and Brooks D. Simpson, eds., *Union & Emancipation: Essays on Politics and Race in the Civil War Era* (Kent, Ohio: Kent State University Press, 1997); and William K. Klingaman, *Abraham Lincoln and the Road to Emancipation, 1861–1865* (New York: Viking, 2001). Perhaps the most controversial perspectives are found in Lerone Bennett Jr., *Forced into Glory: Abraham Lincoln's White Dream* (Chicago: Johnson Publishing, 2000).

2. Sceva Bright Laughlin, *Missouri Politics during the Civil War* (Iowa City: Department of History, University of Iowa, 1921), 59; St. Louis *Missouri Republican,* August 5, 1861; and *Journal of the Missouri State Convention Held at the City of St. Louis, October 1861* (St. Louis: George Knapp, Printers and Binders, 1861), 4 and 17–20.

3. For an excellent overview of the circumstances Lincoln confronted see William E. Parrish, *Turbulent Partnership: Missouri and the Union, 1861–1865* (Columbia: University of Missouri Press, 1963).

4. St. Louis *Republican,* August 5, 1861; James T. Matson to Hamilton R. Gamble, September 13, 1861, and J. W. Wilson to Hamilton R. Gamble, May 23, 1863, Hamilton R. Gamble papers, Missouri Historical Society, St. Louis, Missouri; hereinafter cited as Gamble papers. J. T. K. Hayward to J. C. Fremont, August 10 and 12, 1861; Speed Butler to General Hurlbut, August 10 and 14, 1861; and John S. Phelps to G. M. Dodge, December 2, 1861, *The War of the Rebellion: A Compilation of the Official Records of the Union and Confederate Armies,* series 2, vol. 1, 204–209 and 781; hereinafter cited as *Official Records.* See also Dennis K. Boman, "Conduct and Revolt in the Twenty-fifth Ohio Battery: An Insider's Account," *Ohio History* (summer–autumn 1995): 170–74.

5. Hamilton R. Gamble to Lincoln, August 26, 1861, Gamble papers.

6. Here is a sample of the sources available to Lincoln during the first months of his presidency: Samuel T. Glover to Lincoln, May 20 and 24, 1861, September 20 and 21, 1861, and October 14 and 19, 1861; James O. Broadhead to Montgomery Blair, September 30, 1861; Frank P. Blair to Montgomery Blair, August 15 and 21, 1861; John Poyner to Lincoln, August 27, 1861; Sample Orr

to Lincoln, November 21, 1861; and John W. Dawson to Lincoln, December 14, 1861, Abraham Lincoln papers, Library of Congress Archives, Washington, D.C.; hereinafter cited as Lincoln papers. John S. Phelps to Hamilton R. Gamble, August 8, 1861; Hamilton R. Gamble to Lincoln, August 26, 1861; Edward Bates to Hamilton R. Gamble, October 3, 1861, Gamble papers. For contradictory advice, see Michael Burlingame and John R. Turner Ettlinger, eds., *Inside Lincoln's White House: The Complete Civil War Diary of John Hay* (Carbondale: Southern Illinois University Press, 1997), 29–30.

7. St. Louis *Missouri Republican,* September 11, 1861, and June 2, 1862.

8. Proclamation of John C. Fremont, August 30, 1861; General Order No. 6, J. C. Kelton, August 30, 1861, *Official Records,* series 1, vol. 3, pp. 466–70.

9. Lincoln to John C. Fremont, September 2 and 11, 1861; and John C. Fremont to Lincoln, September 8, 1861, *Official Records,* series 1, vol. 3, 477–78, and 485–86.

10. Ibid. and proclamation of M. Jeff Thompson, September 2, 1861, and of Ben McCulloch, September 10, 1861, *Official Records,* series 1, vol. 3, 693 and 700.

11. J. O. Davis to Hamilton R. Gamble, August 22, 1861, Gamble papers; St. Louis *Missouri Republican,* September 10 and 15, 1861; U. S. Grant to Speed Butler, August 27, 1861, *Official Records,* series 1, vol. 3, 463. Joshua F. Speed to Lincoln, September 1 and 3, 1861; Montgomery Blair to Lincoln, September 14, 1861; and John B. Henderson to James O. Broadhead, September 7, 1861, Lincoln papers.

12. S. M. Breckinridge to Hamilton R. Gamble, August 3, 1861; John M. Richardson to Hamilton R. Gamble, August 10, 1861; and Charles Gibson to Hamilton R. Gamble, September 27, 1861, Gamble papers. Samuel T. Glover to Montgomery Blair, September 2, 1861; James O. Broadhead to Montgomery Blair, September 3, 1861; Winfield Scott to Lincoln, September 5, 1861; Lincoln to David Hunter, September 9, 1861; John B. Henderson to James O. Broadhead, September 7, 1861; John M. Shaffer to Winfield Scott, September 14, 1861; Francis P. Blair Jr. to Lincoln, September 15, 1861; Samuel T. Glover to Lincoln, September 20 and 21, 1861; and John How to Montgomery Blair, October 3, 1861, Lincoln papers. Parrish, *Turbulent Partnership,* 52 and 66–68. For the powerful support Fremont enjoyed see Bruce Tap, *Over Lincoln's Shoulder: The Committee on the Conduct of the War* (Lawrence: University of Kansas Press, 1998), 81–91.

13. See notes 10 and 11 above, and Montgomery Blair to Lincoln, September 14, 1861; Elihu B. Washburne to Lincoln, Lincoln papers. Lorenzo Thomas to Simon Cameron, October 21, 1861; Winfield Scott to John C. Fremont, General Orders No. 18, October 24, 1861; Lincoln to Samuel R. Curtis, October 24, 1861; General Orders No. 28, November 2, 1861; David Hunter to Adjutant General of the United States Army, November 3, 1861, *Official Records,* series 1, vol. 3, 540–49, 553, 559, and 561. Burlingame and Ettlinger, eds., *Diary of John Hay,* 123–24. See also Howard K. Beale, ed., *The Diary of Edward Bates, 1859–1866* (Washington, D.C.: Government Printing Office, 1933), 198–99.

14. Henry W. Halleck to George B. McClellan, November 30, 1861; and Lincoln and William Seward, December 2, 1861, *Official Records,* series 1, vol. 8, 395 and 401.

15. General Orders No. 13, December 4, 1861; General Orders No. 24, December 12, 1861; General Orders No. 32, December 22, 1861; John Pope to Colonel Deitzler, December 29, 1861; Henry W. Halleck to T. Ewing, January 1, 1862; John M. Schofield to Henry W. Halleck, January 1, 1862; Sterling Price to Henry W. Halleck, January 12, 1862; Henry W. Halleck to George B. McClellan, January 14, 1862; and Henry W. Halleck to Sterling Price, January 22, 1862, *Official Records*, series 1, vol. 8: 395, 401, 431–32, 463–64, 475–76, 496–97, 500–2, 514–15; and series 2, vol. 1: 233–37 and 240–41. See also Hamilton R. Gamble to Henry W. Halleck, December 24, 1861; and Henry W. Halleck to Hamilton R. Gamble, December 26, 1861, Gamble papers.

16. *CW,* vol. 3: 497–502; and Jay Monaghan, *Civil War on the Western Border, 1854–1865* (Lincoln: University of Nebraska Press, 1955), 17–116.

17. Charles Robinson to John C. Fremont, September 1, 1861; and Hamilton R. Gamble to O. G. Cates, January 28, 1862, *Official Records,* series 1, vol. 3, 468–69 and vol. 17, part 2, 92. Hamilton R. Gamble to Lincoln, October 18, 1861, Lincoln papers.

18. Henry W. Halleck to Edwin M. Stanton, July 12, 1862; Hamilton R. Gamble to O. G. Cates, November 21, 1861; O. G. Cates to Henry W. Halleck, January 28, 1862; O. G. Cates to Edwin M. Stanton, February 26, 1862; W. W. Sanford to J. C. Kelton, July 7, 1862; Charles R. Jennison to the People of Jackson, Lafayette, Cass, Johnson, and Pettis counties, Missouri, November 27, 1861; and Edward M. Samuel et al. to Lincoln, September 8, 1862, *Official Records,* series 1, vol. 13, 618–19 and vol. 17, part 2, 91–94, and series 2, vol. 1, 231–32.

19. Henry W. Halleck to Edwin M. Stanton, July 12, 1862, *Official Records,* series 1, vol. 17, part 2, 91; and David Herbert Donald, *Lincoln* (New York: Simon & Schuster, 1995), 331–33.

20. Donald, *Lincoln,* 331–33 and 342–48.

21. Message to Congress, March 6, 1862; Lincoln to Henry J. Raymond, March 9, 1862; and Lincoln to Horace Greeley, March 24, 1862, in Michael P. Johnson, ed., *Abraham Lincoln, Slavery, and the Civil War: Selected Writings and Speeches,* the Bedford Series in History and Culture (Boston and New York: Bedford/St. Martin's Press, 2001), 186–89. Randall, *Constitutional Problems,* 365–67.

22. Donald, *Lincoln,* 345–47; and Randall, *Constitutional Problems,* 365–67.

23. John B. Henderson, *Speech of Hon. J. B. Henderson of Missouri on the Abolition of Slavery delivered in the Senate of the United States, March 27, 1862* (Washington, D.C.: L. Towers, 1862), 1–15; Frank P. Blair Jr., *Speech of Hon. F. P. Blair Jr. of Missouri on the Policy of the President for the Restoration of the Union and Establishment of Peace delivered in the House of Representatives, April 11, 1862* (New York: Baker & Godwin, 1862), 3–8; E. H. Norton, *Speech of Hon. E. H. Norton of Missouri on Confiscation and Emancipation delivered in the House of Representatives, April 24, 1862* (Washington, D.C.: n.p., 1862), 2–8; John S. Phelps, *Confiscation of property and Emancipation of Slaves: Speech of Hon. John S. Phelps of Missouri in the House of Representatives, May 22, 1862* (Washington: n.p., 1862), 1–8; and Frank P. Blair Jr., *Confiscation, Emancipation, and Colonization "Indemnity for the Past and Security for the Future": Speech of Hon. F. P. Blair Jr. of Missouri in the House of Representatives, May 23, 1862* (n.p., 1862), 1–7.

24. St. Louis *Missouri Republican,* March 26, 1862, May 1 and 18, 1862, June 1, 5, 7, 10, and 22, 1862, and July 15, 1862.

25. Translated excerpts from local German newspapers, the *Anzeiger des Westons* and the *Westliche Post,* in the St. Louis *Missouri Republican,* May 1, 2, and 13, 1862, and June 6 and 9, 1862.

26. Randall, *Constitutional Problems,* 356–57.

27. St. Louis *Missouri Republican,* June 3, 1862. *Proceedings of the Missouri State Convention Held in Jefferson City, June 1862* (St. Louis: George Knapp, 1862), 72–77.

28. Ibid., 98–100.

29. Ibid., 82–84, 89–94, 103, and 136–37.

30. Ibid., 227 and 239–41; and Parrish, *Turbulent Partnership,* 130–33.

31. St. Louis *Missouri Republican,* June 5, 10, 19, and 20, 1862; and Parrish, *Turbulent Partnership,* 133.

32. Donald, *Lincoln,* 362; Majority Border State Response, July 14, 1862, and Minority Border State Response, July 15, 1862, Lincoln papers.

33. Donald, *Lincoln,* 362–76.

34. Ibid., 375; Parrish, *Turbulent Partnership,* 135–36.

35. *Proceedings of the Missouri State Convention Held in Jefferson City, June 1862* (St. Louis: George Knapp, 1862), 43–71, 95–97, 105–107, 109–13, 119, 130–31, 146, 172, 174–76, 178–79, 200–201, 205–211, 216–18, and 222; St. Louis *Missouri Republican,* October 22, 1862; and Parrish, *Turbulent Partnership,* 136.

36. Parrish, *Turbulent Partnership,* 90–98; Frank P. Blair to Montgomery Blair, August 8, 1862, Lincoln papers; John M. Schofield, *Forty-Six Years in the Army,* forward by William M. Ferraro (New York: Century, 1897; Norman: University of Oklahoma Press, 1998), 56–61.

37. St. Louis *Missouri Republican,* October 9 and 14 and November 17, 18, and 25, 1862; James H. Birch to Hamilton R. Gamble, September 7, 1862, Gamble papers; Samuel T. Curtis to Henry W. Halleck, November 24, 1862, *Official Records,* series 1, vol. 22, part 1, 788–89; and Parrish, *Turbulent Partnership,* 135–36.

38. St. Louis *Missouri Republican,* November 9 and December 13, 1862; Frank P. Blair to Lincoln, November 14, 1862, Lincoln papers.

39. Parrish, *Turbulent Partnership,* 136–37; St. Louis *Missouri Republican,* November 9, 12, and 18, 1862.

40. William G. Eliot to Lincoln, December 18, 1862, Lincoln papers.

41. St. Louis *Missouri Republican,* December 6, 1862, January, 17, 22, and 23, February, 2, 6, and 19, and March 9 and 10, 1863.

42. Ibid., March 13 and April 22, 1863.

43. John B. Henderson to Lincoln, January and March 30, 1863, Lincoln papers; John B. Henderson, *Speech of Hon. J. B. Henderson of Missouri on Emancipation in Missouri: Delivered in the Senate of the United States, January 16, 1863* (Washington D.C.: L. Towers, printers, 1863); Thomas L. Price, *Emancipation in Missouri: Speech of Hon. T. L. Price of Missouri in the House of Representatives, February 1863* (Washington D.C.: n.p., 1863); David Turpie, *Speech of Honorable D. Turpie of Indiana delivered in the United States Senate on Saturday, February 7th, 1863* (Baltimore, Md.: Murphy, 1863); James W.

Wall, *Speech of Hon. James W. Wall of N.J. on the Missouri Emancipation Bill in the United States Senate, February 7th, 1863* (Washington D.C.: M'Gill & Witherow, 1863); and James S. Rollins, *Speech of Hon. James S. Rollins of Missouri, February 28th, 1863* (n.p., 1863).

44. *Journal of the Missouri State Convention, Held in Jefferson City, June 1863* (St. Louis: George Knapp, 1863), 3; St. Louis *Missouri Republican,* February 6, 1863.

45. The St. Louis *Missouri Republican* ran a series entitled the "Spirit of the German Press," in which were provided translations of editorial columns critical of Gamble's administration primarily from the St. Louis *Neue Zeit* and the *Westliche Post.* For attacks on Gamble leading into the convention and Lincoln's reply to the radical meeting's resolutions see St. Louis *Missouri Republican,* May 23 and June 3, 5, 6, 9, 11, and 12, 1863.

46. St. Louis *Missouri Republican,* June 17, 1863; and *Journal of the Missouri State Convention, Held in Jefferson City, June 1863* (St. Louis: George Knapp, 1863), 3–6; hereinafter cited as *Journal, June 1863.*

47. *Journal, June 1863,* 24; and *Proceedings of the Missouri State Convention Held in Jefferson City, June 1863* (St. Louis: George Knapp, 1863), 135–36, 144–45, and 229; hereinafter cited as *Proceedings, June 1863.*

48. James S. Rollins to Lincoln, June 12, 1863; John M. Schofield to Lincoln, June 21, 1863; and Lincoln to John M. Schofield, June 22, 1863, Lincoln papers; and Burlingame and Ettlinger, eds., *Diary of John Hay,* 88–89.

49. *Journal, June 1863,* 12 and 27; and *Proceedings, June 1863,* 34–35, 285–86, 290, and 315–17.

50. *Proceedings, June 1863,* 344 and 367.

51. Hamilton R. Gamble to Lincoln, December 5, 1862, May 2 and July 13, 1863; Samuel T. Glover to Montgomery Blair, December 7, 1862; Samuel T. Glover to Edward Bates, May 15, 1863; Samuel T. Glover to Lincoln, April 13, 1863; Lincoln to Samuel T. Curtis, December 10, 1862; Samuel R. Curtis to Lincoln, December 12, 19, and 20, 1862; John S. Thomas to Samuel R. Curtis, December 16, 1862; John T. Hayward to Lincoln, January 27, 1863; Hamilton R. Gamble to Samuel R. Curtis, February 9, 1863; Charles Gibson to Lincoln, February 23, 1863; Hamilton R. Gamble to Montgomery Blair, September 24, 1862; B. Gratz Brown to John G. Nicolay, November 25, 1862; John B. Henderson to Lincoln, March 30, 1863; B. Gratz Brown to Lincoln, November 25, 1862; Henry T. Blow to Lincoln, March 22 and May 5, 1863; Ozias M. Hatch et al. to Lincoln, March 25, 1863; and Joseph W. McClurg to Lincoln, May 22, 1863, Lincoln papers. Hamilton R. Gamble Jr. to Hamilton R. Gamble, March 6, 1863; John B. Henderson to Hamilton R. Gamble, March 30, 1863; Hamilton R. Gamble to Lincoln, July 13, 1863; and Lincoln to Hamilton R. Gamble, July 23, 1863, Gamble papers.

52. Burlingame and Ettlinger, eds., *Diary of John Hay,* 88–89; and Joseph A. Hay to Lincoln, September 11, 1863, Lincoln papers.

53. Charles D. Drake, "Autobiography," 918–22, Western Historical Manuscripts Collection, State Historical Society of Missouri, Columbia, Missouri; hereinafter cited as Drake Autobiography. Charles Gibson and James S. Rollins to Lincoln, October 11, 1863, Lincoln papers.

54. Drake *Autobiography*, 918–22.

55. Ibid., 923; and Burlingame and Ettlinger, eds., *Diary of John Hay*, 88.

56. Burlingame and Ettlinger, eds., *Diary of John Hay*, 88–89.

57. Lincoln to Charles D. Drake, October 5, 1863, *Official Records*, series 1, vol. 22, part 2, 604–7.

58. Ibid.

59. Ibid., and General Orders No. 101, September 28, 1863, *Official Records*, series 1, vol. 22, part 2, 577.

60. Parrish, *Turbulent Partnership*, 195–96.

61. Ibid., 200–201.

62. Ronald Syme, *The Roman Revolution* (Oxford: Oxford University Press, 1960 [1939]), 4.

63. The extensive number of books and articles written about Lincoln prevent a comprehensive listing of them here. However, three essays by Don E. Fehrenbacher in *Lincoln in Text and Context: Collected Essays* (Stanford, Calif.: Stanford University Press, 1987), 95–112, 129–42, and 197–213, provide a useful analysis of Lincoln historiography. Two other books that repay reading are David Donald, *Lincoln Reconsidered: Essays on the Civil War Era* (New York: Alfred A. Knopf, 1956), and Richard N. Current, *The Lincoln Nobody Knows*, American Century Series (New York: Hill and Wang, 1958). Two recent books representative of the tradition hostile to Lincoln are Bennett, *Forced into Glory*, and Thomas DiLorenzo, *The Real Lincoln: A New Look at Abraham Lincoln, His Agenda, and an Unnecessary War* (Roseville, Calif.: Prima, 2002).

64. Hamilton R. Gamble to Edward Bates, July 14, 1862, Edward Bates papers, Missouri Historical Society, St. Louis, Missouri; and Hamilton R. Gamble to Lincoln, May 2, 1863, Gamble papers.

65. Lincoln to Albert G. Hodges, April 4, 1864, Lincoln papers.

LIST OF CONTRIBUTORS

Dennis K. Boman received his Ph.D. in United States history from the University of Missouri–Columbia and is a freelance writer focusing on antebellum and Civil War history. Currently, he is writing a history of Lincoln's handling of civil-rights issues in Missouri. In addition to articles and essays in journals and other publications, Boman has written two biographies of prominent Missourians. The first, published in 2002, is *Abiel Leonard: Yankee Slaveholder, Eminent Jurist, and Passionate Unionist*. The second, published in 2006, is *Lincoln's Resolute Unionist: Hamilton Gamble, Dred Scott Dissenter and Missouri's Civil War Governor*.

Brian R. Dirck is an associate professor of history at Anderson University in Anderson, Indiana. He specializes in the history of the American Civil War and has a particular interest in the political and legal ramifications of that conflict. He is the author of *Lincoln & Davis: Imagining America, 1809–1865,* and a forthcoming study of Abraham Lincoln's law practice.

Allen C. Guelzo is the Henry R. Luce Professor of the Civil War Era and Director of Civil War Era Studies at Gettysburg College. He is the only two-time winner of the Lincoln Prize, for *Abraham Lincoln: Redeemer President* (2000) and *Lincoln's Emancipation Proclamation: The End of Slavery in America* (2004). He has been featured on C-SPAN, The History Channel, and as a "Great Professor" by The Teaching Company.

Kevin R. C. Gutzman received his J.D. from the University of Texas School of Law and his Ph.D. in history from the University of Virginia. He is the author of articles in numerous journals, including *The Journal of the Early Republic,* the *Journal of Southern History, The Virginia Magazine of History and Biography,* and *The Journal of the Historical Society,* among others, as well as dozens of encyclopedia entries and book reviews. He is currently working on a book on Revolutionary and Early Republican Virginia, a diplomatic life of John Jay, and a biography of John C. Calhoun. Gutzman is an associate professor of history at Western Connecticut State University.

James N. Leiker is a professor of history at Johnson County Community College in Overland Park, Kans. He received his Ph.D. in U.S. social history from the University of Kansas. His research focuses primarily on racial and ethnic relations in the American West, particularly on interrelationships between peoples of color. His articles have appeared in *Western Historical Quarterly, Great Plains Quarterly, Journal of the West,* and *Kansas History*. His book, *Racial Borders: Black Soldiers along the Rio Grande* (2002), was a winner of the T. R. Fehrenbach Award for the best book on Texas history and a co-winner of the Border Regional Library Association Award.

Phillip Shaw Paludan was born in Minnesota and subsequently lived in Canada, Southern California, and Illinois before beginning his permanent teaching career at the University of Kansas where he taught for thirty-three years. In 2001 he moved to the University of Illinois, Springfield, where he is the Naomi Lynn Distinguished Chair of Lincoln Studies. He is the author of four major books: *A Covenant with Death: The Constitution, Law, and Equality in the Civil War* (1975); *Victims: A True Story of the Civil War* (1981, 2005); *"A People's Contest": The Union and Civil War* (1988, 1996); *The Presidency of Abraham Lincoln* (1994). He has been a Guggenheim Fellow, a Fellow of the ACLS, and a Liberal Arts Fellow at Harvard Law School. In 1995 he won the Lincoln Prize for the outstanding book on the Civil War era. His current work focuses on Lincoln's views of race, democracy, and compassion.

Michael Vorenberg, Brown University, is at work on a book about the impact of the American Civil War on citizenship as well as a document collection relating to Civil War emancipation. He is the author of *Final Freedom: The Civil War, the Abolition of Slavery, and the Thirteenth Amendment* (2001).

Kenneth J. Winkle is Professor of History and Chair of the History Department at the University of Nebraska–Lincoln. His first book, *The Politics of Community* (1988), received the Allan Sharlin Award from the Social Science History Association. He has written *The Young Eagle: The Rise of Abraham Lincoln* (2001), a study of Lincoln's development as a national leader and statesman before his election to the presidency, and coedited *The Oxford Atlas of the Civil War* (2004). In addition, he has published numerous articles in *The Journal of Social History, The Journal of Interdisciplinary History, Civil War History, History, The Journal of the Abraham Lincoln Association, Social Science History,* and *Reviews in American History.*

INDEX